THE ANTISEMITISM WARS

How the British media failed their public

Karl Sabbagh

SKYSCRAPER PUBLICATIONS

The Antisemitism Wars

Published by Skyscraper Publications Limited
20 Crab Tree Close, Bloxham, OX15 4SE
www.skyscraperpublications.com

First published 2018

Copyright information:

The Summer of Antisemitism, Viscious (sic) propaganda,
and Conclusion: Karl Sabbagh

The Story So Far…: Tony Greenstein

Giving the Truth a Voice: Cyril Chilson

Smoke and Mirrors: Thomas Suárez

The IHRA definition: The Palestine Return Centre,
Geoffrey Robertson QC, and Stephen Sedley.

Exposing the Vigilantes: Redress Information and Contact

Who Will Edit the Editors?: Kathy-Anne Mendoza,
and the Canary website

Enough Tropes to Hang Themselves: Al Jazeera television,
transcripts of The Lobby

The Conduct of Baroness Tonge: The House of Lords Privileges
Committee report on the conduct of Baroness Jenny Tonge
contains Parliamentary information licensed under the
Open Parliament Licence v3.0.

Labour, Antisemitism and the News: Dr Justin Schlosberg and
Dr Laura Laker of the *Media Reform Coalition*.

All rights reserved. This book is sold subject to the condition that it shall
not be resold, lent, hired out or otherwise circulated without the express
prior consent of the publisher.

A CIP catalogue record for this book is available
from the British Library.

ISBN-13: 978-1-911072-36-2

Cover concept Thomas Suárez

Typesetting by chandlerbookdesign.com

Printed in the United Kingdom by CPI

"It is easier for the world to accept a simple lie than a complex truth."

Alexis de Tocqueville

CONTENTS

PART 1 THE ANTISEMITISM WARS	1
1. The Summer of Antisemitism	3
PART 2 ON THE RECEIVING END	17
2. The story so far… **Tony Greenstein**	21
3. Viscious (sic) propaganda **Karl Sabbagh**	41
4. Giving the Truth a Voice **Cyril Chilson**	55
5. Smoke and mirrors **Thomas Suárez**	63
PART 3 THE DOCUMENTS	75
6. The IHRA 'definition'	83
Origins	83
Defining Anti-Semitism:	85
Anti-Semitism: The IHRA definition and its consequences for freedom of expression	90
7. Exposing the Vigilantes	115
Exposed! How Britain's Anti-Semitism scaremongers operate	115

8.	Enough Tropes to Hang Themselves	139
	The Lobby, Part 1	139
	The Lobby, Part 2	153
	The Lobby, Part 3	167
	The Lobby, Part 4	181
9.	Who will Edit the Editors? **Kerry-Anne Mendoza**	195
10.	The Conduct of Baroness Tonge	213
	Committee for Privileges and Conduct	213
Conclusion		233
Authors		239
Appendices		241
	Appendix 1:	241
	Appendix 2:	242
	Appendix 3	245
Further reading		253
Acknowledgments		255
Endnotes		257

Note on terminology:

I have used the spelling 'antisemitism' throughout. This is the spelling recommended by the IHRA (International Holocaust Remembrance Alliance) and although I do not agree with all recommendations of the IHRA, I accept this one. But since some of the documents I quote use other spellings, principally 'anti-Semitism' – perhaps because this is Microsoft Word's default spelling when the writer's spellcheck is used – I have not always changed the spelling in quoted documents.

Footnotes and endnotes

Notes by Karl Sabbagh are printed as footnotes, using symbols. Notes in material by other writers are printed as Endnotes, from page 243.

All notes in Karl Sabbagh's pieces are identified by symbols and printed at the foot of the page

PART 1
THE ANTISEMITISM WARS

1

The Summer of Antisemitism

On the day I started writing this chapter, the British newspapers were reporting in detail a speech by a former Prime Minister of the U.K., Gordon Brown, in which he urged the Labour Party to adopt in full something called "the IHRA definition of antisemitism"*. I always thought that the job of newspapers was to publish news, and Gordon Brown's speech was as newsworthy as a speech by the Pope praising the Roman Catholic Church. Brown is a passionate supporter of Israel, a member of Labour Friends of Israel and a man who, when prime minister, said "I was incredibly proud to be the first British Prime Minister to address the Knesset and as long as I am Prime Minister Israel will always have the firmest of friends in the British Government."

And a few days before I finished compiling the material for the book, the Labour Party National Executive Committee accepted

---

* The best way to understand the IHRA 'definition' is to read the opinion of Geoffrey Robertson QC, in the Documents section of this book, p. 90 But so as not to disrupt the flow you may take it as read for now that, in the words of the American lawyer who drafted it, "The definition was not drafted, and was never intended, as a tool to target or chill speech."

the entire IHRA 'definition' along with its eleven examples, and rejected a qualifying statement from Jeremy Corbyn designed to defuse some of the worst anti-free-speech effects of the definition if put into action.

The summer of 2018 has seen an extraordinary outpouring of invective against the Labour Party under Jeremy Corbyn, by high-profile people, all of whom have long been supporters of Israel and critics of anyone who supports the Palestinians. This reached its zenith (or nadir) when a former chief rabbi, Jonathan Sacks, said "I know of no other occasion in these 362 years where Jews, the majority of our community, are asking 'is this country safe to bring up our children?'".

Just pause to think about this. What sort of event could instil fears for their own safety in perhaps a quarter of a million British Jews? ("The majority of our community") To ask "Is this country safe to bring up our children?" suggests that antisemites, perhaps many of them, are on the march in anti-Jewish demonstrations, harassing Jewish children as they leave their schools, agitating for laws to discriminate against Jews, and controlling the media to produce a torrent of antisemitic coverage. Consider the Battle of Cable Street in 1936, when Oswald Mosely's antisemitic British Union of Fascists paraded in Jewish areas of the East End. It seems to me highly likely that more Jews asked 'is this country safe to bring up our children?' at that time – and with better reason – than in August, 2018.

In fact, the remark that Sacks claimed has made "the majority of [the Jewish] community" fear for their safety, was made by Jeremy Corbyn about a couple of British Zionists, in a meeting five years ago in 2013, when he said that their hostile reactions to a rather witty speech by the Palestinian Ambassador to the UK suggested that they didn't understand English irony, in spite of living in the UK 'probably all their lives'.

Sacks' comment on this remark raises many questions. Were a quarter of a million Jews really so terrified by the remark, made five years ago, that they got in touch with Sacks to tell him of their fears? And if so, did they explain why an accusation of not understanding English irony was so hurtful that they were thinking of giving up their British citizenship, uprooting themselves and leaving the country they have lived in all their lives? In any case, what on earth is antisemitic about Corbyn's remark? We can be pretty sure that no Jew said in 1936 "at least they are not accusing us of not understanding British irony – that would really make me want to leave the country."

But of course, widespread and flagrant expressions of antisemitism have not occurred. What then is it that British Jews are really complaining about?

This book tries to answer that question, by showing how a determined phalanx of supporters of Israel, ranging from Israeli diplomats and official Jewish organisations to individual freelance agitators recording meetings and roaming social media, distort and misrepresent what anti-Zionists and supporters of Palestine say, and sometimes fabricate reports of antisemitism where none exists. Indeed it is reaching the stage where 'Zionist' as a noun or adjective has actually been given two meanings. It means 'Jewish' if used by a non-Jew, allowing anti-Zionists to be accused of antisemitism, (this was the basis of the attack on Corbyn's 'irony' remark), but a Jew can still call himself a Zionist in the original sense of 'a supporter, Jew or non-Jew, of the right of Israel to take over Palestine' when self-applied by people who hold that particular political view.

Sacks was one of a number of leading British Jews who seized an opportunity presented by the British media to use whatever weapons they could manufacture to attack a Labour Party which, at times over the last year or two, in the light of the disarray among the Conservatives, looked as if it had a chance of forming a government. And a government with Corbyn at its head would destroy the cosy relationship that has endured between British governments and Israel since Israel was established, and usher in a period when the rights of the Palestinians, in particular their right not to be maimed and murdered by Israeli bombs, white phosphorus and bullets, would receive the attention they deserve.

Ironically (sic), as often happens, you can find a more measured assessment of the situation in Israeli media, particularly the daily newspaper *Ha'aretz*. One Israeli columnist, Anshel Pfeffer, quoted a statement by a group called Campaign Against Antisemitism (more about them later) that "more than half of British Jews felt that anti-Semitism today echoed that of the 1930s", and went on to say that if British Jews "actually believe that, then it's hard to take anything they say about contemporary antisemitism in their home country seriously." Pfeffer added that such a belief showed "a disconnect bordering on hysteria ... not only are they woefully ignorant of recent Jewish history but have little concept of what real antisemitism is".[*]

Much of the attack on Labour has been in the name of racism, with Jews as one target. But many Zionists, some of them taking part in the daily media attacks, seem concerned only with antisemitism, while expressing support for bigoted views about other groups, most notably the Palestinians[†] Sacks himself extended a "personal invitation" to Diaspora Jews to join him on a trip to Israel which included "leading" the March of the Flags on Jerusalem Day. This marked the anniversary of Israel's capture of Jerusalem, and marchers vandalized shops in Jerusalem's Muslim Quarter while chanting 'Death to Arabs'. But Sacks made no comment about whether such activities make Palestinians who have lived in Jerusalem for centuries ask "Is this country safe to bring up our children?"

And it is equally difficult to take seriously Sacks' comparison of Corbyn's remarks to Enoch Powell's 'rivers of blood' speech,

---

[*] https://www.haaretz.com/jewish/.premium-disturbing-trend-among-u-k-jews-1.5360394

[†] See Appendix 2

when he (Sacks) wrote in 2017 that one of his 'best books of the year' was one by an author called Douglas K. Walker which quoted favourably Enoch Powell's speech and said that the demographic consequences of Muslim migration would destroy white, Christian Europe.

The subtitle of this book is "How the British media failed their public" and it is arranged as follows:

Introductory material providing some historical background to the issues, and a few examples of how the story believed by many Jews and others of how Israel came about is shaped by a series of lies transmitted by Israel and its supporters.

Personal accounts of the ways in which critics of Israel and Zionism have been hounded and smeared by an antisemitism industry, who, in the words of one of the contributors, have 'weaponised' antisemitism.

Key documents, articles and, in one case, transcripts of a television series, which have shown a side of the story which has rarely been featured in the mainstream media which have often just reprinted with little comment the outpourings of several organisations claiming to represent British Jews. By providing chapter and verse, these documents fill in details missing from mass media coverage which show how much of what we read in the headlines is plain wrong.

In particular, they show that:

- The IHRA 'definition' of antisemitism is a slipshod, unenforceable and sometimes counterproductive statement, accompanied by clauses which are clearly designed to suppress criticism of Israel rather than hatred of Jews.

- There have been no significant examples of antisemitism, defined as 'hatred of Jews as a people', among senior figures in the Labour Party.

- When complaints of antisemitism are brought forward by Zionists and generate newspaper headlines, on being officially investigated they are often rejected, with evidence shown to be fabricated, months after harmful publicity.

- When meetings are organised which are critical of Israel, there are organised attempts to define such meetings as antisemitic and get them banned.

- Many of the statistics about antisemitism which are feature widely in headlines and in statements of Jewish organisations, are gathered by methods which have little or no statistical rigour and are designed to create a climate of fear among Jews.

- The so-called Compliance Committee of the Labour Party which claims to investigate and adjudicate on claims of antisemitism is a kangaroo court, run by someone who has been described as the "Witchfinder-General". Complaints which are often half-baked and erroneous, and describe what are valid criticisms of Israel are pursued in detail, wasting time and money, sometimes to find there is no substance in them.

I hope the reader will excuse some repetition as different people write about this period. I find that, within moderation, reading different accounts of the same events helps to make them stick in the mind, particularly when they are as shocking as some of the events of the Antisemitism Wars.

It is worth drawing the attention of the reader to two further points:

Although, by definition, antisemitism is hatred of Jews, some Jews have themselves been accused of antisemitism because of their criticism of Israel – another English irony?

Many Jews are sickened by what Israel does and by the actions of groups which claim to represent the whole Jewish community, but they don't have the ear of the media or are ignored or insulted by the Zionists.

Confirmation that the UK media have failed their public came in late September 2018, in a report by the Media Reform Coalition, entitled Labour, Antisemitism and the News. The report is summarised in Appendix 3, p. 247, where there is a link to the full report. The Guardian and the BBC turn out to be among the worst purveyors of biased and inaccurate reports.

At the risk of telling readers things they already know, I will give some examples in this chapter of events, decisions, and actions which are often at the heart of the opposition of many of us to the creation and maintenance of the state of Israel. The actions and statements of Zionists up to 1948, and the state of Israel since then, have been politically unjust, deliberately mendacious, and destructive of the culture, society, property and lives of a people, Palestinians, who have as much, if not more, right to a state of their own as the Jews of the world.

This chapter is far from comprehensive since much of the story is covered in my two books *Palestine: A Personal History*, and *A Modest Proposal... to Solve the Palestine-Israel Conflict*.

In the first half of the 20th century, a movement – political Zionism – initiated by European Jews set out to persuade British statesmen that a Jewish state should be established in the small Arab territory, then part of the Ottoman Empire, known as Palestine, a name used for this area between 450 BC and 1948 AD.

At the time this idea was mooted, the population of Palestine was made up of about 632,000 Arabs and 32,000 Jews, with the Arabs therefore forming about 95% of the population. One of the first of many lies used by the Zionists to persuade the British and others that the land should be made into a Jewish state was that it was an 'empty' land. This myth, still propagated on many Jewish websites, was based on no evidence at all, other than the accounts of travellers like Mark Twain, who, in his book *The Innocents Abroad*, published in 1869, is quoted by Zionists as saying:

There is not a solitary village throughout its whole extent [valley of Jezreel] – not for 30 miles in either direction... One may ride ten miles hereabouts and not see ten human beings. ... For the sort of solitude to make one dreary, come to Galilee ... Nazareth is forlorn ... Jericho lies a moldering ruin ... Bethlehem and Bethany, in their poverty and humiliation... untenanted by any living creature...A desolate country whose soil is rich enough, but is given over wholly to weeds ... a silent, mournful expanse ... a desolation ... We never saw a human being on the whole route ... Hardly a tree or shrub anywhere. Even the olive tree and the cactus, those fast friends of a worthless soil had almost deserted the country ... Of all the lands there are for dismal scenery Palestine must be the prince. The hills barren and dull, the valleys unsightly deserts [inhabited by] swarms of beggars with ghastly sores and malformations. Palestine sits in sackcloth and ashes ... desolate and unlovely ... [Mark Twain, *The Innocents Abroad*, 1867][1]

It sounds pretty conclusive, doesn't it, if you are happy to take the word of a penny-a-word humorous journalist? The place was clearly entirely empty of people, and as barren as the Sahara. But here is a description written at about the same time and describing the same place:

Here were evidences of cultivation, an acre or two of rich soil studded with last season's dead corn-stalks of the thickness of your thumb and very wide apart. ... It was a thrilling spectacle. ... The view presented from its highest peak was almost beautiful. Below was the broad, level plain of Esdraelon, checkered with fields like a chess-board, and full as smooth and level, seemingly dotted about its borders with white, compact villages, and faintly penciled, far and near, with the curving lines of roads and trails. When it is robed in the fresh verdure of spring, it must form a charming picture, even by itself. Nazareth is wonderfully interesting... We found here a grove of lemon trees -- cool, shady, hung with fruit. ... It *was* beautiful. ...We lunched, rested, chatted, smoked our pipes an hour, and then mounted and moved on. The narrow canon in which Nablous, or Shechem, is situated, is under high cultivation, and the soil is exceedingly black and fertile. It is well watered, and its affluent vegetation gains effect by contrast with the barren hills that tower on either side. We came finally to the noble grove of orange-trees in which the Oriental city of Jaffa lies buried; we

passed through the walls, and rode again down narrow streets ...
Sometimes, in the glens, we came upon luxuriant orchards of figs,
apricots, pomegranates, and such things...

So, who are we to believe? Mark Twain or ... Mark Twain? Because, of course, both extracts come from the same book, pieced together from across many pages. The ellipses in the first quote reveal what a selective patchwork it is, and the idea that either can be taken seriously as a demographic and economic account of Palestine in the middle of the 19th century is an example of how desperate Zionists have been to make a silk purse out of a sow's ear, knowing that most of their target audience will already be receptive to an account of Palestine as empty, barren and waiting for the talents of the Jews to bring it to life.

Surprising as it may sound, it was data like these, presented by the leading political Zionist at the time, Chaim Weizmann, a Russian chemist, that persuaded Arthur Balfour, then foreign secretary and David Lloyd George, prime minister, to commit Britain to the task of handing Palestine over to "the Jews of the world." The reason I put that phrase in quotes is because there is no such entity. Now, I am not of course saying, as many Zionists, including Golda Meir, have said of the Palestinians, that the Jews don't exist. There are people all over the world who define themselves as Jews. What I am saying is that the closer you look at how Jews define themselves the more confusing the picture becomes and the more difficult it is to find any common characteristic, other than self-definition. This may be OK for a social group but is a very shaky basis for defining a nation or a people which claims the same rights as other nations or peoples round the world.

Let's look at what Jews might be, to qualify for a state of their own:

Are they ethnically related? There is little evidence that all Jews share the same genetic heritage, one definition of ethnicity. In fact, there is strong evidence from genetic studies that some Jews are indistinguishable from Palestinian Arabs. But many other

Jews have no significant Middle Eastern genes but instead show an origin in Central Asia connected with the kingdom of the Khazars, famous for having converted *en masse* to Judaism in the 8th century AD. So in the oft-used phrase "the right of return", who is returning where, and why? Many Ashkenazi Jews, if they have a right to return anywhere after 900 years, a pretty dubious claim anyway, should be boarding planes to Rostov-on-Don in Russia, and heading a few hundred miles south. If anyone has a right of return to what is now Israel, it is the descendants of the 750,000 Palestinians who were expelled when the UN, persuaded by American Zionists, handed over much of Palestine to be transformed into a Jewish state.

How about religion? Only 38% of Jews around the world consider themselves religious.* In fact, they are among the least observant of people polled. What, then, links the rest?

Often when questioned, a Jewish person will say 'culture', a collection of practices which may include a shared language, and shared 'rites of passage' (most Jews will circumcise their male babies, many will make their children go through bar- or batmitzvahs, without believing in Judaism) and so on).

But British, Americans, Canadians, Australians and New Zealanders share a common culture, as do football fans round the world, Harry Potter enthusiasts, and people who do crosswords, but they never argue for being allowed to have a land of their own on someone else's territory. Interestingly – and I think this is very relevant to the antisemitism issue – many Jews who have no religious ties feel a strong bond with Israel. Not strong enough to make them go and live there, but strong enough to act as some kind of focus for their social activities, charitable giving, and media habits. I would say that, in their minds, anyone attacking Israel is attacking their own 'Jewishness' since they associate so strongly

---

* https://www.haaretz.com/jewish/jews-least-observant-int-l-poll-finds-1.5287579

with the state and everything it says about its own legitimacy, right down to the concept of 'the chosen people'. The paradox is that even those who claim no religious affiliation are happy to benefit from the myth that the God they don't believe in gave Palestine to the Jews. And for the religious Jews, the contradictory writings of their bible provide a cast-iron justification for injustice which far outweighs the whole apparatus of modern legislation, definitions of statehood or the Geneva Convention. However, of course, they pick and choose which bits of the bible to believe and which to ignore. Israel's treatment of the Palestinians suggests that they have decided to ignore Proverbs 22, verse 8-9:

> Whoever sows injustice reaps calamity,
> and the rod they wield in fury will be broken.
> The generous will themselves be blessed,
> for they share their food with the poor.

Whether or not you are a Zionist, think for a moment of what the Palestinians must have felt after World War 1, when the British government said: "We are planning to promote the immigration of certain citizens of Britain, Germany, Russia, and the Americas into your country until there are so many that they will form the majority and Palestine will no longer be a country for Palestinians." Certainly, my father's family had great difficulty initially in taking the whole thing seriously. They could trace their ancestors in Palestine back hundreds of years, if not further, and the idea that a Russian Jew, say, who had never set foot in the land and whose family had no connections with it, could take a ship to Haifa, disembark and be given a plot of land and Palestinian citizenship seemed laughable.

But their incredulity was misguided. Slowly but surely, throughout the 1930s and 1940s Zionists set up a parallel administration to the British, insisted on privileges not granted to the Arabs, including what was effectively a standing army, and used terrorism to attack the British, Arabs and even Jews who disagreed with them.

By 1948, the Zionist argument that the Arab state of Palestine should be made into a Jewish state (ideally all of it but they reluctantly accepted the idea of partition), using the Holocaust as an extra justification, had managed to influence enough members of the United Nations, some of whom actually voted against their original stance, because they were bribed or threatened by American Jews and members of the US State Department.

The 1948 Arab-Israeli War ensued, in which Israel determined to acquire the area assigned to the Palestinian Arabs, since it had always said it wanted all of Palestine as a Jewish state. The paltry efforts made by the other Arab states to come to the aid of Palestinians, in the face of a well-organised Israeli army, and weapons which had been smuggled into Palestine, have usually been described ever since by Zionists as the Arabs "trying to push the Jews into the sea." In fact, the intention of the Arab armies was to prevent the Israeli army taking more Palestinian land and so they only went as far as the UN-determined borders, and for the most part they did not enter the areas assigned to Israel. In fact if anyone pushed anyone into the sea, it was the Israeli army in the Arab port of Jaffa, leaving no outlet for the Arab inhabitants to escape but the sea. But truth is the first casualty of war, particularly when lying has become an official policy in Israel. As former terrorist and prime minister, Yitzhak Shamir, declared openly "It is permissible to lie for the sake of the Land of Israel."[*]

Much of what I have written above, and much more that I could write, about the formation of Israel and its subsequent takeover of Palestinian land and persecution of the Palestinians who remain, is taken by many Jews who know little or nothing about the history of the Middle East to be disguised or even undisguised antisemitism. As we will see, many Jews who protest at the telling by people like me of the story of the mistreatment

---

[*] Akiva Eldar, *Haaretz*, November 24, 2003

of the Palestinians in the past and today cannot believe much of what they read, and assume therefore that such accounts are motivated by antisemitism. This is not helped by Israel's own deliberate efforts to blur the edges between the concept of Jews and the idea of Israel itself. Indeed, as the years go by, Israel is more strident in its protests that Israel must be seen as 'the Jewish state', even though its population is 20% Palestinian Arab. The so-called 'Basic Law' passed in July 2018 just reinforces that. If Israel calls itself the Jewish state, why can its actions not be called 'Jewish actions'? It is reaching the point where, even to describe Israel and its supporters as 'Zionists' is being redefined deliberately, helped by the clauses in the IHRA 'definition', as antisemitic. The Al-Jazeera documentary series *The Lobby* has several examples of where supporters of Israel are heard to says with a straight face that someone who has made an anti-Zionist remark is thereby demonstrating their antisemitism

Finally, it is not pointed out often enough how illogical it would be for any intelligent person to hate "all Jews" or "all blacks" or "all Muslims". The human phenotype is so varied, even when there are large genetic similarities – as there are not among Jews – that anyone who could consider an entire group of millions of people deserving of his hatred is clearly deranged or just very stupid. Conversely, I reserve the right to hate, or at least dislike, a whole range of types of people, from CEOs who get multimillion pound payouts for incompetence, or politicians who call for the UK to leave the EEC, people who kill animals for pleasure, to individuals who can't tell the difference between 'may' and 'might', and begin their sentences with 'So.' Any of these might also be Jews, but I would not be antipathetic to them *because of* their Jewishness.

It might be worth considering what real antisemitism might look like. I think many readers would accept that remarks like the following directed at Jews would show strong evidence of antisemitic racism:

"The Jews are like crocodiles, the more you give them meat, they want more."

"[The Jews are] beasts walking on two legs."

"The Jews would be crushed like grasshoppers ... heads smashed against the boulders and walls."

"There was no such thing as Jews, they never existed

"We have to kill all the Jews unless they are resigned to live here as slaves."

"We must use terror, assassination, intimidation, land confiscation, and the cutting of all social services to [get rid of the] Jewish population."

"One million Jews are not worth an Arab fingernail."

In fact, I have taken examples of anti-*Palestinian* bigotry spoken or written by public figures in Israel or the Jewish diaspora, and substituted the word 'Jews' where they said 'Palestinians'. (If you want to see the original quotes and their sources, they are in Appendix 1.)

It may seem that I am making a trivial point here but I think it hints at a great unexplored area – the way in which Israel's actions against Palestinians are motivated by racism. I will finish with a story which I think shows the tip of an iceberg of prejudice which lurks beneath the surface of Israeli society. A friend of mine – we'll call him Aharon – an Israeli who believes in reconciliation between Palestinians and Israelis, was once talking to another Israeli who knew that Aharon was friendly with a lot of Palestinians. "Tell me, Aharon," the man said, "Have you ever seen a Palestinian hug his children?"

Such a depth of ignorance, and a willingness to believe such an extraordinary lie about people who, genetically and linguistically, are his neighbours, shows the depth of the abyss which people seeking peace have to jump over.

PART 2
ON THE RECEIVING END

This section features first person narratives from people who have been persecuted for their views by the Zionist lobby in the U.K., starting with an account by me.

I am including a personal experience I had thirty-five years ago at the hands of the pro-Israel lobby in the UK because it shows two things:

First, the current Antisemitism Wars are nothing new in style and content, only in the intensity with which they have been fought. The issue is the same as it always has been – an attempt to suppress anyone who tries to tell truth to power, when the truth is about the rise of Israel and how that has been achieved, and the power is a state, Israel, which has no interest in truth, and its major supporter on the world stage, the USA.

Tony Greenstein:

No one has been a closer observer and a more assiduous blogger on the Antisemitism Wars than Tony Greenstein. He has been a member of the Labour Party – when permitted – and therefore his account of his own encounters with the antisemitism industry illuminates the broader picture of the onslaught on the Labour Party, and he is well-placed to suggest reasons, other than actual antisemitism, for why it is seen as so important to attack Jeremy Corbyn at every turn, at a time when Labour support is increasing.

Karl Sabbagh:

In 1982, I wrote an article about an atrocity committed in a Palestinian Arab village by the Jewish Irgun and Stern Gang, led by a man called Menachem Begin, in the month before the formation of the state of Israel. At the time I wrote the article, Begin was prime minister of Israel. The aftermath of the article – the abuse I and the editor received, and the organised nature of the protests – bear uncanny similarities to stories told about much more recent attempts to use the antisemitism smear, and that is why I think the story bears retelling today.

Thomas Suárez:

Suárez is an author who wrote a well-researched book on Jewish terror in Palestine during the 1940s[*]. I'm afraid I have to say 'Jewish' because all the people who committed the crimes Suárez describes in his book were Jews and claim to be doing it on behalf of the Jewish people. As often happens when a new book comes out, the author is invited to talk about the book at meetings and, he hopes, sell copies of the book. Suárez describes what happened when he tried to do just that. Anyone who believes that using the full IHRA 'definition' will not threaten freedom of speech in this country will be shocked by Suárez' narrative and realise that this is exactly what the 'definition' is intended to achieve.

Cyril Chilson:

Cyril Chilson is an academic at Oxford University and an ex-Israeli who served as a Captain in the Israeli army. His parents were both holocaust survivors, including his mother who was in Auschwitz concentration camp. His father only just escaped the Nazi invasion of Soviet-occupied Poland and went on to fight in the Soviet army.

He describes how and why he was expelled for two years by the Labour Party on March 20th 2018, as part of its fight against 'antisemitism' in the Party. It is a revealing inside look at how self-appointed, inexperienced and ignorant Party officials wield power within the Labour Party.

---

[*] Thomas Suárez, *State of Terror*, Skyscraper Publications, 2016

2

The story so far...
Tony Greenstein

After an absence of nearly a quarter of a century, I decided to rejoin the Labour Party in October 2015 in the wake of Jeremy Corbyn's election as leader of the Labour Party the previous September. I had already registered as a Labour supporter in July and voted, only to be deregistered and have my vote fished out of the electronic ballot box as Labour's General Secretary, Iain McNicol carried out a purge of thousands of Corbyn supporters.

On a sunny spring day in March 2016 I opened a letter from the Labour Party. How nice, I thought, for them to send new members a welcome letter. However I was soon disillusioned. It was a letter from John Stolliday, Head of the National Constitutional Committee, or Compliance Unit, as it is better known, informing me that I had been suspended. The letter read:

> 'Allegations that you may have been involved in a breach of Labour Party rules have been brought to the attention of national officers of the Party. These allegations relate to comments you are alleged to have made which will be investigated under 2.1.B of the party's rules'

Being none the wiser as to what these comments might be, I phoned and emailed the Labour Party seeking clarification. None however was forthcoming. Two weeks later all became clear after details of my case were leaked to the *Times* and the *Telegraph*. The *Telegraph* article of 2nd April 2016 read *'Corbyn told to 'exorcise' antisemitism in his party.'* The *Times* was even blunter: *'Labour welcomes back blogger who compares Israelis to Nazis.'* Amongst my crimes was to have compared Israel's marriage laws to the Nazi's Nuremberg laws. In fact I was simply quoting from Hannah Arendt's book *Eichman in Jerusalem: The Banality of Evil* which commented on the hypocrisy of the Prosecution's denunciation of the Nazis' marriage laws which prevented Jews and 'Aryans' from marrying.

I had been caught up in the Zionist campaign alleging that the Labour Party was 'riddled' with antisemitism. The nature of this 'antisemitism' was made clear in the *Telegraph* article which referred to an article by Jonathan Arkush, President of the Board of Deputies of British Jews. Arkush alleged that Corbyn had met with 'real dyed-in-the-wool antisemites, including representatives of Hamas and Hezbollah.'

It made sense of course. If the Labour Party was overrun with antisemites, clearly they needed to start expelling Jewish anti-zionists!

When Jeremy Corbyn stood for the leadership of the Labour Party he had to 'borrow' the nominations of Labour MPs who weren't his supporters but who believed that the Left should be represented in the contest. No one in their wildest dreams believed that Corbyn stood a chance of being elected. Under the previous leader Ed Miliband, the electoral system had been changed in order to ensure that the Left could never triumph in such an election.

The theory was that swamping the electoral rolls with ordinary voters would marginalise the Left and its dedicated band of activists. Anyone could register as a Labour Party supporter for a paltry £3 and get a vote. New Labour believed that the Labour Party needed to become like the Democratic Party in the United States where anyone can register as a supporter. The Right were convinced by their own propaganda that the Left were unpopular amongst the wider electorate who preferred 'moderates' such as themselves.

As it became clear over the summer that Corbyn was going to win, panic set in amongst Labour MPs. Many of them, such as John Mann and Barry Shearer, sought to have the whole election annulled on the grounds that Labour had been 'infiltrated' by 57 varieties of Trotskyists, Stalinists and malcontents. However, for interim leader Harriet Harman to cancel the election because the 'wrong' candidate was in danger of winning was a step too far even for the Labour Right. When the election result was declared, Corbyn had won a decisive majority in all sections of the party – existing members, registered supporters and trade union affiliated members. The idea that half a million Trotskyists had become registered supporters was seen for what it was, the invention of desperate people who didn't understand why their prescriptions were unpopular and why their mentor Tony Blair was discredited.

However, it wasn't just amongst Labour MPs that panic set in. Alarm bells must have been ringing all the way from CIA HQ in Langley Virginia to the Israel military's HQ in Kirya, Tel Aviv. The United Kingdom is the United State's closest ally in Europe, something usually expressed as the 'special relationship.' The Labour Party is the UK's alternative party of government. Jeremy Corbyn's whole political career, from President of the Stop the War Coalition to Patron of the Palestine Solidarity Campaign, has been marked by opposition to United States foreign policy and support for the Palestinians. Put quite simply, Corbyn was unacceptable to the British, American and Israeli political establishment. Democracy has its limits and those limits had been reached with Corbyn's election.

As former CIA case officer Phil Agee demonstrated in *Inside the Company,* the CIA's very existence is predicated on the assumption that the United States has the right, if not the duty, to interfere in the internal affairs of other countries where US interests are perceived as threatened. Iran, Guatemala, Chile and Argentina are just a few of the states in which the CIA has practised its talents. What possible reason would there be for the US not intervening in the affairs of its closest ally if a perceived enemy was in danger of becoming Prime Minister?

What we do know, from Al Jazeera's investigative programmes, *The Lobby*,* broadcast in January 2017, is that the Israeli Embassy was heavily involved with Labour Friends of Israel and the Jewish Labour Movement [JLM] in waging war against Jeremy Corbyn.

Israeli agent Shai Masot, who was an employee of Israel's Ministry of Strategic Affairs, which was set up with a $50 million slush fund to wage war against BDS (Boycott, Divestment, and Sanctions), was caught on camera plotting how he might bring down members of the British government, such as Sir Alan Duncan, who was seen as unsympathetic to Israel. The glimpse that Al Jazeera gave us of the activities of Israeli Ambassador Mark Regev showed that he was active in the false antisemitism campaign being waged in the Labour Party. We also saw Joan Ryan, Chair of Labour Friends of Israel, inventing allegations that a Labour Party delegate Jean Fitzpatrick, had spoken about Jewish influence in banking and was therefore antisemitic.

It beggars belief that the US Embassy is not heavily involved in helping to co-ordinate the 'antisemitism' campaign inside the Labour Party. We know from Wikileaks that one key actor, Ruth Smeeth MP, was considered an asset by the US Embassy. Smeeth was the instigator of the witch hunt and expulsion of black activist Marc Wadsworth.

It should be no surprise that 'antisemitism' has been chosen as the weapon with which to attack Jeremy Corbyn. It was carefully chosen to cause maximum confusion amongst its opponents. Most people on the left are horrified by the thought that they are antisemitic. Memories of the Nazi Holocaust and the murder of 6 million Jews are still vivid.

It is the Left which has, through organisations such as the Anti-Nazi League and Anti-Fascist Action, fought against any resurgence

---

* See Documents: The Lobby, pp. 139-193

of neo-Nazism in this country. The Left has been particular active in combating groups such as the National Front and British National Party. The accusation of 'antisemitism' is designed to be hurtful and demoralising. The choice of antisemitism made sense because it divided and confused the very people who backed Corbyn.

It also gave the Right of the Labour Party a sense of a moral purpose. They could pose as anti-racists rather than as supporters of the American war machine. Supporting austerity and cuts to benefits or the NHS are not quite as popular in the Labour Party as being seen to oppose racism. Of course the Right and the Zionists could have attacked Corbyn for his financial profligacy in wanting to abolish student fees, but this would not have sown divisions amongst Corbyn supporters.

'Antisemitism' was thus an ideal weapon in the battle to remove Corbyn. The question was how to employ it to maximum effect. The first task was to ensure that the press, not least the liberal press was onside. This meant, above all, the *Guardian*.

Most Labour Party supporters don't read the *Daily Mail, Express, Telegraph* or *Times* but they do read the *Guardian*, which until recently was the house paper of the left intelligentsia. The naked opportunism of the right-wing press in attacking Corbyn's 'antisemitism' is clear to most people on the left. When the *Daily Mail* and *Sun* condemn 'antisemitism' at the same time as they employ 'journalists' such as Katie Hopkins, famous for calling refugees 'cockroaches', people have difficulty taking their opposition to antisemitism seriously.

We have the absurdity of the *Daily Mail*, the paper which in the 1930's supported the Nazis and which campaigned against the admission of Jewish refugees from Nazi Germany, protesting about 'antisemitism'. It is the same paper which attacked Ed Miliband's Marxist father, Ralph, as an alien who hated his country and which attacked Miliband, Labour's first Jewish leader, for not being able to eat a bacon sandwich properly. The *Sun*, which has been in the forefront of condemning Corbyn for 'antisemitism', had no hesitation in attacking George Soros, as a 'puppet master' for financing the opposition to Brexit, thus employing all the old antisemitic stereotypes of Jewish financiers seeking to manipulate and control the political process.

It is the *Guardian* though under Jonathan Freedland, a senior editor, which has been the backbone of the antisemitism campaign. Freedland, a *Jewish Chronicle* columnist, who Corbyn labelled as 'subliminally nasty' has penned numerous articles alleging that the Labour Party is antisemitic. His article *Yes, Jews are angry – because Labour hasn't listened or shown any empathy*[2], was in defence of the International Holocaust Remembrance Alliance definition of antisemitism. In response to the allegation that the IHRA conflates antisemitism and anti-zionism Freedland wrote that 'This [suggestion] makes plenty of Jews want to slam their heads on their desks in frustration.' According to Freedland the IHRA allows people to 'say everything THE state of Israel has done since its birth has been racist. All it prohibits is branding as a racist endeavour 'A state of Israel.'''

This assertion is a good example of the disingenuousness of those behind the false antisemitism campaign. No sooner had the Labour Party adopted the full IHRA definition at its meeting in September, coupled with a free speech caveat that this would not prevent criticism of Israel, than Israel's propagandists immediately began complaining. Margaret Hodge, the MP who had described Corbyn as 'a fucking racist and antisemite' said it was "an unnecessary qualification" and would "dilute" the adoption of the IHRA's eleven examples of 'antisemitism', seven of which refer to Israel. Simon Johnson, CEO of the Jewish Leadership Council said the free speech caveat "drives a coach and horses" through the IHRA definition. Labour Friends of Israel director Jennifer Gerber called the caveat an "appalling" measure which "totally undermines the other examples the party has supposedly just adopted." Clearly Freedland's friends have engaged in self harm to no useful purpose.

The sheer volume of articles and propaganda relating to Labour's 'antisemitism' strongly suggest that there is a certain level of co-ordination behind what is happening. From 1965 to 1975 the CIA ran its own news service in this and other countries called *Forum World Features*. It employed journalists such as the BBC's John Tusa and its purpose was to ensure that the media was on message when it came to the Vietnam War and the CIA sponsored coup in Chile. We can be sure that the intelligence agencies have been up to their ears in supplying journalists with fake copy.

In years to come, journalists and researchers will no doubt discover, via the Freedom of Information requests and whistleblowers, just how this campaign was organized. One thing, however, is for certain. The campaign is not spontaneous and it is not based on any actual or real antisemitism.

The 'antisemitism' campaign began even before Jeremy Corbyn was elected Leader. On August 7th 2015 the *Daily Mail* ran an article which alleged that Paul Eisen, the British director of the group *Deir Yassin Remembered*, named after a Palestinian village of that name which the Zionist militias wiped out in 1948, was a Holocaust denier and that Jeremy Corbyn had attended some of DYR's fundraising events before it was realised just who Eisen was. Also attending these concerts were liberal Jewish rabbis and Gerald Kaufman MP. Indeed the 2013 concert was held in a liberal Jewish synagogue.

What the *Mail* really meant to say was that Corbyn was indifferent if not sympathetic to Holocaust denial. However libel laws prevent such allegations. The *Mail* therefore had to be content with an article relying on the tried and trusted McCarthyite technique of guilt-by-association.

The *Jewish Chronicle* followed this up on August 18th with an article alleging that Corbyn had attended an event hosted by Eisen in 2013. In fact there is considerable doubt whether the event of 2013 was even staged by DYR. The *Jewish Chronicle* continued to pursue this line of attack up until the time that Corbyn was elected Leader on September 12th.

As the shock of Corbyn's election subsided so too did the antisemitism campaign. Clearly those who had given it a trial run were sitting back and rethinking tactics. The first indication of a renewal of the campaign came when Sir Gerald Kaufman, Father of the House of Common, unwisely suggested that it was 'Jewish money' that had influenced the Conservatives into supporting Israel.[3] This became the first major 'antisemitism' cause célèbre. Gerald apologised for any offence caused and he was duly reprimanded

The allegations of antisemitism were false. The term 'Jewish money' is widely used by Jewish people themselves as a boast about how influential they are today. I did a search in the *Jewish Chronicle* archives and came up with 600 examples of the use of this phrase. Even one of Kaufman's main critics, *Jewish Chronicle* columnist Geoffrey Alderman, had used the same phrase twice within one article.[4]

The Kaufman affair quickly died down. For one thing Gerald Kaufman had long been a critic of Jeremy Corbyn. He had almost certainly not voted for him as leader. Only the rabid Campaign Against Antisemitism, a group formed in August 2014 at the height of Operation Protective Edge, the 2014 Israeli onslaught on Gaza, which specializes in accusations of antisemitism against supporters of the Palestinians, had waged a campaign against Kaufman. The CAA, a registered charity, has played a significant role in the anti-Corbyn campaign. Almost certainly funded by the Israeli state, the CAA is on the far-Right of the Zionist movement.[*]

On its website it published no fewer than 27 articles attacking Kaufman. When he died in February 2017, the CAA published a final article 'Sir Gerald Kaufman MP's Words Have Left A Rotting Stain On Our Institutions'.[5]

---

[*] See *Exposing the Vigilantes*, pp. 115-138

There was then a further hiatus until all hell broke loose in January 2017 with the news that the Chair of the Labour Club at Oxford University, Alex Chalmers, had resigned claiming 'antisemitism'. When one dug a little deeper it transpired that the real reason for Chalmer's resignation had nothing to do with 'antisemitism' and everything to do with Oxford University Labour Club endorsing Israel Apartheid Week.

Instead of calling this out for what it was and robustly rejecting the suggestion that OULC was a hotbed of 'antisemitism' Jeremy Corbyn set up an Inquiry under Baroness Janet Royall. When Royall eventually reported she concluded that 'I do not believe that that there is institutional antisemitism within OULC.'[6] However this was not for want of trying. As Royall confessed to the JLM 'I know that you will share my disappointment and frustration that the main headline coming out of my inquiry is that there is no institutional Antisemitism in Oxford University Labour Club.'

Royall, who had previously visited Israel as part of a Labour Friends of Israel delegation, had clearly done her best to find antisemitism. What kind of person would confess to being '*disappointed*' that they had not found evidence of institutional antisemitism? She should have been delighted with her findings.

In an article for *Electronic Intifada*, 'How Israel lobby manufactured UK Labour Party's antisemitism crisis' Asa Winstanley revealed that Alex Chalmers had been an intern for BICOM, the main Israeli propaganda organization in Britain.[7]

The whole affair of OULC had been a setup from the start, but what happened there set the stage for Jeremy Corbyn's disastrous handling of the false antisemitism crisis. By agreeing so easily to the Royall Inquiry, and by accepting without question the legitimacy of the accusations of antisemitism, Corbyn had made a rod for his own back. Corbyn's behaviour gave the green light for further bogus accusations of antisemitism to be made.

Corbyn's response to the accusations of antisemitism was to repeat that he wasn't an antisemite, which was of course true.

What he didn't seem to understand, though, was that when his Zionist opponents used the term 'antisemitism' they were not talking about hatred of Jews but hatred of Zionism. In other words they were talking past each other.

If Corbyn had stood up to his accusers from the beginning then he would have shot this fox. To a very large extent Corbyn has been the author of his own misfortunes. All he needed to have done was to say that yes, he condemned antisemitism but he *also* condemned those who weaponised antisemitism for their own political advantage. He could also have noted how supporters of Israel repeatedly accuse opponents of Zionism of 'antisemitism'. It was not as if Corbyn was unaware of this. One of his Jewish anti-Zionist friends, the late Mike Marqusee, had written a book about this, *If I Am Not For Myself.*

Jeremy Corbyn of all people should have understood what was happening. He has been involved in Palestine solidarity politics for over 30 years. He cannot be unaware of the fact that the standard go-to accusation of Zionism is to accuse their opponents of 'antisemitism'. There cannot be a Palestine solidarity supporter in the country who hasn't been accused of antisemitism. This is entirely understandable. If you have to defend the theft of land, the demolition of homes, the allocation of 93% of Israeli land to Jews only, coupled with torture, administrative detention and abuse of children, then it is much easier to cry 'antisemitism'.

Prominent Zionists like the Chief Rabbi Ephraim Mirvis, Mick Davies and Alan Dershowitz don't even bother to hide their belief that anti-Zionism equals antisemitism. There really is no excuse for Corbyn's disastrous handling of the antisemitism campaign.

Although Jeremy Corbyn has many good qualities, including a hatred of oppression, a desire to see an end to war, and an instinctive hatred of racism and austerity and those who would make the poor pay for the failures of capitalism, he lacks the determination to face down his enemies. Instead of standing up to his Zionist enemies and assessing why this was happening, he simply repeated like an incantation the fact that he wasn't an antisemite.

Corbyn is surrounded with advisers yet the advice he seems to have received has verged on the disastrous. This was seen very early in the leadership campaign when he was the subject of accusations that he was a 'friend of terrorists'. In particular at one meeting which he chaired he called the representatives of Hamas and Hezbollah his 'friends'. Of course no one seriously believed that they were his personal friends but this was used as a stick to beat him with. There was one particularly angry interview on *Channel 4 News* about this with Krishna Guru Murthi.[8] Corbyn found it difficult to explain that he was engaging in a simple matter of courtesy. What he could and should have said was what he had previously said, namely that Hamas and Hezbollah were not 'terrorist' organisations but groups that represented their own people. He could also have compared these groups to the ANC who had also been called 'terrorists' by Thatcher and Reagan. Every anti-colonial political movement has been called terrorist by the colonial power.

The affair of OULC set the antisemitism hare running. On March 18th I was suspended from the Labour Party and in May Jackie Walker, the black Vice-Chair of Momentum, was also suspended. Jackie's offence had been to refer, in a private Facebook discussion, to Jews as 'the chief financiers of the sugar and slave trade...' The Israeli Advocacy Movement had broken into her conversation and on the basis of omitting one word, Jackie was suspended. As a result of the furore which greeted her suspension, Jackie was reinstated after three weeks.

At the end of April, Ken Livingstone, the former leader of the Greater London Authority, in the course of an interview with Vanessa Feltz on 28th April 2016,[9] remarked that Hitler had supported Zionism as a means of ridding Germany of its Jews. Livingstone's comments, which referred to the Nazi-Zionist trade agreement Ha'avara, were correct. In August 1933 the Nazis and the Zionist Organisation concluded an agreement which meant that the wealth of German Jews, which the Nazis had frozen, could be used in Palestine to buy German industrial goods and equipment. This would increase German exports and also benefit the Zionist economy. It resulted in 60% of capital investment in the Zionist economy between 1933 and 1939 coming from Nazi Germany.[10] It also destroyed the international Jewish boycott of Nazi Germany which had threatened the very existence of the Nazi regime. The Zionist movement had one concern. Saving the wealth of Germany's Jews. The agreement itself saved hardly any Jews.

Livingstone was subject to an enormous campaign of denigration for telling the truth about the record of the Zionist movement in the 1930's. This included being confronted by a loud mouthed bully, John Mann MP, in a staged confrontation outside the BBC Westminster studios.[11] After Livingston was suspended for a year, the previous General Secretary Iain McNicol, as his last act of retribution, extended the suspension indefinitely. Livingstone was forced into resigning after a call for his expulsion on television by Baroness Chakrabarti. My understanding is that Livingstone agreed to resign after a personal request to this effect was made by Corbyn. However, throwing supporters like Livingstone to the wolves has not helped Corbyn quite the opposite. Livingstone was a valuable ally.

Livingstone had been suspended in the course of defending Labour MP Naz Shah who had, during Israel's attack on Gaza in 2014, joked that the problem of Israel's aggressive behaviour would be solved if Israel was moved to the territory of its main benefactor the United States. This was a humorous remark, a joke, which no one with a sense of humour could possibly mistake for a serious proposition. What Naz Shah was doing was using the professed love that United States' politicians have for Israel and saying 'why don't you make Israel into your 51st state.' Naz accompanied this meme with a map of Israel inside the United States, a map incidentally that derived from the site of the Jewish Virtual Library, which Israel's Yad Vashem sponsors. Everyone understood perfectly well that this was a joke, with the possible exception of Labour's humourless bureaucrats. It was an imaginary solution to the very real problem of Israel's addiction to war and mass murder. The Zionists transformed it into Jews being 'transported' to the concentration camps because they imagine themselves as Jewish victims of the Palestinians whose sole intention is to repeat the Holocaust. Zionists find it difficult to understand that Palestinian hostility to Zionism stems from their expulsion and oppression rather than hatred of Jews as Jews.

In April Corbyn set up another Inquiry, this time chaired by Shami Chakrabarti, the former Director of *Liberty*, into Antisemitism and Racism. There were two vice-chairs, Professor David Feldman and Janet Royall. However, as was made clear to me when giving evidence, the Report was Chakrabarti's alone. The Report itself was strong on procedural issues and the need for natural justice and due process but politically it was very weak. Corbyn compounded his problems by making Chakrabarti a member of the House of Lords very soon after the Report was published.

On June 1st at the press conference to launch the Report, a long-standing black anti-racist activist Marc Wadsworth spoke to complain of the lack of black representation. The media was there in force as were right Labour MPs. Wadsworth, in the course of his speech, criticised Ruth Smeeth MP, a right-wing Zionist member and officer of the JLM, for trading information with the *Daily Telegraph*. Smeeth stormed out, allegedly in tears (although no one ever saw them) and Wadsworth's verbal attack was described as 'antisemitic'. This allegation was eventually withdrawn when the evidence showed that nothing Marc had said was antisemitic. Instead the catch-all charge of 'bringing the party into disrepute' was substituted.

The decision to reinstate Jackie Walker was never accepted by the Zionists and the JLM, an offshoot of the racist Israeli Labor Party, campaigned for her resuspension. In September 2016 John McDonnell shared at platform with Jackie at a meeting in Brighton at the TUC Conference. For this he was bitterly criticised by Jeremy Newmark, Chair of the JLM.[12] As I wrote in an article *The Jewish Labour Movement and its Political Lynching of Jackie Walker*,[13] on September 17 2016, over a week before the Labour Party conference, the JLM was intent on seeing Jackie suspended again. At the Labour Party conference Jackie walked into a honey trap when she attended a JLM 'training session' on antisemitism.

As I had often remarked, having the JLM take a training course on antisemitism was much like asking the late Dr Harold Shipman to give a lecture on medical ethics.

Jackie's interventions in the meeting were secretly recorded by Adam Langleben, the JLM Campaigns Officer, and remarks such as that she hadn't found a definition of antisemitism that she could work with and that Holocaust Memorial Day should cover all Holocausts and not just the Jewish one, were met with a carefully stage-managed headlines in the press.

The result of this was that Jon Lansman, the unelected Chair of Momentum, the main pro-Corbyn group in the Labour Party, attacked Jackie in the press and in early October he successfully moved that she be removed as Vice-Chair of Momentum. Lansman told the *Independent* that:

> I spoke to Jeremy Newmark of the Jewish Labour Movement this morning, he's very upset and I can understand that – I work closely with Jeremy, I've been meeting with Jewish organisations to talk.[14]

In this comment Lansman, a key figure on the Labour left, let slip his close relationship with Jeremy Newmark, the Chair of the organisation which had led the antisemitism witchhunt against Jeremy Corbyn and his supporters.

We therefore had the crazy situation whereby the leader of the 40,000 strong pro-Corbyn organisation, Momentum, is a Zionist who was actively working with the very organisations seeking the overthrow of Jeremy Corbyn. Throughout these attacks Lansman has remained silent, failing to give any support to Corbyn and effectively supporting the Zionist attacks.

On October 4th, at a meeting picketed by Free Speech on Israel, Momentum's Executive voted narrowly to remove Jackie as Vice-Chair, with the support of Jill Mountjoy of the Zionist Alliance for Workers Liberty group.

During the succeeding two years, the false antisemitism campaign has ebbed and flowed. As soon as Labour pulled ahead in the polls a new set of allegations could be guarantee to be in the offing.

The nature of the 'antisemitism' campaign has recently changed. Until the local election campaign this year the Zionists did not attack Jeremy Corbyn himself as antisemitic, rather they alleged that it was the Labour Party itself that was 'overrun' with antisemites. I spent much of the past three years going around the country arguing that Jackie Walker, Ken Livingstone, Marc Wadsworth and myself were merely collateral damage. The real target was Corbyn.

In March this year a long-erased mural, dating back six years was resurrected by Zionist Labour MP Luciana Berger. The mural had depicted six bankers, two of whom were Jewish, dining out on the backs of black sweated labour. Honest people could differ as to whether this mural was antisemitic or anti-Masonic. However, Corbyn had defended the mural on free speech grounds and this was held to be antisemitic. This furore occurred, quite conveniently just as the local election campaign were starting and on March 26th the Board of Deputies called for a demonstration outside Parliament on the theme of 'Enough is Enough'.

About 1,000 people attended this 'anti-racist' demonstration, the first such demonstration to be attended by MPs from the Democratic Unionist Party, Norman Tebbit and various Tory MPs. The main chant was 'Jeremy Corbyn is a racist' and it was opposed by about 250 from Jewish Voice for Labour, Labour Against the Witchhunt and assorted anti-Zionist groups.

As if a six-year old mural wasn't sufficient, the next saga was an eight-year old meeting with Auschwitz survivor Hajo Meyer which Corbyn chaired. Hajo Meyer's offence was to compare his own experiences with those of the Palestinians, a comparison that Marek Edelman, the last Commander of the Warsaw Ghetto was also fond of making. Instead of standing up to his critics, Corbyn once again apologised and thus weakened his own position.

Joining in with the attacks on Corbyn was none other than Benjamin Netanyahu.[15] Fortunately on this occasion Corbyn responded, pointing out that only a few weeks previously Netanyahu's military had murdered 160 unarmed Palestinians in Gaza. This marked a break in Corbyn's record of apologising. Repeatedly during the false 'antisemitism' campaign Corbyn has strengthened his critics by apologising to his opponents.

When in March Jonathan Arkush of the Board of Deputies issued a statement attacking Corbyn he made it clear that his main concern was not antisemitism but Corbyn's support for the Palestinians.[16] Together with Jonathan Goldstein of the Jewish Leadership Council he wrote "Again and again, Jeremy Corbyn has sided with antisemites rather than Jews. At best, this derives from the far left's obsessive hatred of Zionism, Zionists and Israel." The pretence that the concern about 'antisemitism' had anything to do with hatred of Jews, was now being dropped. Arkush emphasised what his real concerns were with his condemnation of Jewdas, a dissident Jewish group that Corbyn had spent Seder night with. Arkush accused Jewdas of being a 'source of virulent antisemitism'.[17] On this occasion Arkush, who had warmly welcomed Donald Trump's election as President,[18] praising "America's standing as a beacon of progress, tolerance and free thinking", had overstepped the mark.[19] Accusing a Jewish group of being a source of antisemitism had given the game away. Arkush's initial refusal to meet Corbyn without a series of preconditions being met fell away.

Someone has clearly been very busy in researching into Corbyn's past speeches and comments. The hatred of the British state and its journalistic appendages for Corbyn led to a recording of a meeting in which Corbyn had told two far-Right Zionists that they lacked a sense of British irony despite having lived in the country for most or all of their lives.

This generated another Zionist attack when the former Chief Rabbi Jonathan Sacks accused Corbyn of being an antisemite who was no different from Enoch Powell, the racist Tory MP. Sacks himself is a right-wing figure, bitterly hostile to Jewish gay organisations, highly sectarian towards Reform Jews (refusing to attend the funeral of Rabbi Hugo Gryn, an Auschwitz survivor) and a supporter of the far-Right in Israel.[20] None of this however prevented the British media from reprinting Sack's worthless comments whilst omitting minor details such as Sack's sponsoring of the annual pogrom-like march of thousands of Jewish settlers through the Arab quarter of Jerusalem.[21]

It was thus inevitable that, when the new Labour Party General Secretary, Jennie Formby, drew up a Code on Antisemitism, it should be met with vociferous opposition from the Zionist lobby. The reason for their opposition was that the Code didn't simply copy verbatim the 500+ word International Holocaust Remembrance Alliance definition of antisemitism which had been discarded by Europe's Fundamental Rights Agency in 2014.

After Theresa May had adopted the whole IHRA definition of 'antisemitism' Jeremy Corbyn made a rod for his own back by only adopting the 38-word introduction to the IHRA initially and not the eleven 'examples' of antisemitism, seven of which refer to Israel, and the damage was done.

Professor David Feldman, Director of the Pears Institute for the Study of Antisemitism, described the IHRA definition as 'bewilderingly perplexing.'[22] The definition has been slated by eminent legal authorities such as former Court of Appeal Judge Sir Stephen Sedley, Hugh Tomlinson QC and Geoffrey Robertson QC. Sedley wrote how the IHRA 'fails the first test of any definition: it is indefinite.'[23] Hugh Tomlinson QC described how it had a 'potential chilling effect' on free speech.[24] and in the latest critique, renowned human rights lawyer Geoffrey Robertson QC slated it as 'not fit for purpose' and, echoing Tomlinson, he wrote how it was 'liable to chill legitimate criticisms of the state of Israel and coverage of human rights abuses against Palestinians.'[25]

Unsurprisingly in the face of this unanimity of opinion over the IHRA's threat to basic civil liberties the Zionists demanded that the Labour Party adopt it wholesale. Jon Lansman, who had previously defended Labour's Antisemitism Code of Conduct as a 'gold standard' lobbied in favour of adopting all the examples.[26] The leader of Momentum thus threw his weight behind the IHRA and its eleven examples, which effectively equates anti-Zionism and antisemitism. In the process he rejected Jeremy Corbyn's attempt to strengthen the free speech safeguards by way of an accompanying statement which included the provision that:

"It should not be considered antisemitic to describe Israel, its policies or the circumstances around its foundation as racist because of their discriminatory impact." [*Jewish Chronicle* 17.7.18.] [27]

Instead Labour's National Executive Committee adopted a far weaker proviso that adoption of the IHRA will not 'in any way undermine freedom of expression on Israel or the rights of the Palestinians." Of course, even this weaker caveat undermines the central purpose of the IHRA, which is to equate criticism of Israel and anti-Zionism with antisemitism. Thus it is no surprise that Jennifer Geber of Labour Friends of Israel called the NEC's decision "appalling" and claimed the "freedom of expression" clause "totally undermines the other examples the party has supposedly just adopted".[28] The JLM claimed that 'The only speech that IHRA definition seeks to limit is antisemitism.' which is as dishonest as it is absurd since a rejection of the notion of a Jewish supremacist state has nothing to do with a hatred of Jews.[29]

It is unfortunate that Corbyn's effective deputy, John McDonnell MP, has been even more eager than Corbyn to placate Labour's Zionist lobby. When interviewed in the *Jewish News* he accepted that 'It is antisemitic to oppose a Jewish state, of course it is.' Labour's leaders are still unable to understand that opposition to a Jewish supremacist state, which relegates its own Palestinian citizens to the status of resident aliens, has nothing to do with antisemitism.

It is the political weaknesses of Labour's left leadership that has caused the Zionist attack on them to increase. It remains to be seen if the popularity of the left programme of Corbyn and McDonnell can overcome the Establishment narrative on Zionism and Antisemitism.

Perhaps the best comment on the situation that Corbyn finds himself in is that of Jonathan Cook, a journalist based in Nazareth in northern Israel:

> as he has lost all sense of how to respond in good faith to allegations made in bad faith, he has begun committing the cardinal sin of sounding and looking evasive – just as those who deployed the antisemitism charge hoped. It was his honesty, plain-speaking and compassion that won him the leadership and the love of ordinary members. Unless he can regain the political and spiritual confidence that underpinned those qualities, he risks haemorrhaging support.[30]

3

Viscious (sic) propaganda
Karl Sabbagh

In September, 1981, I was director of a charitable foundation, the MSD Foundation, which produced teaching material for trainee general practitioners. I was also known as a free-lance writer with a monthly column called *Mere Words* in the doctors' magazine, *World Medicine*. The topic I chose to write about that month, and the article I wrote, set in train a series of events which showed in its most naked form the way in which a pressure group tries to curtail press freedom, when it comes to criticising Israel and Zionism. That simple little article also became a small thorn in the sides of the Presidents of the Royal Colleges of Physicians and General Practitioners, an aspiring President-to-be of the Royal College of Surgeons, several Regional Advisers in General Practice, and some of my best friends, as well as being alleged to have affected the future of *World Medicine* itself and a medical Foundation.

That month, I chose to write about the massacre at Deir Yassin in Palestine in 1948, carried out by the Irgun and the Stern Gang led by Menachem Begin. The fuss that followed was a particularly vivid example of how Zionists can organise themselves, and pressure others, to rally to the cause when they read something they don't like. In this case, there was an additional factor, the political naivety of doctors who knew little of the background to the Middle East dispute and were therefore readier to believe what they were told by the Zionist organisations that orchestrated the protest.

It so happened that October, 1981, was a month when a group of British doctors were due to go out to Israel to take part in a so-called 'Medical Olympics', designed to attract doctors to visit Israel and play golf and tennis. I decided to write an open letter to those doctors, and anyone else who cared to read it, telling them a few things about the former Palestinian Arab population and the terrorist activities under the command of Menachem Begin, then the Prime Minister of the country they were planning to visit. It seemed a good idea at the time...

Here is the article I wrote:

THE BLOOD ON BEGIN'S HANDS

While you are in Israel you may find that you are invited as a doctor to visit the Government Hospital for Mental Diseases at Kfar Sha'ul, an outer suburb of Jerusalem. Some of the patients with a range of severe psychiatric illnesses are housed in a compound of old stone buildings which is charming but unremarkable. It's only if you know the history of the area that those buildings take on a macabre significance.

As Kfar Sha'ul is near the highway from Tel Aviv to Jerusalem it is likely that the Prime Minister of Israel, Menachem Begin, passes the spot quite often. I wonder if it reminds him of his younger days as a 'freedom fighter' for the Jews who desired a state of their own as a refuge from the centuries of persecution that culminated in the Nazi holocaust. As an elder statesman now, Mr Begin can look back with satisfaction over the fifty-odd years that have turned Arab Palestine into Jewish Israel. When Begin arrived in Palestine from his own country, Poland, where his fellow Jews were being slaughtered, he set about planning how to kill Arabs, and some British, so as to persuade the British authorities that he and his colleagues deserved to govern the beautiful land of Palestine, a land that, annoyingly, had been inhabited for the last few centuries by Palestinian Arabs. Young (well, late thirties, really) and impetuous (well, a cold-blooded killer, actually) Begin and the other terrorists (sorry, "freedom-fighters") saw no alternative to violence against the Arabs whose land they coveted.

As you take time off from running, jumping, and playing golf, your hosts may show you their beautiful country. However, as they take you through village after village with Hebrew names they may neglect to point out that, in Moshe Dayan's words to his compatriots: "Jewish villages were built in place of Arab villages. You don't even know the names of these Arab villages, and I don't blame you because these geography books no longer exist. Not only do the books not exist, the Arab villages are not there either ... There is not one single place built in this country that did not have a former Arab population."

One of those villages is Kfar Sha'ul, the site of the government mental hospital. Kfar Sha'ul had an Arab name that most Israelis do know, although they may try to forget it. It was called Deir Yassin and was the scene of one of Mr Begin's most memorable exploits, which greatly assisted the Zionist takeover of Palestine. In 1948, Deir Yassin was a small Arab village of about 400 inhabitants, mainly masons at a nearby quarry, and their families. Just over a month before the end of the British mandate, 132 men of the Irgun and Stern gangs descended on the sleeping village early in the morning and murdered two thirds of the inhabitants, men, women and children. Commanded by Menachem Begin, your genial host at the Medical Olympics, the raiders had killed 254 people by noon with the loss of four of their own men killed by the "murderous" fire of some old Turkish muskets wielded in self-defence. Begin, in a book he wrote some years later, explained that his men had "sought to avoid a single unnecessary casualty". Here are details of some of the, presumably, *necessary* casualties:

- Salhiyah Eid, nine months pregnant, a bullet in the neck and her womb cut open with a butcher's knife.

- Aisha Radwan. killed trying to extract the unborn baby from the dead mother's womb.
- Young girls raped.
- Women's ears slit to remove earrings.
- Kadri Zidan, aged four. a bullet in the head.
- Mohammed Zidan, aged seven, a bullet in the chest.
- Families blown up by grenades thrown into their houses.

But what were these casualties 'necessary' for? Well, the events which followed demonstrated a justification for the massacre in Zionist eyes. As a result of the slaughter, many Palestinian Arabs drew the understandable conclusion that they might be unwise to stay in their own villages when the British mandate ended. Deir Yassin was, after all, a particularly peaceable village with no history of anti-Zionist activities; hundreds of thousands of Arabs fled in the following months, somehow failing to believe in the sincerity of Jewish requests to stay.

Does any of this matter now? Isn't it all water under the bridge, the harsh facts of history but irrelevant to modern political realities? Well, just suppose, fancifully I admit, that Mrs Thatcher had in her youth been a militant supporter of the Protestants in Northern Ireland. Suppose she had led a group of terrorists into a sleeping Catholic village in Northern Ireland and massacred 250 men, women and children to warn the Northern Irish Catholics of what would happen unless they all scuttled south. Suppose further that during the following thirty years she consistently justified the massacre, seeing it as a necessary political act. Would anyone nowadays see it as other than a grim joke if she were to continue to profess a belief in peaceful solutions to the problems of the area?

And yet this grim joke is acted out in the world's political arenas, as Mr Begin, still from time to time up to his old terrorist tricks, tries to persuade the world that he seeks a just and peaceful solution to the Arab-Israeli dispute. I ask you to think about these matters as you board your El Al flight to Tel Aviv and to bear in mind, as you pass through Israeli villages, Moshe Dayan's words quoted above: "There is not one single place built in this country that did not have a former Arab population."

Oh. and one other thing. If you happen to be taken to Safad and, in particular to the now rather chi-chi "artists' quarter" originally called in Arabic "Haret al Nasara", you might look out for a house called "Qabu Isa". an old stone house with a courtyard and cool living rooms with domed ceilings. That's where my father's family lived before 1948. They're not there any more. Bon voyage.

After my article, the following things happened:

(i) The British branch of an organisation called the Israel Medical Association wrote to all its members asking them to send back future copies of *World Medicine* unopened with letters of complaint to the editor. The members were not sent a copy of the article but that didn't stop them obeying instructions. Indeed, one doctor wrote to protest about the article and, in the same letter, asked for a copy of it since he hadn't read it.

(ii) The I.M.A. also wrote to advertisers in that issue of *World Medicine* requesting that they withdraw their support until an undertaking was given that *World Medicine* would never again publish blatant "PLO propaganda". In fact much of the article was based on accounts written before the PLO existed, indeed before Israel existed.

(iii) Several pharmaceutical companies wrote to *World Medicine*, threatening reprisals.

(iv) The I.M.A. wrote to the Governors of the MSD Foundation and suggested that the Governors dissociate themselves *en masse* from my views. The article had actually been written in my private capacity, with no reference made to my employers.

(v) Jewish doctors from round the country wrote letters to the editor, sometimes using identical phrases, complaining about the article. Their letters reflected almost unanimous distress and annoyance that it had been published but furnished little or no evidence of any alternative version of the facts, or of any alternative interpretation of them.

(vi) Jewish doctors wrote to Merck, Sharp and Dohme, the pharmaceutical company which funded the foundation, saying that they would no longer prescribe that company's drugs to their patients. Remember, this was a company which funded a foundation that was directed by someone who wrote an article in his private capacity that annoyed individual G.P.s

(vii) The I.M.A wrote to the President of the Royal College of General Practitioners, who was one of the Governors of the Foundation I worked for, and asked that he reassure them I would not write similar things in the future. He was, of course, not in a position to do so.

(viii) According to one of the Governors, Dr Donald Irvine, MSD told him that if I was still Director of the foundation when my contract next came up for renewal they would discontinue funding the Foundation. (Barely a month before the article a decision had been taken by the Governors, including Irvine, with the support of the company, to renew my contract for another three years with a twenty percent pay rise and the grateful thanks of all concerned for my work for the foundation.) Several of the executives of the company, including the American managing director of the British company, were Jewish.

(ix) The Governors of the MSD Foundation met and passed a motion criticising me for a serious error of judgement in writing in my private capacity an article about Israel that offended some Jewish doctors.

What on earth was going on? Why had doctors, Presidents of Colleges, and leading medical administrators responded so readily to a tiny pressure group, extreme in its support of Israel right or wrong? It is of course entirely understandable that the Israel Medical Association or any other Zionist organisation would not wish anyone to be reminded of the deeds of the Irgun or the Stern Gang or indeed of the rights of the Palestinian Arabs. What is odd is that they were able to influence intelligent, sophisticated British doctors in positions of power who failed to see how they were being manipulated.

In trying to understand quite why my former colleagues and friends were reacting in the way they were, I got tired of hearing all of them preface their remarks with "We're not saying that the article was inaccurate but...", and the 'but' usually led to a warning about the unwisdom of offending Jewish doctors. As I've said, most of the offended doctors never accused me of inaccuracy. Indeed, many of them seemed to know little or nothing of the events of the 1940's in Palestine, preferring to rely on the word of the Zionist I.M.A that Jews had never been terrorists. (Dr Mann of Bolton wrote: "I write to express my disgust at the article by Karl Sabbagh..." and added later "Incidentally whether or not Mr Sabbagh's remarks are based on fact, I cannot say.") It was this observation that led me to try to understand what it was that aroused such anger in the doctors.

I had thought initially that these doctors were angry because they thought they knew the history of that period and therefore believed that I had got things wrong. But it became clear from the letters that most of the writers had no idea what went on in the name of Zionism thirty years beforehand. In fact, they could not believe that what I wrote could possibly be true of Jews. Jews just don't kill women and children in cold blood, and anyone who suggests that any Jew did, particularly if he involves the Prime Minister of Israel in his accusations, is obviously fabricating. This is probably why many doctors got straight to the point in their letters, not bothering to analyse the issues but launching straight into abusive questioning of my motives:

"What on earth is this anti-semitic nonsense doing in a magazine such as *World Medicine*?" (Dr Marcus Latner, London)

"... another vicious anti-semitic (oops antizionist) diatribe of the sort usually associated with 'Bulldog' or 'Spearhead'..." (Dr B.I. Chazan, Sunderland)

"...viciously bigoted..." (Mr R.R. Domb, Dentist, Cambridge.)

"...pure viscious (sic) anti-Israel propaganda of the crudest kind and indeed totally false and inflammatory..." (Dr Alan Fox, Edgware)

"...blatantly political and viscious (sic, again) article..." (Dr Gerald Jesner, Glasgow.)

"Your rabid anti-Jewish contributor Sabbagh..." (Dr S. Alder, Brighton)

"The editor and staff of *Der Sturmer* would have been proud to publish Mr Karl Sabbagh's article..." (Dr Eve Hammer, Wembley)

There were also letters sent to the home of Michael O'Donnell, the editor of *World Medicine*, and a great supporter of my writing. Some years later, in an article in the British Medical Journal, he wrote

> Well over a hundred anonymous letters arrived at my home, many of them airmailed from the USA. Each had to be opened to confirm the diagnosis of anonymity and my wife and I took to opening them together. We both suffered from the same behavioural quirk. Once we opened a letter we felt compelled to read it. Reading them together allowed us to use humour as an antidote to venom. Some particularly nasty letters were addressed to our children. We managed to intercept these, thanks to a friendly postman who agreed to hand the post only to us.

I should now remind you of the date that all this took place. October, 1981, was several months before Israeli guns started bombarding Palestinian homes in Lebanon, and nearly a year before the massacres in Sabra and Chatila refugee camps while they were under Israeli control. In the following year, anything I said in my article had paled into insignificance beside the critical comments made throughout the world press, culminating in an editorial attack on Begin in the *Jewish Chronicle* which I would have been proud to have written myself. And of course in the nearly four decades since then, there has been no shortage of innocent Palestinian lives lost at the hands of the Israeli army.

But for many Jews the facts about Israeli actions are irrelevant. *Anyone* criticising Israeli aggression is clearly motivated by antisemitism.

Some correspondents boiled over into incoherent expressions of annoyance, including my favourite from Dr and Mrs Gilbert of Romford who finished their short letter to the editor with "we are referring the matter to the appropriate authorities from whom you will, no doubt, hear in due course." We never did.

As the letters came in and I read these sad offerings from very angry doctors, it became clear that most of them did not want to believe that what I had said might be true. Their long-standing support of Israel and Zionism was threatened by the possibility that right was not entirely on the Jewish side. Some of the actions carried out on both sides were unpleasant during the years leading up to 1948, when the Palestinians were trying to hold onto their land and the Zionists were trying to take it away from them, but these doctors appeared only to have heard of Arab terrorism, thanks to the skill over the years of organisations like the Israel Medical Association and the Board of Deputies. Now we can add to them the Campaign Against Antisemitism and the International Holocaust Remembrance Alliance.

There is no doubt, from the evidence of the letters and of the actions of the I.M.A. that these people actually believed that it is right and proper to prevent articles you disagree with being published. It is also, of course, a function of Zionism to prevent discussion of the past in case people realise that the Palestinians have a case. By closing the ranks of Jewish doctors and playing upon their easily roused indignation, the Zionist lobby thought that it might be able to achieve another small victory in its never-ending campaign to suppress unpalatable arguments.

But why did some uncommitted non-Jewish doctors, some of them quite senior figures, respond so readily to the blatantly organised lobby? The Governors of the MSD Foundation, all very busy people, met several times to discuss what to do about the letters of complaint from Jewish doctors. If they had been letters from Catholics about an article on abortion or from Jehovah's Witnesses about blood transfusion they would have kept quiet and accepted these as the predictable responses to be expected when these subjects are raised. But these equally predictable responses to a subject outside their knowledge were obviously less easy to deal with. "The Jewish lobby is very powerful", these Princes of the profession would say to me, shaking their heads, and I would want to ask "But what can they do to you? Why are you so worried?" It seemed to me that they had never asked themselves *why* the Jewish lobby is powerful, and got the, correct, answer "Because they know that people like you behave like this when threatened." Committed to a quiet life, disliking fuss or criticism, these senior doctors, and the companies involved with them, never thought for a moment about the freedom of the press. All along, their argument was "You should have known that this article would offend some people, and that should have been enough to stop you writing it."

Thirty-five more years of the Palestinian-Israeli dispute has not changed the situation. In fact, it has become clearer than ever that many Jews are able to ignore all criticism of Israel because they are persuaded that antisemites are on the rampage again. It does no credit to a people who have contributed in a major way to the world's cultural and intellectual reserves that they swallow such a shoddy explanation without reservations. For as Karl Popper might have pointed out, it is an invalid explanation in scientific terms. How could you ever disprove that criticism of Israel is founded on antisemitism if that criticism is itself *prima facie* evidence of antisemitism? Of course Jews must be on the lookout for a resurgence of crude racial hatred, and of course they must consider this as one possible explanation for criticism of Jews. But they must not stop there. They must look at the issues in their own terms and consider whether by remaining quiet about Israeli actions they encourage Israel to believe that it can get away with murder. In the long term, such unwavering support can only lead to the flourishing of extremism and an ever-worsening situation.

There were several postscripts to the *World Medicine* incident. Several years after these events I was in New York discussing a television project with an American Jewish producer friend of mine. We wanted to work together on a film, and he was seeking funding for it. One day, out of the blue, he said:" Do you mind if I ask you something? Did you ever write an article in a magazine that attacked Israel and caused a fuss?" "Yes," I said to my friend," I did." "Well," he said, "I was discussing our project with someone who might have put money into it and he reached into a filing cabinet and handed me a piece of paper, saying 'Do you know about this?'" Bad news has wings and this particular piece of news had flown 3000 miles to nestle for years in an American businessman's filing cabinet.

The second postscript was the demise of *World Medicine* itself. In the months after I wrote my article, Michael O'Donnell left the magazine after an apparently unrelated argument with McGraw Hill, the American publisher that owned it. Another editor came along and produced a greatly inferior magazine for a while, and finally the magazine was closed. The details are murky but there is some evidence that the fuss over my article played a part in closing it down.

And finally, another bit-player in the drama, Dr Donald Irvine, the man who appeared to see nothing odd about the fact that the major pharmaceutical company Merck, Sharp and Dohme would close down a charity that was doing a good job because its director wrote an anti-Zionist article, became Sir Donald and one of the most important doctors in the land, when he was made President of the doctors' regulatory body, the GMC.

It's worth making the point that, although these events happened 35 years ago, the willingness of British doctors to make themselves look stupid (and to harm freedom of speech) is unchanged in the 21st century. In 2008 I was given the opportunity to analyse emails that were set to the *British Medical Journal* after it published an article by Derek Summefield about the effects of Israeli actions on the health of Palestinians in Gaza.* Some of them were aimed at the writer and some at the Acting Editor at the time, Kamran Abbasi, whose Arabic name seemed to annoy some people.

The point I want to make here is that the emails received by the BMJ bore uncanny similarities to the letters sent to *World Medicine*. The first similarity was that many of them had no interest in the truth of the research reported in the original article. Their sole aim was to impute antisemitism to the writer, often in childishly abusive terms.

The second was the way in which many of them actually gave their names and addresses, revealing how years of medical education followed by working as doctors had not taught them rationality, the ability to assess data, civility, or the ability to spell. Internal evidence suggests that many of these came from doctors in the United States.

It also became clear that the writers of many of the emails were obeying the suggestion of a Zionist website, called *HonestReporting* (sic) which said:

"If you agree this article is inappropriate for a respected medical journal, send comments to *British Medical Journal* editor Kamran Abbasi: click here"

Here is a brief sample of the 1000 or so emails I categorised:

> I think Sumerfield's article was disgracefull. It is packed with lies and distortions. I ma surprised that a reputable, Proffesssional publication wouls print such rubbish withouts carefull investigation as to the true facts.

---

* *BMJ* 2009; 338: a2066 (Published 25 Feb 2009)

it amazes me that the limey attitude that precedes your rotting teeth still lives on in your shithole corner of the world. are you jealous of israel? i mean, if you had to build a wall around your pathetic island to keep your citizens alive and safe from terrorist attacks, then maybe you could comment. but to condemn israel is bogus and bullshit. piss off you limey wankers.

your involvement with politics as a medical journal is terrible. amments concerning your interprtation that Israelis kill palastinians with impunity is ridiculous and should not be in the journal. would you like to have a terrorist as a neighbor???

I am deeply appaulded at your journal's recent publication of the artilce by Dr. Derrick Summerfield. To politicize the health conditions of that region and for those people as he did is reprehensible and grossly unetheical. It is your professional repsonsibility to retrack Dr. Summerield's inflamitory remarks and apologize to your readers for publishing politically motivated garbage. If you are not completely embarrassed by Dr. Summersfield's article being published in your journal, you should yourself resign as editor.

He [Summerfield] hates the jews because they have more in their little finge than ha ha in his whole brain.

since bmj is one of the most reputable med journals in the world it behooves you to verify the info in print, especially since your target audience represent the leading religions in the world.

what does the fictional country of balestine have to do with a medical journal? Now everything in your magazine is suspect.

Because reading this sort of stuff is wearying after a while, I have put a longer selection of the emails in Appendix 2 section of this book. Those of us who speak and write of the Palestine-Israel conflict regularly will find them all too familiar. In 1982 it was letters; in 2005 it was emails; these days it is social media, but the intention is always the same – to smear critics of Israel and supporters of Palestine as lying antisemites, in the hope that this will seem such shameful accusation that people will stay away from the topic in future. In fact, for many of us, it makes us more determined than ever to insist on the freedom to be anti-Zionist without being considered antisemitic.

4

Giving the Truth a Voice
Cyril Chilson

In 2015, I started publishing online tweets which were collected as 'evidence' by an anonymous *agent provocateur* who submitted them to Labour's National Constitutional Committee (NCC), accusing me of 'Antisemitism'. These tweets had in common a stark criticism of the State of Israel, focusing on its atrocious policies against the Palestinians in the occupied territories and refutation of the accusations which Jewish organisations, individuals and the henchmen of Hasbara (i.e. the Israeli State-sponsored propaganda system), were spreading all over the social media. Following this complaint (the identity of those who submitted it remains concealed), my membership was suspended in August 2016 while the characters who had taken upon themselves the task of assessing whether my tweets were antisemitic did not seem too keen to get their act together.

After an extended period of incubation, the NEC and the NCC suddenly became quite anxious to get things done. I was contacted in November 2017 and was given three weeks to respond and find legal representation. The NCC rejected my request to have Tony Greenstein[*] as my legal representative,

---
[*] See Tony Greenstein's piece on pp. 21-39

despite his legal qualifications. When Daniel Bennett, a barrister from the Doughty Street Chambers, volunteered to act on my behalf, the NCC agreed at last to defer the hearing. Having been forced to accept that being represented by a lawyer would deprive me of the right to speak during the hearing, I decided to represent myself and give up Mr Bennett's kind offer, with my wife as my 'silent friend'.

We arrived at the hearing venue, the Jurys Inn Hotel in Oxford where the NCC panel met.

The panel was chaired by one Maggie Cosin. Her lieutenants were Emina Ibrahim and Douglas Fairbairn. The 'prosecutor' (appearing here under the bureaucratic euphemism: 'presenter') was a certain Dan Hogan from the so-called Compliance Unit. A young trainee-apparatchik with a title to match: 'Investigations Officer'. He was accompanied by Louise Withers-Green, an even younger 'silent friend'.

The session began with Mr Hogan's presentation of the charges against me. He homed in on an assortment of my tweets which were the sole material used as 'evidence' by the NEC industrious investigators. He pulled out of nowhere the Chakrabarti Report into Ken Livingstone and Naz Shah and I tried to question the relevance of this report, particularly since the official status of the document remains unclear.

At this point the Chair, Ms Cosin, started to shout at me: "If you go on like this, you will have to leave the room." Hogan 'apologised' for not having added the said report to the bundle and dispatched Jane Shaw, Secretary to the NCC, to photocopy its pages. The same thing happened with Hogan's reliance on the IHRA definition which was called into question by me. I referred Hogan and the panel to the resolution of the last Party conference whereby the endorsement of the definition for antisemitism which was laid down by the IHRA in 2016 was limited to the preamble, not to the examples which follow it. Once again, the Chair chided me: 'Keep this for your own presentation'. When I tried to clarify that this was a procedural issue, given that this material did not appear in the bundle and the Party's own rules make it clear that no further evidence can be accepted after the deadline of evidence submissions, I was once again facing a threat from the Chair: "Enough of this. I have been very tolerant up until now".

Hogan's presentation was chequered with personal insults and mendacious statements. He did not refrain from character assassination by association aimed even at those who were already expelled from the Party during the present witch hunt: "Mr Chilson", announced Hogan in dramatic pathos, "wanted to be represented by Tony Greenstein. This was followed by Mr Chilson dismissing Mr Daniel Bennett, a barrister who volunteered to act on his behalf. One wonders why". Mr Hogan seems to have forgotten that innuendo based on the lawyer-client relationship (which is meant to be confidential), is unacceptable. What I wondered in this context is how Mr Hogan knew that I had 'dismissed' Mr Bennett? He wasn't briefed by Mr Bennett, surely?

This was followed by a failure of Hogan's reasoning: "Mr Chilson refused to engage with the NEC investigation". When I reminded him that I answered the questionnaire which was sent to me and asked him how this could be squared with my attendance at the hearing, which on the face of it contradicted his postulate, he ignored my question and instead the Chair again reprimanded me: "Don't talk over him!" despite the fact that I never did. In fact, Ms Cosins herself kept interrupting me time and again.

One of the charges against me arose from one of my tweets about Zionism and the *Haavara* Agreement, whereby I reminded my interlocutor that following the boycott of German goods which the Jewish leadership in the US had organised after the Nazis came to power in 1933, the Nazis had swallowed their racist pride for fear of the impact on Germany's frail economy and agreed to negotiate with the Zionist Federation, being forced to treat the Zionist representatives as their equals. Hogan tried to liken this to an act of Holocaust denial, dubbing it 'historical revisionism'.

When I mentioned that I was a son of Holocaust survivors and therefore could not be anti-Semitic let alone a Holocaust denier, Hogan said "I only refer to the evidence, I don't know you". I went on to ask him if he was a trained historian with an expertise on the history of the Zionist movement in Nazi Germany. He admitted he was 'no expert'. At this stage the Chair intervened: "I know everything about the history of Nazi Germany and everything about Jewish history - and I want this to stop and I want it to stop now! We are not here for a history lesson!"

Was the Chair of the Kangaroo Court becoming concerned as Dan Hogan was losing ground?

Another contention which demonstrates the falsehood of the charges and the way in which they were looked at by the panel revolved around my tweet about the pro-Israeli lobby in the UK and those who run it. I highlighted the pivotal role of two individuals connected with the arms trade, and Hogan tried to portray this as an attempt to present the UK Jewish community as a collective whose loyalty to the UK is questionable. Hogan went on to refer to it as a 'typical anti-Semitic trope'. Likewise, drawing on one of my tweets in which I argued that 'Jewish solidarity is not a sentiment but an investment' he tried to develop this theme and claim that by criticising certain British Jews I was employing an anti-Semitic stereotype whereby Jews around the globe are collectively responsible for the policies and acts of the State of Israel. 'The investment' theme, declared Hogan, 'is a typical reference to Jewish greed and manipulative behaviour'.

When I reminded Hogan that even a broken clock shows the correct time twice a day, he was struggling with the meaning of this metaphor. I had to explain to the puzzled 'presenter' that the existence of anti-Semitic tropes does not exclude the existence of Jewish individuals who sadly behave in a way reminiscent of those repulsive generalisations. If we were to refrain from criticising them because they happen to be Jewish, we betray the truth and by remaining silent we actually join the oppressors. 'No one should be beyond reproach, even if he or she happen to be Jewish'. I also reiterated a claim which Hogan tried to dispute and found himself in a pickle due to his ignorance of Jewish contemporary history: the leadership of the Jewish communities in the western world (particularly in the US and the UK), adopted a policy of 'my country right or wrong' vis-à-vis the State of Israel especially since the coming to power of Likud Party in 1977. This is not a 'trope' or a 'stereotype' but a historical fact.

I referred Hogan to an article by the American Jewish columnist Jonathan Weissman on this specific issue, published only four days beforehand in the *New York Times*. Weissman criticised the American Jewish leadership for being, in his own words, 'obsessive' about Israel. So much so, that the community leaders had neglected domestic Jewish-American issues such as the rising home-grown anti-Semitism. They also refrained from criticising the rise of far-right anti-Semitism in Europe as this did not suit the current Israeli foreign policy and its chummy relations with several European neo-fascists. As regards Anglo-Jewry, Hogan kept ignoring my references to a study by a Jewish sociologist from London City University which corroborated my claim that the majority of Jews in Britain regard the State of Israel as an essential part of their self-identity. Among these, 71% accept (to a variable extent) Israel's policies in the occupied territories even if they are unhappy about parts or all of them. All of this was labelled as 'typical anti-Semitic conspiracy-theories'.

Hogan asked me or rather stated at some point: "So like most anti-Semites you think that all the Jewish community in the UK are in Israel's pocket or collaborators of Hasbara!" (the Israeli state-sponsored propaganda system) to which I answered: 'No. No one could say such a thing about the late Sir Gerald Kaufman or the late Harold Pinter or the excellent members of Jewish Voice for Labour or Labour against the Witch Hunt, but these are, alas, the exception. Let me remind you that certain dignitaries in the Jewish community called not to vote Labour in 2015 because

'Ed Miliband' as they put 'is not one of us'. Was it the bacon bap that he ate in public or rather his (fairly moderate) criticism of Israel that made Miliband fall afoul of them?'

When I was suspended I used to tweet headlines concerning atrocities committed by Israel in the Palestinian territories. I added to those headlines the rhetorical question: 'Is reporting this anti-Semitic?' Hogan tried to claim that by doing so I was mocking the very concept of anti-Semitism and thus "denying the Jewish people the language to describe their persecution by a deliberate attempt of hijacking the definition of what antisemitism is". Hogan failed to realise that he was actually conflating criticism of Israel with anti-Semitism contrary to his own admission that 'criticising Israel is not anti-Semitic' and therefore he himself was actually denying me any language to describe the unpleasant truth. Certain Israeli Jews have become persecutors and certain Jews abroad support them by trying to gag anyone who dares to tell this simple and horrible truth.

"Are you denying", asked Dan Hogan, relishing his freshly-baked scholasticism, "that by sending those tweets you were distracting from actual anti-Semitic acts which deserve redress and indeed, by doing so you were denying Jewish people the language to describe the prejudice, discrimination and hatred they are subject to? And if you do deny it, why should a reasonable person send these questions? Who was meant to answer them?"

Here I had to remind the already ecstatic Mr Hogan that rhetorical questions were not meant to be answered. The Chair interjected: "we all know what a rhetorical question means."

"Apparently not" I replied.

"Well, answer then: what was the purpose of all of this?"

"Telling the truth and opposing the gagging by false accusations of anti-Semitism" I replied.

Mr Hogan wanted to continue but the Chair signalled him to stop. She seems to have realised that even in a Kangaroo Court, silly questions must be asked in a measured manner.

Mr Hogan's 'cross examination' featured repeated insinuations such as: "Have you been aware of the inflammatory nature of your tweets?", "Can you understand that your tweets come across as offensive?" "How do you feel about causing pain to Jewish members of Labour?" "Do you think that comments such as yours would make Labour an attractive and safe place for Jewish voters?"

I stressed time and again that I never meant to hurt anyone. I likewise apologised for any feelings which might have been hurt but at the same time I expressed my belief that mature and constructive politics must not involve sentiment. Rather, it must be realistic, truthful and logical. I then told the panellists how I was abused by one of the most active pro-Israel accounts on Twitter whose handle is @GnasherJew. This hitherto anonymous operator (whose identity has since been revealed as one David Collier[*]) did not refrain from appealing to the Oxford College in which I teach, requesting the College to sack me while adding an abusive description of myself.

My account of the abusive and slanderous behaviour of @GnasherJew was simply ignored. The above are of course only snippets from what went on during my hearing. I concluded my summations by saying: "I never imagined, when I proudly joined the Party, that I, son of Holocaust survivors, would have to defend myself against allegations of anti-Semitism against other Party members who have chosen to weaponize anti-Semitism to achieve their political targets. You may disagree with me but expelling me from the Party will be tantamount to spitting on the non-existent graves of the Holocaust victim, including those of my extended family."

The Chair asked me after my concluding remarks: "Do you think your hearing was a fair one?"

"I think this question is unfair. I do have some misgivings about what went on here today, but I hope to be proven wrong", I replied,

---

[*] This character seems to crop up in a number of incidents of false accusations of antisemitism. See Thomas Suárez' piece starting on p. 63

trying hard to maintain a calm tone, hoping I was not showing my indignation and disgust at this ostensibly innocent question.

There was a break of thirty minutes. When we returned to the room the Chair said: "The panel has decided that the charges against you have been proven. I want to remind you that we are able to expel you and would like to ask you whether there were any mitigating circumstances?"

So, I was not proved wrong after all. This was indeed a kangaroo court that was apparently one-track-minded.

At this point, I decided that this farce had to be brought to an end. I grabbed my briefcase and said: "This was a colossal waste of time. Goodbye!"

"Hang on! Don't go! We haven't reached a decision yet!" shouted the Chair in a last attempt to keep a façade of fairness. My wife and I kept walking and did not look back.

The letter with the decision to expel me for two years arrived on the following Saturday. I found particularly repulsive the concluding paragraph: "If you apply to re-join you will not be eligible to have your join date backdated to give you continuity with an earlier period of membership."

5

Smoke and mirrors
Thomas Suárez

What follows is an account of my entanglement with the word "antisemitism". It is one person's experience, but it is a microcosm of how British democracy has been held hostage by those six syllables. As with the vast majority of people with similar stories, it is my involvement with human rights in Israel-Palestine that brought me face to face with the ugly word.

A decade ago, my interest the British Mandate period in Palestine led me to Britain's National Archives. Several years' study of that great institution's relevant source documents culminated with the October 2016 publication of my book, *State of Terror: how terrorism created modern Israel*. A US edition followed in December, and Arabic and French editions were published in 2018. I continue to monitor the National Archives for newly declassified material related to the topic, and continue to request release of such material slated to be locked away for some years.

My first university talk based on this research took place a couple of weeks after publication, at London's School of Oriental and African Studies (SOAS). The lecture was intended for students, but two well-known pro-Israel activists, David Collier and Jonathan Hoffman, gatecrashed and commandeered the event. Security was called; but instead of removing the saboteurs, the saboteurs 'removed' Security. Amidst screams of 'antisemitism', Hoffman feigned assault by a guard, at which point the Security personnel, not wanting to be in the morning's headlines in a fabricated story of an 'antisemitic attack', walked away. The 'antisemitism' pandemonium brought the meeting to an untimely close.[31]

The guards 'escaped' without harm, except for a rough online video falsely labelled as one of them "assaulting" Hoffman. My own keepsake was an article in the popular tabloid, the *Daily Mail*, whose headline announced "Israeli Embassy's fury after anti-Semitic hate speaker gives talk at a top London university."[32]

The two ringleaders have been active in stopping even top academics like Richard Falk from speaking, and Collier in particular has been in the news regarding the crusade against Jeremy Corbyn. Everything that happened to me from that point on links directly back to this SOAS talk and the 'news' story they fed the *Daily Mail*. That tabloid piece would become gospel and propagate in myriad guises to create a network of pseudo-corroboration. Across the Atlantic, the two antisemitism merchants would morph into academics and professors, and be trusted and quoted by real academics.

In today's climate, the charge of antisemitism is its own proof. There is no exorcism that can entirely rid someone of its ghosts. Like the McCarthyism of 1950s United States, being identified as an antisemite is akin to having the plague: you are shunned even by people who don't believe it, for fear of being contaminated and shunned as well. Yet 'antisemitism' is ultimately a more sinister witch hunt. The word 'communism' was exploited by regimes both flaunting and criminalising it, but communism itself is simply a political and economic theory. Antisemitism, in stark contrast, is itself a great evil.

Since the antisemitism industry is ultimately a weapon in Israel's war against Palestine, Palestinians and their supporters are in its crosshairs by definition. Fear leads vulnerable students in university Palestine clubs to behave as though they were guilty.

One student group at a major UK university uninvited me with obvious fear when the *Daily Mail* article was compounded by a swastika that appeared on a dormitory door. 'Antisemitism' was waiting for an opportunity to squash the student organisation, and I would give it the excuse.

Another student group, aware of my *Daily Mail* infamy, first declared that my Israel Apartheid Week talk would go ahead no-matter-what, even if the venue had to be changed. But as the date neared, the organiser was so unnerved by an IAW campus crackdown that she abruptly broke contact.

The actual scale of destruction is far greater than the paper trail would suggest. There is no way to tally academic events that are never even proposed, because of fear. Nor is there record of self-censorship; for example, I cancelled a talk at a struggling human rights organisation out of worry that I might put their already challenged funding in danger.

When the SOAS duo filed a complaint against me with the university, I contacted the administration and offered to face my accusers in their presence. SOAS is accustomed to charges of antisemitism and assured me there was no need, but the accusers exploit their 'news' of their own complaints to frighten students from further projects.

Their complaint to the Charity Commission was also dismissed, but simply lodging the complaint enabled them to 'corroborate' it with their own headline in the *Jewish News*: "Charity Commission investigating anti-Semitic Suárez meeting at SOAS". The *Independent* repeated the story.[33] Their next brainstorm was a Freedom of Information request, a shot-in-the-dark to find 'dirt' on me, which I learned about only from the disappointed reference to the outcome on one of their blogs.

Neither disrupter was invited when I spoke at the House of Lords the month after SOAS, but nonetheless Hoffman filed a formal complaint with the Lords about that talk's 'antisemitism', citing a barely intelligible list of alleged falsehoods in my book. His complaint proved spurious and was entirely dismissed three months later (HL Paper 142).

Quakers first held meetings in Jesus Lane in Cambridge in the 1650s. When Cambridge PSC (Palestine Solidarity Campaign) asked me to give a talk at Jesus Lane Meeting House (the original parts of which date from 1777), I was honoured and marked it down in pen.

On a Friday, six days before that talk, Jesus Lane received a letter from the Board of Deputies of British Jews, the self-appointed representative of 'the Jewish Community', telling them to cancel my talk. The next day, Hoffman called Jesus Lane and "demanded" (his word) that the booking be cancelled, and reinforced this 'demand' by email. There was no explanation as to why he and the Board of Deputies waited until the eleventh hour to demand cancellation of a talk that had been publicised for two months, and the short notice made it impossible for Jesus Lane to address the issue through its own internal processes.

As a consequence, the issue was raised at a Meeting for Worship for Business on Sunday. "Under pressure of time and with incomplete information," as Jesus Lane elders later explained the result, it was decided to err on the side of caution and cancel the booking.

The next morning, a *Jewish Chronicle* headline announced "Board halt Israel hate author talk".[34] I was "accused of peddling antisemitic theories on Israel and Judaism," and "rose to notoriety after an hour-long rant on Jews and Zionism" [SOAS]. Repeating the tabloid lies, the article quoted me as saying that Zionist leaders "encouraged antisemitism in Germany to force Jews to move to Palestine."

PSC Cambridge found an alternate venue for my talk but kept it confidential to avoid further problems. Hoffman tried to find out, and cited PSC's refusal to let him know to prove his allegations — what he and Collier sometimes frame as 'Jews not being allowed'.

Some Jesus Lane Friends *were* among the audience, and Jesus Lane Meeting scheduled its own showing of a video of the talk.

Meanwhile, Jesus Lane Local Meeting wrote to the *Jewish Chronicle* requesting corrections to its misstatements about them. Not only was no response whatsoever received, but the Quakers' cancellation was seized upon as a self-corroboration prize: 'the Quakers' – not even just Jesus Lane, but *the Quakers* — were now said to be of the same mind. On social media and on Amazon, Hoffman now invoked the Quakers to corroborate the lies. Unable to stop the abuse through direct communication, in September Jesus Lane Friends Meeting's elders issued a public statement that read in part:

> Elders of Jesus Lane Friends Meeting (Quakers) are concerned at the continuing misrepresentation by Jonathan Hoffman and others regarding the decision made by Cambridge Jesus Lane Quaker Meeting to cancel a talk by Tom Suárez in May 2017 ... Friends (Quakers) who have read the book or seen the video recording of Tom's talk have no reservations about Tom Suárez or his work.

Yet the Board of Deputies and the *Jewish Chronicle* responded with even greater fabrications at the next opportunity: Bath.

When Hoffman tried to block a talk I was scheduled to give in Bath, the venue — the Bath Royal Literary & Scientific Institution — stood firm. Outraged, the Board of Deputies used a new *Jewish Chronicle* piece to further embellish the inventions about me and about Jesus Lane that it had already refused to correct the year before.[35]

The Board of Deputies feigned outrage that I had been allowed to speak at BRLSI after Jesus Lane Meeting — which it described as a "similar institution" — had already "banned" me. But there was a glitch: BRLSI is not a Quaker institution. To fix this, the *JC* named an individual (unknown to me or Jesus Lane) who in turn cited Edmund Rack, a Quaker who died in 1787, thirty-seven years before BRLSI was founded but who was involved in forerunner societies. The *JC*'s 21st century gatekeeper decided on Rack's behalf that he would have opposed my being allowed to speak at BRLSI (had it existed while he was alive), and he was a Quaker, therefore ... it all made sense.

But the crowning insult against Jesus Lane was the headline's invention that the scandal of my speaking had precipitated a "Quakers row". Jesus Lane immediately wrote to the *JC*. They had never "banned" me, and neither the Board of Deputies nor the *JC* had any right to allege a non-existent "row" in their name. When no response came, Jesus Lane wrote again. The *JC* kept its impenetrable silence.

At that point I turned to the Independent Press Standards Organisation (IPSO) to challenge the *JC*'s reporting and its refusal to allow me to respond to its allegations.[36] When the paper was unable to substantiate either the 2017 or 2018 articles, it still stood 100% behind both stories — by changing subjects. The issue was no longer accuracy, nor indeed even my talks, but what the *JC* called "the tone and treatment of the story." For that "tone and treatment" it relied exclusively on a 59-page so-called *Report* about my book co-authored by, yes, the original two saboteurs who were the *JC*'s and the Board of Deputies' sources in the first place. The *Report* now gave their allegations the facade of published 'fact' in pseudo-intellectual format.[37]

In a final, extraordinary stroke of self-corroboration, the *JC* then defended its reporting by arguing that its views are "shared by many JC readers." The *JC* readership's sole knowledge of me is what comes from the same two sources of the tabloid story, whether directly or via the Board of Deputies; yet the *JC* seriously proposed that the fact that these correspond is proof that they are true.

IPSO's final request to the *JC* for evidence brought a two-part reply. First was: "I'm not sure how much I can add but have a call in as I write to the writer of the original." But several days later, the *JC*'s source had still failed to come up with the goods. The *JC*'s final words to IPSO: "I'm not I can [sic] add anything further. I think I'll let matters rest there." That was the end of it. Yet still it admitted no inaccuracy whatsoever. All the lies, all the defamation, serve to protect the Israel state from accountability. What F16s can't do, 'antisemitism' can.

The Collier-Hoffman *Report* added one new lie to the mix: Holocaust denial. It concluded that I have "disdain ... for the Holocaust and Jewish life in general," and stated that I question the truth of a survivor of Josef Mengele, the Nazi doctor who used Jews for sadistic experiments. In fact, I have never written or spoken about Mengele, nor was he ever a part of my research. In various online media and Twitter, its two authors advertised how my "hatred of Jews runs through the book. Like blood in an animal, the book has no life without it." Collier's site included an apparent threat: "We see you. We know what you are."

Terrorism, like antisemitism, is amorphously defined to serve political need. Certain ethnicities, certain nationalities, commit terrorism; others commit defence. It was thus eminently efficient to enlist PREVENT, the British government's counter-terrorism initiative, to add another layer of corroboration.

Being neither Arab nor Muslim, my heart did not sink too deeply when I learned that PREVENT had been alerted to my activities. I was on the train to Portsmouth, where I was to speak in a few hours, when Portsmouth & South Downs PSC informed me that I had been banned from public venues city-wide. Undeterred, my hosts whisked me to the back room of a hotel pub in a neighbouring town, along with an audience of people known to them. The quaint hotel made me feel as though I'd stepped back to the 1950s, and we could just as well have been whispering about Marx. But here we were in Britain, trying to discuss British source documents from Britain's own archives about the British Mandate, closed down by a British institution with British tax money at the orders of individuals acting in the interests of a foreign pariah state.

My sponsors were not intimidated. They demanded to meet with the local PREVENT Coordinator, Charlie Pericleous, and when that meeting was set I returned to Portsmouth. Mr Pericleous refused to state the evidence against me, and refused to reveal who my accusers are. Yet he also refused to issue any statement clearing my name of suspicion, despite repeated requests from me, from Portsmouth PSC, and from the main PSC organisation.

Nor do we know how Portsmouth MP Flick Drummond got involved. The *Daily Mail* reported that she alerted the police to block me, but when I contacted her she replied that she was concerned not about me, but about "some trouble from people" who were opposed to me.

The *Daily Mail* took advantage of the 'news' that I had been closed down for hate speech to condemn, by association, another man who is a magnet for the six-syllable plague: Jeremy Corbyn. I have never met nor had any contact with Mr Corbyn, but the *Daily Mail* lined us up with side-by-side mug shots. The headline read: "Corbyn is urged to cut links with Palestine charity after it hosts anti-Semitic speaker..." Their slurs against me corroborated their campaign against Corbyn.[38]

The plague-word now sought corroboration overseas. When three professors at the University of Massachusetts at Amherst learned that I was to speak there, they organised a letter-writing campaign to stop it, accusing me of "supporting 'identity-based hate' against Jewish people." But the President stood firm. The talk went ahead.

In the days following my talk, it was again Collier-Hoffman, five and a half thousand kilometres to the east, not my talk right in the university, that determined what I had said. The reporter for the 125-year-old Massachusetts *Daily Collegian* had not attended, but was sufficiently sure of what I'd said to jump to antisemitism right in the headline and subheading: "The anti-Semitism of the Suárez talk is not the way to discuss the Israeli-Palestinian conflict – Suárez's rhetoric is a detriment to the Jewish student body on campus." As proof that UMass is not the first university where I received a "backlash from local Jews", he cited the SOAS talk, perhaps not even aware of the irony. Rather, he invoked the very fact that I had spoken at SOAS, with its "history of anti-Semitism", as corroboration. Even when I gave the journalist a link to a video clip from the talk itself, proving that I had said the opposite of what he had reported, nothing changed.[39]

An article in the *Amherst Wire* used my talk to argue that (as the headline read) "Hate does have a home at UMass," and used alleged verbatim quotes from the talk to prove the point: "Zionists allowed or enabled or directly dealt in creating the Holocaust so they could profit off the Middle Eastern Israeli venture"; and "if we wipe Israel off the map, then the entire region will be at peace..." I was most fortunate, however, that Professor of Communication Sut Jhally, executive director of the Media Education Foundation and an expert in communication, advertising, and propaganda, attended the talk, along with Interlink Books publisher Michel Moushabeck. Professor Jhally had a video of the complete talk and Q&A transcribed, presented it to the *Amherst Wire*, and asked them to find anything remotely resembling the quotes. The *Wire* removed the online article, the sole instance in which a paper has shown any responsibility for what it has published about me.[40]

Professor Jhally obtained a copy of the letter that had been confidentially circulated in an attempt to block me. The sole source it cited to support the professors' case was, yes, the Collier-Hoffman *Report*. The professors had now invested themselves in the antisemitism pyramid scheme. In a final commentary by a *Collegian* columnist, Messrs. Collier and Hoffman have suddenly become academics, Collier is now 'Professor' Collier, and they, along with the UMass professors who relied upon them, now constituted "a variety of academics" who have "debunked" me.[41]

The *Washington Free Beacon*, which self-describes as "dedicated to uncovering the stories that the powers that be hope will never see the light of day," carried the three professors' statement and the usual Collier-Hoffman slurs, describing me as "dripping with racial hatred against Jews."[42] Meanwhile, the conservative American political site *HotAir* declared me to be a "particularly odious speaker" and wondered in its headline: "Is it time for conservatives to 'shut down' anti-Israel campus speakers?"

There was a recurrent subplot to the 'antisemitism' charade that also appeared in new form overseas: my musical life. The original SOAS *Daily Mail* article was accompanied by an 'informational' box entitled "VIOLINIST TURNED 'HATE SPEAKER' THOMAS SUÁREZ". Describing my talk as a "rant on Jews and Zionism," the box included a reference to what the writer apparently (but wrongly) thought was an important employer, the American Symphony Orchestra. It was an odd choice; but to a non-musician searching my history on the internet, the ASO's name would seem to be of consequence. Whatever the *Daily Mail*'s intent, there is no benign explanation for why the *Daily Collegian* embedded 'American Symphony Orchestra' as a *metatag* in the article. That metatag was not inserted to help searches for the article's actual topic. It was inserted in the hope of harming my career.

Roger Waters has said that musicians are afraid to speak up about Israel and Palestine. If they are merely "afraid" in his musical circles, they are altogether terrified in the classical music world. Among the eager distributors of the original *Daily Mail* piece was the popular music critic Norman Lebrecht, whose music blog *Slipped Disc* is widely read in Britain and the US. An avid Zionist, he has used his site to "out" musicians critical of Israel. When he seized on the original tabloid story to "out" me, he prefaced it with a list of every ensemble he could find that I have ever been associated with (including one I never was).[43] It is not hyperbole to state that if I were still in the US relying on the violin to pay the rent, I would have woken up to find life suddenly different.

I never figured out how the plague word got to the mayor of Bronxville, an affluent suburb north of New York City. A long-planned talk I was to give in Bronxville was abruptly cancelled in response to an email by Mayor Mary Marvin invoking 'antisemitism'. I offered to meet the mayor at her convenience, but she refused, and nor would she agree to sample a video of previous lectures. I do not know Mayor Marvin, but I do not believe that concerns about what Bronxville citizens might hear from my mouth was what worried her.[44]

One particularly effective use of 'antisemitism' is to claim that the person is a danger to young people — students. News articles in the *Independent*, *Evening Standard*, and *Mancunion* reported that Jews do not feel safe in school, and all cited me as evidence.[45] Not one of these British papers replied to my attempts to respond. When *Haaretz* grouped me with a supporter of female genital mutilation and a Salafi preacher, the reporter quickly responded to my email and apologised, but offered no correction. Nor were parents' fears eased when an article in the *Jewish Press* quoted me as saying that "the only good Jew is a dead Jew."[46]

At other universities I was unaware of trouble. I spoke at Columbia on the fourteenth anniversary of Edward Said's death — without incident. I spoke at a socially involved restaurant in Washington, DC, whose owner had fended off a barrage of harassing UK phone calls from Hoffman, who threatened to organise a mass demonstration and boycott of his establishment. The owner was all the more happy to have me: *Please, fly over, I need the publicity*, he laughed back. A troll's Twitter photo of me at the lectern with a nasty caption was the meagre spoils.

The cynical exploitation of antisemitism threatens to compromise — *has* compromised — the democracies of the United Kingdom, mainland European nations, the United States, and Canada. Cutting away all the obfuscation, all the propaganda, all the lies, the Antisemitism Wars are one thing only: a front in Israel's war against Palestine, trivialising true racism against Jews in order to continue its racism against the Palestinians. Zionism has weaponised antisemitism. It cannot succeed without the media's acquiescence.

PART 3
THE DOCUMENTS

The following documents, most of them written over the last couple of years while the Antisemitism Wars were unfolding, give detailed evidence for many of the criticisms I and others have made of the IHRA 'definition', the Zionist Lobby in the U.K., and individual 'useful idiots'* as they are sometimes called, who provide unthinking support for Israel whatever it does.

The documents section starts with two analyses of the IHRA definition. First, an account originally published in the *London Review of Books* by a leading judge, Stephen Sedley, describing the IHRA definition and its arrival on the British scene after being kicked around in different forms by various obscure international organisations.

Second, a legal opinion of the IHRA 'definition' of antisemitism, commissioned by the Palestine Return Centre from Geoffrey Robertson QC. Robertson is one of the country's leading Human Rights QCs and with forensic skill he takes apart the so-called definition and demonstrates how it is entirely unfit for purpose. In particular, he describes 'the ineptitude of its drafting' and analyses one by one the eleven conditions which many supporters of Israel have insisted be adopted by the Labour Party. He shows how three of them in particular would restrict or eliminate freedoms which have been taken for granted in this country up to now, to criticise the existence, the history, and the conduct of Israel, and its self-definition as a Jewish state.

One of the mysteries of the Antisemitism Wars is how insignificant, erroneous or tendentious information is treated seriously by the media, and indeed magnified by the habit newspapers have of quoting themselves or other newspapers rather than investigating

---

* "In political jargon, a useful idiot is a derogatory term for a person perceived as a propagandist for a cause of whose goals they are not fully aware and who is used cynically by the leaders of the cause. The term was originally used to describe non-Communists regarded as susceptible to Communist propaganda and manipulation." Wikipedia

the origins of the information they are fed. The Campaign Against Antisemitism (CAA) is an organisation which has as its *raison d'être* the aim of demonstrating how widespread antisemitism is in the UK, and the effects this has on UK Jews.

In an article on the US website *If Americans Knew*, a journalist, Eve Mykytyn, investigated the CAA in a way which no British journalist seems to have had the courage to do. She shows the origins of some of the spurious accusations and dubious statistics that are alleged to demonstrate the spread of antisemitism throughout the Labour Party and beyond. Often mentioned as an authoritative source of statistics about antisemitism in the U.K., the CAA is rather less impressive that it might seem from its grand-sounding title, as this article reveals. Aimed at an American readership, this article provides a lot of information which has not been published in the U.K.

In January 2017, the Al-Jazeera television channel transmitted four documentaries called *The Lobby*, which used secret filming to investigate the way Israel, through its Ministry of Strategic Affairs, attempts to influence opinions in the UK by infiltrating Israeli embassy staff and freelances into British organisations. The programmes were produced and narrated by Clayton Swisher. The Documents section includes transcripts of these four documentaries, and the original programmes can be seen at https://www.aljazeera.com/investigations/thelobby/

It's worth looking at an incident described in detail in Programme 3 because it gives a good idea of how Chinese whispers turn a normal conversation about Israel and Palestine into an "antisemitic incident." It is important because it suggests that many of the claimed thousands of incidents of antisemitism start as a simple discussion critical of Israel and the organisations it supports and are turned by the Zionist listener into an 'antisemitic trope.' We even have the chair of the Friends of Israel misreporting to her colleagues what a Labour Party member says to make it sound more like the 'antisemitic trope' she keeps going on about, by introducing an idea that Jews influence the financial sector when, as the secret recording shows, the Labour Party member said nothing of the sort. One participant filmed secretly in the programme seems to define anything which makes him feel uncomfortable as 'antisemitic: "Yesterday ... I was made to feel uncomfortable and although nothing anti-Semitic was said I'm sure there were undertones of it" And so he is well on the way to chalking up another antisemitic incident.

In 2018, Al-Jazeera made another documentary series, *The Lobby - USA*, using undercover filming to reveal the activities of the Israel lobby in America, coordinated by an organisation called the Israel Project. It showed how, in a similar way to activities in the UK, the Israel Lobby in the USA spied on American citizens in coordination with Israel's Ministry of Strategy Affairs.

Among the revelations was the fact that after a meeting of Israeli diplomats in the US, who were filmed complaining about the pro-BDS activities of an organisation called Black Lives Matter, attempts were made to infiltrate and disrupt Black Lives Matter activities, including leaning on the owner of a nightclub to cancel a planned fundraiser.

The U.S. documentary series also shows an official of the Emergency Committee for Israel teaming up with the right-wing Hoover Institution to pay protesters to heckle a 2016 conference of Students for Justice in Palestine.

As usually happens, these people were proud of the suppression of free speech they had organised. Eric Gallagher, the development director of The Israel Project, boasted of how the cancellation had been achieved. "I don't know if you saw that this club ditched a Black Lives Matter event," Gallagher said to the undercover reporter. "One of our donors, we just put in a call to him and he put in a call to the place."

When *The Lobby – USA* was ready to be screened in the USA, pressure was put on Qatar, the Arab state which funds and hosts

Al-Jazeera, to suppress the documentary series. One factor was said to be Qatari fear that the US would withdraw its military base from Qatar, at a time when the country was under diplomatic attack from Saudi Arabia and the United Arab Emirates, both allies of the US.*

Who will Edit the Editors? provides a rare example of a journalist working in this area who is willing to speak out against some of the activities of his employer. In July, 2018, three U.K. Jewish newspapers, *Jewish News*, the *Jewish Chronicle* and the *Jewish Telegraph*, published a joint front page describing Labour leader Jeremy Corbyn as an "existential threat" to British Jews. Stephen Oryszczuk, foreign editor of *Jewish News,* was appalled by this action and in a rare display of conscience he agreed to an interview with Kerry-Anne Mendoza, editor of *The Canary* website about his disgust with his employers..

The Conduct of Baroness Tonge is the title given to a thorough investigation of several complaints of antisemitism in a meeting hosted by Baroness Jenny Tonge in the House of Lords (at which I was one of the speakers). The complaints were made by a range of people, but they started with a Zionist blogger who crops up quite a lot whenever false accusations of antisemitism are made, and who within hours of the meeting wrote an account which – to be charitable – contained lies, and sent it to major newspapers. These reports led to official complaints being made to the House of Lords Privileges Committee, and part of their final report follows. You can read the whole of the report, including appendices, which contain much juicy material, at the reference in the footnote. The report covered two sets of complaints from outside Parliament, that Baroness Tonge had breached the parliamentary code of conduct:

---

* A fuller account of the *The Lobby – USA* series can be found at: https://grayzoneproject.com/2018/09/05/censored-documentary-exposes-the-israeli-governments-attack-on-black-lives-matter/amp/?__twitter_impression=true

1. That she had hosted a meeting that was "very antisemitic".

2. That she had hosted a book launch, which is forbidden in the Palace of Westminster. (The book in question, *State of Terror*, by Thomas Suárez, is about Zionist terrorism in the 1930s and 40s. I suspect that if it had been a book about flower arranging, no one would have complained even if it had been a launch.)

In the course of investigating the meetings, the Commissioner for Standards added a third charge after she came across the fact that one of the meetings was recorded, and that Baroness Tonge may have breached rules by agreeing to this.

The only charge that was upheld was this last one, which Baroness Tonge admitted was a mistake, because she thought that the Al-Jazeera film crew had applied for and received permission. The other two charges, relating to antisemitism at the first meeting, and the possibility of the second one being a book launch, were decisively dismissed.

Paradoxically, the most serious complaints about the first meeting – that it was "very anti-Semitic with the usual comments made about non-Israeli Jews"; was an "anti-Jewish litany and holocaust deniers' rant"; that Baroness Tonge "did not rebuke her speakers or stop them at any time"; and that "blatant racism and anti-Semitism was made ... public by her meeting and her speakers" – could only be shown to be fabrications because the (illicit) recording of the whole meeting was available to the Committee.

I have omitted material about the 'TV recording' complaint, which is irrelevant to this book, and the 'book launch' complaint, because it turned out that it wasn't a book launch. I have also omitted most of the footnotes, which generally referred to appendices in the full report which can be read online, on the Parliament website. You may also read the 3000-word rant about the meeting by the blogger in question, all of whose complaints of antisemitism were rejected by the Commission.

But the analysis of the first meeting is worth reading in detail for two reasons. First, it is an indication of how the media can be manipulated by Zionists to create headlines out of candy floss, and when it turns out months later that not a word of what was printed was true, there is no redress which will undo the harm caused by the original reports.

Second, the report reveals how ready defenders of Israel are to jump into the arena without establishing whether there is any basis in fact for what they are alleging. From peers of the realm down to the Israeli ambassador who, in the old definition, is a man 'sent to lie abroad for his country', people who were not at the meeting were prepared to complain in public to the House of Lords about events which didn't happen, words which were never said and even applause that never took place.

What is sad about this Report is the realisation after reading all of it, that a huge amount of time, energy and money was wasted as a result of the hobby of a couple of bloggers who roam the halls of academe, parliament and churches to find material they can then claim as antisemitic. It was their largely fabricated reports of the meeting in question that set the ball rolling, all the way to its measured and well-argued conclusion that none of the complaints they made against Baroness Tonge had any substance.

You would think that when their actions were dismissed so roundly and comprehensively by the Privileges Committee Report, the complainants might pause and consider whether to take up another hobby. But no – several months later, I stood behind one of them in a queue to get into another meeting about Palestine in a room in the House of Common, and was pleased to see that he was denied entry because he had not been granted a ticket.

6

The IHRA 'definition'

The article *Defining Anti-Semitism* in the *London Review of Books* was followed by correspondence, leading Sedley to add a piece about how the IHRA definition came to be written and adopted by the British government. I think it is helpful to put that piece before the main article.

Judge Stephen Sedley

Origins

In 2005 a working party of the European Monitoring Centre on Racism and Xenophobia, an EU institution, produced a forty-word 'working definition':

> Anti-Semitism is a certain perception of Jews, which may be expressed as hatred towards Jews. Rhetorical and physical manifestations of anti-Semitism are directed towards Jewish or non-Jewish individuals and/or their property, towards Jewish community institutions and religious facilities.

It was followed by a series of examples, of unknown authorship, which, depending on their context, might constitute acts of anti-Semitism. Of the 11 examples, seven referred to Israel rather than to Jews. But both the definition and the illustrations were rejected by the EUMC, and in 2013 its successor, the Fundamental Rights Agency (FRA), removed the entire text from its website as part of a clear-out of non-official documents.

In May 2016 the same text was adopted by the International Holocaust Remembrance Alliance (the IHRA), a Berlin-based association of 31 states, at its meeting in Bucharest. To it were added, in the IHRA's press release, the list of 11 examples.

What I did not appreciate then was, first, that the IHRA text was not original but had been retrieved from the files of two other bodies which had never adopted it; second, that the 'examples' had been added to the adopted text; and, third, that the content of the versions adopted by UK institutions and bodies (and by governments such as those of Austria and Romania) has itself been variable.

In December 2016, a press release from the Department for Communities and Local Government and the prime minister's office announced that the UK had 'formally' adopted the IHRA's working definition of anti-Semitism, setting out the forty-word definition without any of the associated examples. It is not known what 'formal' adoption means in constitutional terms: either a text has to take legislative form, with all that this entails, or it remains simply a policy. On the same day Jeremy Corbyn announced that the Labour Party was adopting the definition.

In neither of these announcements were the tendentious illustrations included. But central government has cited them as grounds for rejecting the advice of the Home Affairs Committee that the 'definition' should be qualified by spelling out that in the absence of additional evidence of anti-Semitic intent, it is not anti-Semitic to criticise Israel's government, to hold it to the same standards as other liberal democracies or to take a particular interest in its policies or actions. A number of municipalities, including London, Manchester and Birmingham, have adopted the list wholesale – London, among others, using a version which omits the proviso that the listed examples depend on their context.

What is at issue is suggested by the prime minister's contemporaneous speech, quoted in the government's press release: 'Israel guarantees the rights of people of all religions, races and sexualities, and it wants to enable everyone to flourish.' From this it isn't far to the first of the 'examples' of anti-Semitism: 'Manifestations could also target the state of Israel, conceived as a Jewish collectivity.' Leaving aside the difference between targeting and criticism, one asks: conceived by whom? The world at large, millions of Jews included, conceives of Israel as a state with the same rights and obligations as any other state, including an obligation not to extend its territory by incremental colonisation or to occupy and administer the land of others under military law. It is hardline Zionism and hardline jihadism which coincide, as extremes tend to do, in regarding Israel as a 'Jewish collectivity' – jihadism by seeking to identify Israel with all Jews (making every Jew a legitimate terrorist target), Zionism by seeking to identify all Jews with Israel (whence the description of Israel's Jewish critics as 'self-hating').

None of this is addressed by a definition which sets the bar needlessly high by stipulating hatred rather than simple hostility as the defining characteristic of anti-Semitism, nor by tendentious examples which look to immunise Israel from sharp criticism. Those who seek to make use of such material in the UK should perhaps remember that public authorities are bound by the Human Rights Act to give effect to Article 10 of the European Convention on Human Rights, which guarantees the right of free expression subject only to restrictions prescribed by law – which the IHRA definition is not.

Defining Anti-Semitism:

Shorn of philosophical and political refinements, anti-Semitism is hostility towards Jews as Jews. Where it manifests itself in discriminatory acts or inflammatory speech it is generally illegal, lying beyond the bounds of freedom of speech and of action. By contrast, criticism (and equally defence) of Israel or of Zionism is not only generally lawful: it is affirmatively protected by law. Endeavours to conflate the two by characterising everything other than anodyne criticism of Israel as anti-Semitic are not new. What is new is the adoption by the UK government (and the Labour Party) of a definition of anti-Semitism which endorses the conflation.

In May 2016 the International Holocaust Remembrance Alliance, an intergovernmental body, adopted a 'non-legally-binding working definition of anti-Semitism': 'Anti-Semitism is a certain perception of Jews, which may be expressed as hatred towards Jews. Rhetorical and physical manifestations of anti-Semitism are directed towards Jewish or non-Jewish individuals and/or their property, towards Jewish community institutions and religious facilities.' This account, which is largely derived from one formulated by the European Monitoring Centre on Racism and Xenophobia, fails the first test of any definition: it is indefinite. 'A certain perception of Jews, which may be expressed as hatred' invites a string of questions. Is anti-Semitism solely a matter of perception? What about discriminatory practices and policies? What about perceptions of Jews that are expressed otherwise than as hatred?

These gaps are unlikely to be accidental. Their effect, whether or not it is their purpose, is to permit perceptions of Jews which fall short of expressions of racial hostility to be stigmatised as anti-Semitic. Along with the classic tropes about a world Jewish conspiracy and Holocaust denial or dismissal, the IHRA's numerous examples include these:

> Manifestations might include the targeting of the state of Israel, conceived as a Jewish collectivity. However, criticism of Israel similar to that levelled against any other country cannot be regarded as anti-Semitic.
>
> Applying double standards by requiring of [the state of Israel] a behaviour not expected or demanded of any other democratic nation.

> Denying the Jewish people their right to self-determination, e.g. by claiming that the existence of a state of Israel is a racist endeavour.

The first and second of these examples assume that Israel, apart from being a Jewish state, is a country like any other and so open only to criticism resembling such criticism as can be made of other states, placing the historical, political, military and humanitarian uniqueness of Israel's occupation and colonisation of Palestine beyond permissible criticism. The third example bristles with contentious assumptions about the racial identity of Jews, assumptions contested by many diaspora Jews but on which both Zionism and anti-Semitism fasten, and about Israel as the embodiment of a collective right of Jews to self-determination.

In October 2016 the Commons Select Committee on Home Affairs published a report entitled 'Anti-Semitism in the UK' in which it broadly accepted the IHRA's 'working definition' but proposed that two qualifications be added in the interests of free speech:

> It is not anti-Semitic to criticise the government of Israel, without additional evidence to suggest anti-Semitic intent.
>
> It is not anti-Semitic to hold the Israeli government to the same standards as other liberal democracies, or to take a particular interest in the Israeli government's policies or actions, without additional evidence to suggest anti-Semitic intent.

The government in its published response adopted the IHRA definition but brushed aside the select committee's caveats, taking the exclusion of 'criticism of Israel similar to that levelled against any other country' to be part of the IHRA definition and to be a sufficient safeguard of free speech.

A recent opinion obtained from Hugh Tomlinson QC, a prominent human rights lawyer, by a group of NGOs concerned with Palestine and Israel, concludes that the IHRA definition is unclear and confusing (it could be suggested, in fact, that it is calculatedly misleading), that the government's adoption of it has no legal status, and that the overriding legal duty of public authorities is to preserve freedom of expression. He also argues that, even taken on its own terms, the definition does not require characterisations of Israel as an apartheid or colonialist state, or calls for boycott, disinvestment or sanctions, to be characterised as anti-Semitic.

Policy is not law. At most it is a guide to the application of legal powers where these include exercises of discretion or judgment. For central government the impact of the IHRA policy may well be imperceptible, but for local authorities and educational institutions, and for the police in a number of situations, the policy is capable of having a real impact. Its authors may be pleased about this, but policy is required to operate within the law.

One law of central relevance is section 43 of the 1986 Education Act, passed after campus heckling of Conservative ministers and speakers but of continuing application to tertiary institutions in England and Wales. It places a duty on such institutions to 'take such steps as are reasonably practicable to ensure that freedom of speech within the law is secured for members, students and employees ... and for visiting speakers'.

A second, and fundamental, law is the 1998 Human Rights Act, which makes it unlawful for a public authority to act incompatibly with rights that include the right of free expression under article 10 of the European Convention. The right is not absolute or unqualified: it can be abrogated or restricted where to do so is lawful, proportionate and necessary for (among other things) public safety, the prevention of disorder or the protection of the rights of others. These qualifications do not include a right not to be offended.

The European Court of Human Rights has not helped here. In a judgment handed down in 2016, it upheld the order of a Swiss court requiring an organisation which campaigned against anti-Semitism to withdraw its criticism of an academic commentator for writing '*Quand Israël s'expose sur la scène internationale, c'est bien le judaïsme qui s'expose en même temps.*' It is disturbing that the court failed to protect a publication which contended that propositions like these '*glissent carrément vers l'antisémitisme*' ('are clearly edging towards anti-Semitism'). Why were both the article and the critique not equally protected by article 10? The upholding of the Swiss judgment is another in a long line of cases, starting in 1976 with the Little Red Schoolbook case against the UK, in which the Strasbourg court has tolerated intolerant decisions of national courts on freedom of expression by giving them the benefit of a 'margin of appreciation'.

Although the abstentionist nature of Strasbourg jurisprudence does little to prevent official intervention aimed at muting criticism of Israel, it can be readily seen why it may be contrary to law in the UK to bar a speaker or an event because of anticipated criticism of Israel's human rights record, or of its policies and practices of land annexation. If so, the bar cannot be validated by a policy, much less one as protean in character and as open-ended in shape as the IHRA definition.

In recent times a number of institutions, academic, religious and social, have stood up to pressure to abandon events critical of Israel. What are less easy to track are events which failed to take place because of such pressure, or for fear of it[*]; but the IHRA definition offers encouragement to pro-Israel militants whose targets for abuse and disruption in London have recently included the leading American scholar and critic of Israel Richard Falk, and discouragement to university authorities which do not want to act as censors but worry that the IHRA definition requires them to do so.

When a replica of Israel's separation wall was erected in the churchyard of St James, Piccadilly in 2013, the *Spectator* denounced it as an 'anti-Israeli hate-festival' – a description now capable of

---

[*] Thomas Suárez's piece on pp. 63-73 describes such events.

coming within the IHRA's 'working definition' of anti-Semitism. In such ways the official adoption of the definition, while not a source of law, gives respectability and encouragement to forms of intolerance which are themselves contrary to law, and higher education institutions in particular need to be aware of this.

Anti-Semitism: The IHRA definition and its consequences for freedom of expression
Geoffrey Robertson Q.C.

1. I am asked to advise the Palestinian Return Centre as to the interpretation and impact on free speech, of the British Government's acceptance in 2016 of an extended definition of anti-Semitism promulgated by the International Holocaust Remembrance Alliance (IHRA).

Freedom of Expression

2. The English writer George Orwell, in his introduction to Animal Farm (which his left-wing publisher turned down because it was insulting to Stalin) remarked that "if liberty means anything at all, it means the right to tell people what they do not want to hear." That is an apt definition of free speech in the UK today, in terms of our common and statute law and the long-stop protection of speech in Article 10 of the European Convention of Human Rights. The Common Law in past centuries punished certain kinds of writing (libel) and speech (slander), namely blasphemy (now abolished), sedition (now a dead letter) and obscenity – that which "tends to deprave and corrupt" its potential audience, subject to a "public good" defence and (by judicial definition) some real prospect of harm. More recent criminal statutes have outlawed the stirring up of hatred against those identified by a personal characteristic: their race or religion or sexual orientation. But as the Crown Prosecution Service guidelines emphasize, "Hatred is a very strong emotion" and "stirring up racial tension, opposition,

even hostility may not necessarily be enough to amount to an offence".[47] Anti-Semitic utterances, unless intended or likely to foment hatred against Jewish people, do not amount to an offence under English law. But this discreditable and indeed contemptible behaviour may result in disciplinary action, expulsion from organisations, and a loss of the right to practice certain employments or professions. To accuse someone wrongly of anti-Semitism is defamatory and would incur damages in a civil action.

3. This position taken by British law differs from that in some European countries with historic experience of Nazi repression, which have stricter laws against racism and genocide denial. Even so, all European countries are subject to the Convention, Article 10 of which lays down:

"Everyone has the right to freedom of expression. This right shall include freedom to hold opinions and to receive and impart information and ideas without interference by public authority and regardless of frontiers."

This principle may only be overborne a) by a precise law, which is b) necessary in a democratic society either in the interests of national security, the prevention of disorder or the protection of the reputation and rights of others, and c) counts as a proportionate measure to achieve these legitimate aims. But the need for restrictions must be established convincingly and they must be "clear, certain and predictable" – i.e. formulated with sufficient precision to enable citizens to regulate their conduct. The European Court of Human Rights has also held that they must also be a proportionate response to a pressing social need. The right may be availed of by those whose utterances "offend, shock or disturb." The scope for criticism of states and statesmen is wider than for private individuals because of the need for free and open discussion of politics.

4. These principles were most recently applied by the European Court to strike down the conviction by the Swiss Courts of a rabid Turkish nationalist for proclaiming at a small and unreported conference that "the Armenian genocide was a lie." The Swiss genocide denial law, the Court declared, was too broad: it should not have permitted his conviction unless there was evidence of intention to arouse, or likelihood of, violence or disorder. The 'idea' that there had been no Armenian genocide, although it flew in the face of the facts, was nonetheless protected unless its utterance posed some danger to the public by encouraging or justifying violence, hatred or intolerance.[48]

5. Another case in the European Court was brought by CICAD (Inter-community Coordination against Anti-Semitism and Defamation) which had described an academic as "anti-Semitic:" for criticising the State of Israel, calling it Judaism with "the morality of dirty hands" because of its policies of "closure of territories, destruction of civilian homes and targeted assignation of alleged terrorist leaders."[49] CICAD had been convicted of defamation and fined, but the court ruled that this punishment did not infringe free speech: such criticisms of Israel did not make the academic "anti-Semitic", and the accusation was false and libellous.

6. These cases demonstrate that Article 10 will serve to protect expression of hostile opinion about the conduct of the Government of Israel, however exaggerated or baseless, unless communicated for the purpose or with the result of stirring up disorder or hatred of Jews in general.

7. So, what is "anti-Semitism?" The Oxford English Dictionary gives as its meaning "hostility to or prejudice against Jews." This is both simple and accurate, so long as it is understood that the hostility and prejudice must be against Jews as such, or in

general, because of some sort of presumed racial characteristic – and not against an individual Jewish person or a particular organisation. Wikipedia, with reference to *Encyclopaedia Britannica*, Paul Johnson and Bernard Lewis, defines anti-Semitism as "hostility to, prejudice or discrimination against Jews." The addition of "discrimination" is acceptable, (if unnecessary, because its motive will generally be a feeling of hostility or prejudice) but again, so long as the unfavourable treatment that constitutes discrimination is inflicted because the victims are Jewish.

8. The word seems to have been coined in German literature in the late nineteenth century, although it could be applied to the persecution of Jewish communities ever since the third century BC. It has taken various forms of negative stereotyping in ideologies and myths and of course reached its apotheosis in the Nazi genocide, although recent surveys show that it still manifests in the UK and may be increasing - often on social media or in the vandalism of Jewish tombstones and synagogues. It is a particularly vicious form of racism, criminal when it reaches the pitch of inciting hatred and unacceptable in public institutions, employment and most organisations. It is defamatory to wrongly accuse a person of being anti-Semitic. It might be thought that the word needs no further definition.

9. That is not the view of the UK Government, which in December 2016 "adopted" an extended definition which had previously featured in the "Hate Crime Manual" for police officers and had been recommended – with important changes to protect the freedom to criticise Israel – by the House of Commons Home Affairs Select Committee. It was never debated in Parliament and perhaps not even discussed in Cabinet: it was announced by the Prime Minister at a Conservative Party luncheon, and has no legal effect. It was a definition that had originated as a "working definition" in an obscure European Union agency, the European Monitoring Centre on Racism

and Xenophobia, in 2005. This agency did not formally adopt it and in due course abandoned it, but it was picked up – again as a "working definition," in 2016 by the International Holocaust Remembrance Alliance (IHRA), which as its name implies works on research into the Holocaust. It is not part of the European Union, although it has 31 country affiliates, mainly from Europe. Its version attracted the attention of the Home Affairs Committee which recommended it but only with "caveats" i.e. necessary conditions, to protect free speech.

10. The IHRA, at its Bucharest Conference in 2016, issued this "non-legally binding working definition of anti-Semitism" which comprises what may be described as a core meaning, followed by eleven examples of how that meaning might be applied. That core meaning is:

Anti-Semitism is a certain perception of Jews, which may be expressed as hatred towards Jews. Rhetorical and physical manifestations of anti-Semitism are directed toward Jewish or non-Jewish individuals and/or their property, toward Jewish community institutions and religious facilities.

The definition is avowedly "non-legally binding": were it to become so, or to be adopted for any disciplinary or regulatory purpose, it would be seriously deficient. The second sentence seems surplusage[*]: of course, manifestations of anti-Semitism are directed towards such persons and institutions (and notably, the "State of Israel" is not listed as a target at this point) but they need not be directed to anyone (e. g. anti-Semitic comments and cartoons on the internet). The first sentence is question-begging: what perception, and in whose eyes – those of the Jewish community, of Zionists or anti- Zionists, or is this a reference (as it should be) to the objective impression of the

---

[*] A legal term meaning "a useless statement completely irrelevant to the cause" [KS][*]

reasonable bystander?[50] The use of the conditional word "may" lends vagueness and imprecision: obviously it can be expressed as "hatred towards Jews," but how else "may" anti-Semitism be expressed and if there "may" be other definitions, why are they not identified? As a "working definition," it needs a lot more work before it attains the precision which Article 10 requires for a ban on speech which is "required by law." It may be useful for purposes akin to the context in which it arose for the IHRA in Bucharest, where it was being used as a guide for the police in Romania (a country which had initially collaborated with the Nazis) to identify attitudes unacceptable to the job of law enforcement, but standing alone it lacks the precision required of a definition or rule. It is not clear whether it was adopted as a free-standing core definition by the IHRA at its Bucharest Conference, or whether the eleven "examples" were adopted at the same time. In the latter case, it would not serve as a "definition" at all, but rather as a discussion of whether certain conduct can be identified as anti-Semitic.

12. There is one aspect which I find remarkable, but which does not seem to have engaged the attention of critics or proponents. Despite its imprecision, it does pivot upon manifestations of "hatred towards Jews." As I point out in paragraph 2 above, "hatred" is a very strong word. It is the emotion that can be deduced in those who daub abhorrent slogans on tombstones and Synagogues, but it falls short of capturing those who express only hostility or prejudice, or who practice discrimination. "I don't like Jews and never employ them, but I don't hate them" – this speaker is anti-Semitic, but it does not seem included in this definition. Similarly, "I am prejudiced against Jews because they are not 'one of us' and their religious practices are ridiculous, but I don't hate them." Or "I think we should deport all Jews to Israel, because they would be happy there. It would be in their own interests – I certainly don't hate them, I just think they

don't fit in here in England." Under the IHRA definition, these anti-Semitic comments would not be deemed "anti-Semitic." This consideration, above all others, convinces me that the definition is not fit for purpose, or any purpose that relies upon it to identify anti-Semitism accurately. By pivoting upon racial hatred (a crime to stir up in this country) it fails to catch those who exhibit hostility and prejudice – or apply discrimination – against Jewish people for no reason other than that they are Jewish. It fails Jewish people, most of all, by its inability to detect many who harbour hostility towards them – for example, those who insinuate racial prejudice politely (remember Enoch Powell's "rivers of blood" speech, with its classical allusions).

13. There have been suggestions in the media that the definition and its examples were drafted with the "hidden agenda" that they could be used to chill or ban criticism of Israeli policy and to label the nascent BDS movement as "anti-Semitic".[51] While there have been attempts to use it in this way, this was not the original intention according to its lead draftsperson, a US attorney named Kenneth Stern from the American Jewish Committee against Anti-Semitism, who worked with the European Monitoring Centre on Racism and Xenophobia to study an upsurge in race hate crimes in Northern Europe. It was discovered, in the course of collecting data from various countries that they had different definitions of anti-Semitism, or none at all. So, as Stern testified to the US Congress in 2017:

> "The definition was drafted to make it easier for data collectors to know what to put in their reports and what to reject... because the definition was drafted with data collectors utmost in mind, it also gave examples of information to include regarding Israel... The definition was not drafted, and was never intended, as a tool to target or chill speech."

14. Mr Stern's evidence to this effect is credible, especially as he has spoken out strongly against the misuse of "his" definition at British universities to ban an "Israel Apartheid Week" and in ways he describes as "McCarthy-like."[52] The definition was never formally adopted by the EU Committee: it was placed on its website in 2005, from which it was later removed and was adopted (for want, it may be, of any alternative) by other bodies, and was taken down in 2013.[53] However, in 2016 the core definition was picked up and promulgated in a press release by the IHRA after it was endorsed by representatives of 31 state members at its Bucharest Conference. It is not clear whether they endorsed the eleven examples as well as the core definition, although these examples have always been treated as an extension of that core definition. It is by reference to several of them that some Jewish activists have asserted that BDS activities are anti-Semitic, as well as the EU exercise of labelling Israeli products from the disputed West Bank and occupied Golan. This is not only wrong, as I shall explain, but a perversion of the original intention of the extended definition. Although one of the American drafting team had Israeli Government affiliations and this was at the time when Natan Sharansky identified "the new anti-Semitism" as "aimed at the Jewish State" through "double standards, demonization and delegitimisation", I have found no real evidence that the definition was produced in 2005 with the secret intention of being used as a weapon against Israel's critics. That it has been, is a measure of the ineptitude of its drafting (or of the fact that it was drafted for the innocuous purpose of data collection) rather than as part of some alleged Zionist conspiracy. Although it may be odd that an EU instrumentality should ask Americans to write its definitions, Mr Stem (a self-declared Zionist) has made continual and credible criticisms of the subsequent misuse of his words.

The Examples

15. Having stated at the outset in bold type that the definition itself is a **"non-legally binding working definition"** the examples are prefaced by an assertion that they are "to guide IHRA in its work" - and its work of Holocaust research and commemoration does not include proposing laws or rules. It goes on "the following examples may serve as illustrations: ...anti-Semitism frequently charges Jews with conspiring to harm humanity, and it is often used to blame Jews for "why things go wrong." It is expressed in speech, writing, visual forms and action, and employs sinister stereotypes and negative character traits." This is true and unexceptional. However, it adds (in the place denoted by the ellipsis above):

> "Manifestations might include targeting the State of Israel, conceived as a Jewish collectivity. However, criticism of Israel similar to that levelled against any other country cannot be regarded as anti-Semitic."

The importance of this passage is that the British Government identified it as sufficient to ensure that the definition it adopted would not infringe free speech, after the House of Commons Committee had warned that the definition should only be adopted with additions ("caveats") "to ensure that freedom of speech is maintained in the context of discourse about Israel and Palestine."

16. The Government refused to "adopt" the suggested additional conditions, on the ground that the introductory passing comment – that "criticism of Israel similar to that levelled against any other country cannot be regarded as anti-Semitic" was "sufficient to ensure freedom of speech." This is wrong, or at least naive. The comment makes no reference to freedom of speech, for a start, and Israel is unlike any other country. It was established by resolution of the Security Council in 1947, to compensate for the Holocaust, granting over half of Palestine – a country which

at the time contained 1.3 million Arabs and a small minority of Jewish settlers. It won independence from British rule partly as a result of a terrorist campaign; it turned hundreds of thousands of Palestinians into refugees; it acquired territory (the Gaza strip and the West Bank) through war and refused Security Council demands to withdraw its armed forces; it has persistently been criticised by Britain and by the Red Cross and respected Human Rights NGOs like Amnesty International and Human Rights Watch for policies which have had a "catastrophic" effect on the Palestinian economy and on the health, wealth and wellbeing of its people, for its Parliament (the Knesset) passing various laws that discriminate against Arab Israelis (20% of the population) and for military occupation which stifles political development and has involved frequent lethal attacks with disproportionate civilian causalities, and for encouraging "Settlements" on Palestinian land. As recently as last month, its "One Nation" Basic Law was widely condemned as consigning Palestinians to second-class citizenship, and many commentators described it as "a form of apartheid." It points out, differentiating itself from other countries, that it has been at various times subject to terrorist atrocities – suicide bombing campaigns, routine rocket attacks and armed confrontations with a political organisation – HAMAS – which refuses to recognise its right to exist.

17. All member-states of the UN are bound to comply with international human rights law (notably the International Covenant on Civil and Political Rights) and criticism of Israel on that score could not be regarded as anti-Semitic. Unlike most countries, it is engaged in military operations in occupied territory, and so is subject to International Humanitarian Law (the laws of war) and may be open to legitimate criticism for breaches. It has what fits the definition of a displaced indigenous minority (the Palestinians) and is under an obligation, which it may legitimately be criticised for disregarding, to protect them

from discrimination and to respect their dignity. Therefore, criticism of Israel and its government of the kind mentioned in para 13 above is likely to be dissimilar to criticism levelled against other countries, but is not for that reason anti-Semitic.

18. To suggest that the IHRA definition is internally protective of free speech is mistaken: criticisms may be made of Israel that are not made of other countries, but this of itself does not constitute anti-Semitism. Moreover, the test (if it is used as a test) is confusing. For example, Dr Manfred Gerstenfeld, an anti-Semitism scholar, writes in *Arutz Sheva* of the "huge importance" of the IHRA definition: "Using the IHRA definition it becomes clear that BDS activities are anti-Semitic as they are only applied against Israel."[54] This is plainly wrong, not only because sanctions are applied to other countries (Russia, Iran, North Korea, and formerly apartheid-era South Africa) but because the impression from the IHRA wording has led this commentator to think that criticism of Israel can be defined as anti-Semitic simply because it targets Israel and does not include other countries. This is just one example of how the loose words in the definition have been misunderstood and misapplied, in a way which could be used to besmirch legitimate political action as "anti-Semitic."

19. The eleven examples are prefaced by the statement:

    "Contemporary examples of anti-Semitism in public life, the media, schools, the workplace, and in the religious sphere could, taking into account the overall context, include, but are not limited to: "

    This is an ambiguous way to introduce what are meant to be concrete examples: they "could" (but they presumably could not). This is discussion, not definition. What is not clear, (although it should have been made clear) is whether the core definition requirement of a perception of "hatred towards Jews" is a prerequisite before any example is deemed anti-Semitic. This is an important, but unaddressed, question.

Example 1

"Calling for, aiding, or justifying the killing or harming of Jews in the name of a radical ideology or an extremist view of religion."

20. This is motivated by hatred and obviously anti-Semitic (and, as incitement to violence, is also a hate crime punishable under British law).

Example 2

"Making mendacious, dehumanizing, demonizing, or stereotypical allegations about Jews as such or the power of Jews as collective – such as, especially but not exclusively, the myth about a world Jewish conspiracy or of Jews controlling the media, economy, Government or other societal institutions."

21. Here, the need to find hatred, or at least hostility, towards Jews becomes important. "The power of Jews as a collective" – for example, the power of the American-Jewish Public Affairs Committee (AIPAC) – is often referred to in political discourse as "the Jewish lobby," so described in books and newspapers by reporters and commentators who are not in any sense anti-Semitic. Similar descriptions could be used of the combined efforts of rabbis, Jewish newspapers and organisations who condemned the conduct of the Labour Party executive in altering some of the examples when Labour adopted most of the IHRA definition. There should be no constraint on describing some Jewish organisations or organisers as working towards a shared aim, unless of course it is done with hostility towards Jews in general. If "the Jewish lobby" is used in promoting the longstanding conspiracy theory (promoted by many anti-Semitics) that Jews control the government or media or economy, and the comment displays hatred or hostility to Jews generally, then in that context it would be anti-Semitic.

Example 3

> *"Accusing Jews as a people of being responsible for real or imagined wrongdoing committed by a single Jewish person or group, or even for acts committed by non-Jews."*

22. This is unexceptional.

Example 4

> *"Denying the fact, scope, mechanisms (e.g. gas chambers) or intentionality of the genocide of the Jewish people at the hands of National Socialist Germany and its supporters and accomplices during World War II (the Holocaust)."*

23. Anti-Semitism is frequently manifested by Holocaust denial, which is not a crime in the UK but is outlawed in some European countries. Given the undeniable proof of the Holocaust, denials are usually intended to offend and denigrate the Jewish people, although it is possible that a few may be the product of stupidity rather than malice.

Example 5

> *"Accusing the Jews as a people, or Israel as a state, of inventing or exaggerating the Holocaust."*

24. This is similar to Example 4, although it slips in, as an illustration, the example of criticism of the State of Israel, whether or not it is a manifestation of hostility to Jews generally. There are many grounds on which Israel is criticised – exaggerating the Holocaust (which is difficult to exaggerate, given proof that it took 6 million lives) is not one that is much heard.

Example 6

> *"Accusing Jewish citizens of being more loyal to Israel, or to the alleged priorities of Jews worldwide, than to the interests of their own nations."*

25. Israel, as in recent legislation, claims to be the true homeland of Jewish people wherever they are born, and grants citizenship to all members of its diaspora whether they want it or not.

This does not make it acceptable to treat Jewish people as synonymous with Israel or assume all Jewish people are loyal to and have an affinity with Israel. Accusing Jewish people of being loyal to the priorities of Jews worldwide is likely to promote the anti-Semitic conspiracy theory described in para 21 above. Other countries (Australia, for example) treat dual citizenship as a disqualification for standing for Parliament, presumably for fear of divided loyalties. There may be rare individual cases where a Jewish citizen is in a situation of conflict of interest where their state of birth or nationality is at diplomatic odds with Israel (for example, where a Jewish citizen of Britain returns to Israel for military service and participates in military action in support of the occupation of Palestinian territory). Jewish MP's who oppose their party's or their government's policy on Israel may be made the subject of criticism on this score, which would be anti-Semitic if it expresses a hatred or insinuates suspicion of all Jews, or e.g. that they are "political traitors" because they are Jews. Anti-Semitic abuse of these MPs is notable for viciousness, an indication of hatred.

Example 7
"Denying the Jewish people their right to self-determination, e. g., by claiming that the existence of a State of Israel is a racist endeavour."

This example plainly trespasses on political speech, or at least brands as anti-Semitic what may be statements, supportive of the Palestinian people's right of self-determination, or a reasonably held view about the history of the Balfour declaration, which in 1917 offered to establish a "national home" (not a "nation state") for Jewish people in a land of 400,000 Arabs and 30,000 Jewish settlers. "Nothing shall be done which may prejudice the civil and religious rights of existing non-Jewish communities in Palestine" the declaration added, but in 1947 those rights were certainly prejudiced by partitioning the country and giving more than half of it to Jewish settlers and immigrants and forcing hundreds of thousands of Arabs into exile. Whether the State of Israel is a "racist endeavour" is open to question given its racially discriminatory laws and its new nation state Basic Law which is frequently said to make Palestinians second class citizens and likened by some reputable commentators to a form of apartheid. The claim that Israel has no right to exist is often made by anti-Semites but can be argued dispassionately by historians and others who say that a portion of Germany should have been set aside for a Jewish homeland to compensate for the Holocaust.

27. For the record, the position in international law was pithily summarised by the British judge, Dame Rosalyn Higgins, in the International Court of Justice case about the Wall:

"Israel is entitled to exist, to be recognised and to security, and the Palestinian people are entitled to their territory, to exercise self-determination and to their own State."

Unless made with the intention of arousing hostility against Jews in general, attacks on Israel for "racist endeavours" by denying Palestinians their territory and their right to self-determination cannot be assumed to be anti-Semitic. The example is in any event liable to confuse. The "right of self-determination" is a complex question of international law, which is (in Article 1 of the Covenant on Civil and Political Rights) declared to be the right of "peoples" – the majority of whom were, at Israel's inception, Palestinians. That was not a problem for advocates of Theodore Hertzl's political ideology of creating a Jewish state in Palestine for Jews from anywhere in the world. However, it is not anti-Semitic to be critical of the ideology of Zionism unless this is part of a hate campaign or unless this criticism is expressed in a way that displays prejudice or hostility towards Jewish people generally. Nor is it anti-Semitic to identify some Jewish people who espouse this ideology as Zionists: the Home Affairs Committee notes that 57% of Jewish people in the UK support Zionism (the founding philosophy of the State of Israel) but many do not, here and in Israel itself. But it also noted that "Zionist" and the colloquial "Zio" are frequently used in anti-Semitic discourse as terms of abuse, so the word must be used accurately and in an appropriate context.

Example 8

"Applying double standards by requiring of it a behaviour not expected or demanded of any other democratic nation."

28. This begs the question of what behaviour is being objected to, and why. It focuses on political and diplomatic argument, which often shows double standards (Soviet and US accusations against each other during the Cold War, for example) but it cannot logically be concluded, as this example does, that double standards in criticising Israel denote anti-Semitism. The example could be used against the UN Human Rights Council, which notoriously makes more criticisms of Israel than of other nations where behaviour may be as bad, in moral or legal terms, but is nonetheless different. It would be wrong to accuse the Council members of anti-Semitism, unless their votes are dictated by hatred of Jews generally rather than distaste for the human rights violations allegedly perpetrated by Israel. There is, in any event, a UN country-specific mandate on Palestine, partly because of the history of human rights abuse by Israel – another fact that makes its position different to that of other democratic countries and therefore open to particular scrutiny. Israel, unlike most democratic nations, has not ratified the Treaty for the International Criminal Court and does not accept the jurisdiction of the Human Rights Commission: this also sets it apart and makes criticism of its policies, unless attended by incitement to hatred, unexceptional.

Example 9

"Using the symbols and images associated with classic anti-Semitism (e.g., claims of Jews killing Jesus or blood libel) to characterize Israel or Israelis."

29. This is unobjectionable, although these hateful symbols manifest anti-Semitism irrespective of whether they are applied to Israel or Israelis.

Example 10

"Drawing comparisons of contemporary Israeli policy to that of the Nazis."

30. This is more complicated. The writer or speaker may have no hostility towards Jews in general but may intend merely to draw a dramatic comparison. It will usually be an exaggeration, or else inappropriate, and will invariably give offence to many Jewish people, but that does not necessarily make it anti-Semitic unless the Nazi comparison was intended to show contempt for Jews in general. In the early years of Hitler governance, Nazi anti-Semitic policy took the form of discrimination which made it more difficult for Jews to find employment or enter the professions: it would not be anti-Semitic to liken current Israeli policy to these measures (however inappropriately) unless it displays hatred to all Jews or the intention was to manifest hostility to all Jews, and not just the present Government.

Example 11

"Holding Jews collectively responsible for actions of the state of Israel."

31. Israel is a democracy and its government is by definition endorsed by a majority of voters. But it would be absurd to hold all Jews responsible for its policies and its military actions: they are contested by an opposition in Israel and by many in the diaspora. So the example will usually be evidence of anti-Semitism. However, where such policies have led to human

rights violations to which a blind eye is turned by its courts and law enforcement in Israel and to which little opposition is offered by the opposition in the Knesset (other than by its Palestinian representatives) then it may not be anti-Semitic to criticise "Israelis" for turning a blind eye – unless, of course, the criticism is intended to arouse racial hatred.

General Observations

32. It must be said that all eleven examples are of conduct that "could" amount to anti- Semitism, so long as the core definition is applied, namely that they express hatred towards Jewish people as a race. One problem is that this is not made clear. If the extended definition (i.e. core definition plus examples) were ever put into a law, a court would doubtless find that the core definition must control each example. It would also emphasise the introductory paragraph which makes the examples contingent - they "could" be examples of anti-Semitism, but "could not" if they did not express hatred of Jews as a race. The trouble is that this is not clear, and many commentators, both those concerned to emphasise its danger to free speech and those concerned to use it to endanger free speech, have interpreted the examples as if they were intended to protect the state of Israel from criticism. This is the problem with loose drafting, and it is a problem in the UK because the government promulgated the definition without adding the caveat:

"It is not anti-Semitic to criticise the Government of Israel, without evidence to suggest anti-Semitic intent."

33. It must be remembered that the definition was drafted in 2005 for an EU exercise in data collection about anti-Semitism incidents, and was dropped by that organisation, then called the Fundamental Rights Agency, and removed from its Website in 2013 because of its inutility. It was resurrected by the IHRA at its Conference in 2016, held in conjunction with the highly respected *Elie Wiesel National Institute for the Study of*

the Holocaust in Romania, which was involved in teaching police officers about anti-Semitism and Holocaust denial. It cannot be doubted that the extended definition would be useful for such an exercise, and there could be no objection to its use for similar purposes by police forces in the UK (so long as it is made clear that anti-Semitism is not a criminal offence unless it stirs up racial hatred).

34. In relation to the examples which refer to Israel, special caution is required. According to the Home Affairs Committee, most anti-Semitic utterances come from right-wingers and UKIP is the political party which is most infested. That said, there is no doubt that dyed-in-the-wool anti-Semites may exploit human rights concerns over Israeli policy to whip up anger against Jews generally. There is evidence however, that some politically involved people (in the Labour and Liberal Democrat parties in particular) have allowed their anger at human rights violations by Israel to boil over into utterances and posts that reveal or can reasonably be interpreted as meaning a hatred towards Jews. There can be no objection to political parties, or other membership-based organisations, expelling or disciplining such persons by reference to the IHRA definition, so long as the offending statement does express hatred of Jewish people generally. As pointed out above, I consider this is too limited a definition: such organisations should consider adopting broader definitions that allow them to discipline members who express hostility or prejudice towards Jews in general.

35. UK Courts have not had occasion to consider the IHRA definition, although one very recent decision of the Court of Appeal (August 2018) in *Jewish Human Rights Watch Limited v Leicester City Council* does indicate the likely approach. The Council had passed a motion "to boycott any produce originating from illegal Israeli settlements in the West Bank until such time as it complies with International Law and withdraws

from Palestinian occupied territories." Jewish Human Rights Watch, an organisation formed to challenge anti-Semitism, claimed that condemnation of Israel was being used as a means to attack British Jews and that the BDS movement, which it claimed had the long-term aim of destroying Israel, only increased the level of hatred experienced by Jewish people in the UK. Reflecting Example 8 above, it was argued that by passing the resolution, the Council "singled out Israel for different treatment than that adopted in respect of other countries." The Court rejected these arguments:

> "The condemnation was in line with a respectable body of opinion, including the UK Government, the European Union and the International Court of Justice… there is a legitimate scope for criticism of Israel without that implying anti-Semitic attitudes. There was nothing in the context to suggest the resolution was in fact being proposed as a cover for incitement or anti-Semitism. Calling for boycotts of goods is a well- known gesture of political solidarity with oppressed groups overseas…"

36. This is how I would expect UK Courts to approach the IHRA definition were it deployed by a University, say, or local council to ban protest meetings or to discipline students for criticising Israel. There would have to be evidence that the offending speech or action was a pretext or cover for inciting hatred of Jews generally before the core definition could be applied. Much of the concern about its "chilling" consequences seems misplaced, until it is realised that the very vagueness of the extended definition with its examples of anti-Israel conduct which "could" metamorphose into anti- Semitism, is likely to confuse decision-makers and encourage complaints that are intended to chill legitimate speech. There are already examples of Universities banning meetings because they associate discriminatory Israeli policies with apartheid. These decisions would be likely to be reversed if taken to court.

37. Where the definition most acutely threatens freedom of speech is that by Palestinians resident in or visiting the UK and supporters who may show their opposition and anger at the establishment of Israel against the wishes of its indigenous majority of Palestinians, or the expulsion of 750,000 of them in 1948 (albeit after an unsuccessful attack by Arab States*). Such people are entitled, under international human rights law, to set out their case against the State that they perceive as their oppressor, so long as their expression does not conduce to actual violence against its Jewish citizens, or against Jewish people anywhere – in which case their speech would be contrary to UK law against stirring up racial hatred. If their speech did not go so far, it might nonetheless be characterised (although not under the IHRA core definition) as anti-Semitic, if for example it aroused hostility to Jewish people by praising Palestinian armed action against Israel. The Institute of Race Relations has argued that minority communities "have a right to be heard, to make... information public, while others have the right to hear them, and the arguments based on these facts." That right should be enjoyed by speakers who criticise Israel for being a racist endeavour, unless they step over the red line and encourage attacks on Jewish people by military action or terrorism. I should add that it is not anti-Semitic to criticise the Israeli security service for assassinating terrorist suspects without trial – this has incurred criticism from Human Rights bodies and from countries whose passports have been forged to assist the movements of assassins.

38. I have, necessarily in this opinion, concentrated on the definition of anti-Semitism in respect to critics of Israeli policy. I should add that by far the most common expression of it is in

---

* In fact, the Arab states did not attack the area assigned to Israel but tried, unsuccessfully, to stop Israel taking over land that had been allocated by the UN to Palestine. [KS]

tweets, demonising Jewish MPs and public figures. To judge from those discussed in the Home Affairs Committee report and in newspapers, these are malevolent and vicious outbursts (in no more than 280 characters) evincing hatred or contempt for pro-Israeli commentators or (in particular) for critics of Jeremy Corbyn's alleged pro-Palestinian sentiments. They do not warrant detailed analysis: any identifiable sender of such messages could justifiably be expelled (e. g. if a member of the Labour Party) under any definition of anti-Semitism it chose to adopt. If that party does revert to the full IHRA definition, it should also adopt the Home Affairs Committee recommendation of inserting a provision to protect freedom of speech.

Application of the IHRA Definition

39. As I have made clear, this extended definition might be useful for purposes of discussion but should not be adopted as a rule or standard to be applied in any qualitative or quasi-judicial decision-making by any public authority. Nonetheless, it has been adopted by some universities and local councils and applied or threatened as a ban on public meetings – e.g. "Israeli apartheid week" at various universities, and a proposal to refuse the BDS a meeting place by Barnet Council Hall. Public bodies in the UK are all subject to the Human Rights Act, with its Article 10 freedom of expression protection, (as explained above), so I do not think that such unlawful actions would survive court challenge. They are not even anti-Semitic under the IHRA definition as properly interpreted. So is the adoption of this definition likely to chill free speech? The answer is "yes," but in two non-legal senses. Firstly, the definition, by so often referring to certain criticisms of Israel, is likely to encourage pro-Israeli organisations to urge that they be applied to ban criticisms of Israel. And correspondingly likely to discourage human rights groups and others from organising such protests.

40. Secondly, while it is true that the European Convention protects free speech, that is a protection offered by the courts in what is termed "judicial review" of the actions of public authorities. Like all cases that end up in court, this can be very expensive even if you win – costs only cover part of your legal expenses. For cash-strapped NGOs and student organisations, this is obviously a deterrent when faced with threats of legal action which require an expensive legal defence to protect their fundamental right to criticise Israel when it is unjustifiably limited by the application of the IHRA definition and its examples. Universities and Councils which desire to avoid the costs of a legal quagmire would be well advised not to adopt this confusing and litigation-prone definition, and – if they need one – to use the Oxford Dictionary and add in all cases a provision protecting free speech of the kind recommended by the Home Affairs Committee.

41. In the case of Universities and polytechnics there is a special statutory duty in the Education Act "to ensure freedom of speech," i.e.

> "to take such steps as is reasonably practicable to ensure that freedom of speech within the law is secured for members, students and employees... and visiting speakers."[55]

This duty is compulsory and binding and can be enforced by judicial review. There are also duties under "Prevent" legislation to avoid incitements to terrorism (which are not in any event "within the law") so they would only be entitled to ban speakers or events likely to advocate violence against Jewish people, in Israel or outwith. Intelligent discussion of whether discrimination against Palestinians by the Israeli Government amounts to apartheid, or whether the settler movement is colonialist, or meetings which call for Universities and Councils to adopt BDS policies, cannot be considered anti-Semitic under the IHRA definition or any other, in the absence of evidence that the event is being organised for the purpose of inciting hostility to all Jews. It must be emphasised – as the Court of Appeal in *Jewish Human Rights Watch Limited v Leicester City Council* emphasised – that there must be evidence of anti-Semitic purpose. Despite Natan Sharansky's fears that the hidden agenda of BDS is to cause anxiety in the Jewish community, evidence that goes no further than this will not be sufficient to show even a prima facie case.

Conclusion

42. It is my opinion, for the reasons set out above, that:

   (1) The IHRA definition of anti-Semitism is not fit for any purpose that seeks to use it as an adjudicative standard. It is imprecise, confusing and open to misinterpretation and even manipulation. It does not cover some insidious forms of anti-Semitism.

   (2) It was originally drafted, in the absence of any other definition, as a tool for collecting data and is useful for purposes of discussion, but should not be used (or be used with great caution) as a measure for discipline or in ways which have consequences for political speech.

   (3) The UK Government was wrong to adopt it without the "caveat" recommended with reason by the Home Affairs Committee, namely:

   "It is not anti-Semitic to criticise the Government of Israel, without additional evidence to suggest anti-Semitic intent."

   Any public body or other organisation (including the Labour Party) that is contemplating adoption of the IHRA definition in full should add this provision to it.

   (4) As a matter of internal construction, the examples appended to the IHRA core definition should be read as

incorporating a) the fact that they "could not" amount to anti-Semitism and b) in particular, unless they exhibited to reasonable people a hatred of Jewish people.

(5) The Government's "adoption" of the definition has no legal effect and does not oblige public bodies to take notice of it.

(6) The definition should not be adopted, and certainly should not be applied, by public bodies unless they are clear about Article 10 of the EHCR which is binding upon them, namely that they cannot ban speech or writing about Israel unless there is a real likelihood it will lead to violence or disorder or race hatred.

(7) Universities and Colleges should be particularly careful about adopting or using the definition, as they have a statutory duty to protect freedom of expression.

(8) A particular problem with the IHRA definition is that it is likely in practice to chill free speech, by raising expectations of pro-Israeli groups that they can successfully object to legitimate criticism of their country and correspondingly arouse fears in NGOs and student bodies that they will have events banned or else have to incur considerable expense to protect themselves by legal action. Either way, they may not organise such events.

(9) Whether under human rights law or the IHRA definition, political action against Israel is not properly characterised as anti-Semitic unless the action is intended to promote hatred or hostility against Jews in general.

Geoffrey Robertson AO QC
Doughty Street Chambers, 27th August 2018.

7

Exposing the Vigilantes

Exposed! How Britain's Anti-Semitism scaremongers operate

Eve Mykytyn

This article about the British charitable organisation, the Campaign against Anti-Semitism (CAA), and its officers, Gideon Falter and Steve Silverman, examines events in England but ought to serve as a cautionary message for Canadians and Americans.

The article will delve into the corrosive methods of the CAA; review the manner in which this ultra Zionist group "discovers" anti-Semitic "incidents"; examine their inaccurate statistical "studies" and see how they seek to intimidate political parties, venues, the press and others; and look at the court cases which the CAA has prosecuted. In the guise of fighting anti-Semitism, the CAA has managed to manoeuvre British society into abdicating its core liberal values, intimidate the prosecutorial and judicial system, and silence criticism of Israel in both social media and the mainstream media.

The CAA does not just attempt to limit speech; it openly follows a scorched earth policy "that if someone commits an anti-Semitic act in the UK (including criticism of Israel)" the CAA "ensure[s] ruinous consequences, be they criminal, professional, financial or reputational".

For example, in the last 18 months Britain's largest political party, the Labour Party, has suspended and expelled over a hundred of its members for expressing their views on Israel or Jewish history. Presumably these dismissals act as a deterrent to others who might also wish to express their opinions. Hard as it is to believe, in 21st century Britain people have been imprisoned for trying to be funny...

The CAA's "success" in Britain is not irrelevant to Americans. Despite the First Amendment, rules limiting speech have been creeping into our society, notwithstanding our constitutional protections.

Organisations not unlike CAA have been operating in the US for some time. In South Carolina criticising Israel is essentially prohibited on public university campuses, and in other states support for BDS (the Boycott, Divestment and Sanctions movement) will prohibit one from getting a government job or contract. Similar laws have been proposed in the US Congress. It is crucial that we resist this slide into controlled speech at the expense of our crucial values of free expression and tolerance.

Rowan Laxton

In 2006 Rowan Laxton was using an exercise bike alone on the mezzanine floor of a London gym when he saw a television report about an elderly Palestinian man killed by the Israeli assault on Gaza. Laxton allegedly exclaimed: "F.....g Israelis! F.....g Jews!" Gideon Falter (now head of the CAA) and William Lemaine, who were on a lower floor using weights, claimed to have overheard Laxton, and complained to staff at the gym.

The police were going to let Laxton off with a caution but, before it could be arranged, Falter found out that Laxton was a senior Foreign Office official and brought the story to half a dozen newspapers. The police decided to proceed with a prosecution.

Laxton was initially found guilty of "using threatening, abusive or insulting words or behaviour, or disorderly behaviour... within the hearing or sight of a person likely to be caused harassment, alarm or distress thereby..." aggravated by using abusive words that had a racial or ethnic element. Laxton was fined and removed from his Foreign Office position.

Laxton exercised his right to an appeal and a rehearing wherein the Crown Court found that Laxton did not say "f.....g Jews", the comment on which the prosecution was based and which he had always denied. The court also found, as an alternative ground, that Laxton would have thought no one was within earshot.

The Daily Mail played a key role in ensuring that the case received national attention and went to trial, but seems not to have reported the appeal and acquittal at all. It is an open question of how Falter heard Laxton's alleged outburst, if at the time no one was within earshot of Laxton. One reasonable assumption is that the court did not believe that Falter actually heard Laxton's statement.

Eight years after the Laxton incident, Gideon Falter founded the Campaign Against Anti-Semitism, a hardcore Zionist charity that advocates zero tolerance of, and vows to ensure "criminal, professional and reputational consequences", to those it decides are anti-Semites.

Stephen Silverman

Stephen Silverman is the CAA's "Director of Investigations and Enforcement" and has dedicated much of his time to ruining the intellectual and artistic careers of others. Silverman is himself a musician wannabe, and runs a music school in a London suburb.

In the last few years Silverman and the CAA have engaged in a relentless assault against artists, intellectuals, religious leaders and elected politicians operating in or visiting England. The "Director of Investigations" does not like ex-London Mayor Ken Livingstone, nor does he approve of a list of academics or church ministers who care for human rights or dare to disagree with Israel. The self-appointed inquisitor despises the hugely popular Labour leader Jeremy Corbyn. Silverman has made a number of attempts to ruin the music careers of both Alison Chabloz and Gilad Atzmon. In addition, Silverman takes it upon himself to write and call music venues demanding that they cancel Atzmon concerts claiming that Atzmon is a notorious anti-Semite.

Stephen Silverman was exposed in open court in December 2016 as having been the Twitter troll @bedlamjones. As a Zionist troll, Silverman abused anti-Zionists, particularly women. His sadistic posts called for arrest and imprisonment in response to what he considered to be "anti-Semitic" comments.

Silverman has also determined that Gordon Nardell, the man who has taken on the unenviable job of policing anti-Semitism within the Labour Party, is insufficiently sensitive to anti-Semitism. Apparently, according to Silverman, "Nardell has also turned his sights on Campaign Against Anti-Semitism, stating that our work to combat hatred directed at Jews by Labour members is 'revolting' and results in anti-Semitism being 'abused and belittled'.

For Nardell's sin of distrusting the CAA, the CAA has demanded that "an independent and transparent disciplinary process... be instituted in the Labour Party". The CAA's website does not explain why the Labour Party need justify its own campaign against anti-Semitism to the CAA.

What is anti-Semitism?

UNESCO's definition of racism is that it is "a theory of races hierarchy which argues that the superior race should be preserved and should dominate the others.* Racism can also be an unfair

---

* It's interesting that in a speech at Dimona, Israel's nuclear bomb research centre, in August 2018, Binyamin Netanyahu said "True peace can be achieved only if our hands strongly grasp defensive weaponry. In the Middle East, and in many parts of the world, there is a simple truth: There is no place for the weak. The weak crumble, are slaughtered and are erased from history while the strong, for good or for ill, survive." Some might argue that this fits exactly the UNESCO definition of racism. [KS]

attitude towards another ethnic group. Finally racism can also be defined as a violent hostility against a social group." The traditional definition of anti-Semitism is the "criticising of, or discriminating against Jews for being Jews". This definition is not substantially different from UNESCO's definition of racism.

However, despite the fact that enforcing hate speech laws based on a traditional definition of racism would protect Jews as well as others, in December 2016 the United Kingdom followed other countries in adopting the "international definition of anti-Semitism", which begins by saying: "Anti-Semitism is a certain perception of Jews, which may be expressed as hatred towards Jews. Rhetorical and physical manifestations of anti-Semitism are directed towards Jewish or non-Jewish individuals and/or their property, towards Jewish community institutions and religious facilities."

The new "international definition" is troubling because it specifically targets speech and thoughts and fails to define what a "certain" perception of Jews is, and an expression of hatred towards Jews is cited, not to make the definition more precise but only as one possible example.

It is well worth reviewing the "examples of anti-Semitism" included in the "international definition" which are extremely broad and include, among other things, accusing a Jewish person of valuing Israel or his fellow Jews over his home country and the seemingly paradoxical provision prohibiting speech denying that Jews have the right to self-determination through Israel.

But if racism against one group is to be fought on a broader basis than other forms of racism, that extra protection ought to be to aid a group uniquely needing the state's protection – an allegedly poor, downtrodden and persecuted group. It is of note that, in contrast to the downtrodden, Jews as a group have been extraordinarily successful at utilising the media and the courts and obtaining the power to "hold the feet of the government to the fire".

If UNESCO's definition is aimed at defining racism as a universal problem, the "international definition" adheres to the idea that Jews are not a part of the universal, they are somehow different, their plight is unique.

Why do the Jews in particular need a broader definition of racial hatred? Why do Jews see a need to create a category of hatred that applies only to them? What is lacking in the UNESCO definition that is covered by the "international" one? The answer is that the "international definition" serves to restrain speech and restrict thought. It conflates the Jewish State of Israel with Jews as it vets a range of discourses such as criticism of Israeli politics, Jewish culture, Jewish history and Zionist ideology.

It is not surprising that this definition is espoused by some Zionist institutions. However, its adoption by so many countries is perplexing and begs an explanation. In a world in which free speech, freedom of association and freedom of religion are valued, there is a real question of why such a broad definition of anti-Semitism is appropriate and what exactly it is designed to accomplish.

Then there is the CAA, for whom the international definition is only a starting point. Their accusations of anti-Semitism go beyond even the very broad and over-inclusive definition of the "international definition". If you find anti-Semitism in t-shirts, major party political gatherings or stupid pet videos, then the definition is very expansive indeed. Why would an organisation dedicated to fighting anti-Semitism be so interested in finding anti-Semitism in every possible utterance? It is clear that the CAA wants to stop any discussion of Jews, Israel or Jewish history in any but its prescribed manner. In its aggressive policing of speech, the CAA and others work to enforce Jewish power precisely as it is defined by Gilad Atzmon: "the power to suppress criticism of Jewish power".

Freedom of t-shirt

While freedom of speech may be evaporating throughout the English-speaking world, at least we are assured that freedom of t-shirt is still protected in England.

Last year, the CAA's website bemoaned that Edinburgh-based law graduate Sophie Stephenson won't face criminal charges for wearing a Hezbollah t-shirt. The CAA wrote that: "On 1 July 2017, Stephenson tweeted a photograph of herself wearing a Hizballah t-shirt, explaining: "Went out to dinner with my family tonight wearing a Hizballah t-shirt." And then, even worse, Stephenson confirmed: "I have a flag too."

The CAA, in its zeal to fight anti-Semitism, reported Stephenson to the police, alleging that she had committed an offense under Section 13 of the Terrorism Act 2000. But despite the CAA's urging, Scottish Police declined to act against the young "rebel".

The CAA "considered undertaking a private prosecution" against Stephenson. However, its website lamented, "we were unable to secure enough funding to do so". Following its report of the supposedly anti-Semitic/terrorist-loving Stephenson, the CAA called upon the public to "consider making a monthly donation to help fund Campaign Against Anti-Semitism" presumably to allow it to continue to harass Britons, accusing them of anti-Semitic behaviour, and interfering with their elementary freedoms including the right to wear rebellious t-shirts. Disturbingly, asking for donations in this context suggests that the CAA is attempting to cash in from its dubious anti-Semitic claims. Not exactly the ethical conduct you might expect of a charity.

Methodology, it is not!

The CAA claims to run "methodological" "research into anti-Semitism in British political parties". Trolling and spying on elected British politicians on social media and public meetings, the CAA keeps a "record" of allegedly "anti-Semitic discourse and discourse that enables anti-Semitism, by officials and candidates in political parties". This means that a Jewish organisation with a clear political agenda endeavours to monitor the British political discourse to restrain certain political opinions. The CAA's actions prosecuting its farfetched "findings" are dangerous enough, but more troubling is its success in terrorising the British political universe into compliance with its dictates.

What are some "examples" of discourse that the CAA has claimed enable anti-Semitism and the dissemination of anti-Semitic ideas?

Ken Loach

Internationally acclaimed film-maker and Labour supporter Ken Loach told the BBC's *Daily Politics* programme that he had been attending Labour meetings for 50 years and had "never in that whole time heard a single anti-Semitic word or a racist word", and that allegations of anti-Semitism were a fallacy "without validation or any evidence".

The CAA claimed that Loach's statement brought to light a "discourse that enables anti-Semitism and the dissemination of anti-Semitic ideas". How is Loach's statement racist? Does it target Jews, identify Jews as a collective or advocate discrimination against Jews or anyone else? Is there even a criminal category or a showing of bias in which "not witnessing" conduct implicates one in that very conduct? How does not witnessing anti-Semitism make one into an anti-Semite? Does not witnessing a murder make one a murderer? Under the CAA's "rationale" anyone who fails to see the anti-Semitism they do is an anti-Semite.

Diane Abbott

Abbott ran afoul of the CAA when she said: "It's a smear to say that Labour has a problem with anti-Semitism. It is something like a smear against ordinary party members." The CAA claimed that "Abbott's comments were widely condemned. The overwhelming majority of UK Jewish community bodies have expressed public concern about anti-Semitism in the Labour Party, including the chief rabbi." Whether or not this statement is accurate, how is it that Abbott's statement was misinterpreted as a criticism of Jews when it is clearly a defence of the Labour Party?

Ken Livingstone

The CAA has a long file on former London Mayor Livingstone, beginning in 1982 when the paper, the *Labour Herald*, of which Livingstone was co-editor, ran an unfavorable cartoon of the then Israeli Prime Minister Menachem Begin. According to the CAA, Livingstone's most egregious anti-Semitic remark was his claim that that in 1932 (Hitler came to power in 1933) Hitler had championed Jewish emigration to Israel (actually, then Palestine) and was "supporting Zionism before he went mad and ended up killing six million Jews". The United States Holocaust Museum website generally supports Livingstone's statement and reveals that until 1941, Germany encouraged Jews to emigrate and that 60,000 Jews left Germany/Austria for Palestine, a number second only to the number of Jews who went to the United States.

Livingstone rejected claims that he had brought the Labour Party into disrepute and said he was not guilty of anti-Semitism, but resigned from the party and acknowledged that his comments had upset Jews and offended others. "I am truly sorry for that," he said.

Some of Livingstone's critics were not satisfied with his apology for his truthful statement. Ruth Smeeth, a Labour lawmaker, described his behaviour as "grossly offensive to British Jews". MP Smeeth's reaction is bizarre. Is it anti-Semitic for Livingstone to discuss Jewish history? The Transfer Agreement between Hitler's Germany and the Zionist Congress may be embarrassing for some Jews, but how is recounting history hate speech? MP Smeeth, the CAA and others claiming to be offended managed by ousting Livingstone to enforce their ironclad rule that certain Jewish history is "off limits".

War on Labour

Following its anti-methodology, the CAA came to the conclusion that the British Labour Party is "eight times worse than any other party". Not 5, 6 or 8.3 but exactly 8. What "evidence" supports this "finding?"

The CAA's website publishes an "enemies list" of sorts, chronicling the alleged anti-Semitism of 39 members of the Labour Party. A striking number of the CAA's complaints address statements about Israel, not about Israel as Jews, but about the actions of the country. To date, about 150 members of the Labour Party have been expelled for alleged anti-Semitism and there is a backlog of cases.

Dubious cases such as those cited here are treated by the CAA as "anti-Semitic incidents" that help the CAA feed the idea that England is rife with anti-Semitism. The British media have failed to do their job of investigating alleged incidents of anti-Semitism, and instead accept the CAA's claims without questions.

Fiddling with numbers

Fiddler on the Roof may be emblematic of Eastern European Jewish folklore but fiddling with numbers is a symptom of contemporary Zionist politics in general and of the CAA in particular. The CAA compiles and disseminates information on anti-Semitism, basing its claims on methodology that is patently unreliable.

The "anti-Semitism audit" produced by the CAA purports to track incidents of anti-Semitism on an annual basis. The audit is a deeply flawed document, relying on data known to be unreliable and subjected to no proper statistical analysis.

Even the CAA's use of the term "audit" is inappropriate. An "audit" is defined as "an official inspection of an… organisation's accounts, typically by an independent body". The CAA has no official or professional status as an auditor, nor would its methods be accepted by anyone in a position to conduct a professional audit.

The CAA has been advised by police forces that comparing police reports across jurisdictions and years leads to misleading results. The CAA's anti-Semitism audit was heavily criticised in the Jewish media by statistics experts who noted that the CAA's "methodology" was "flawed", "amateurish" and "misleading". But none of that stopped the CAA from promoting its manufactured "findings" in the mainstream media.

The CAA based its audit on gathering data from the police. But the CAA doesn't enjoy free access to police files. Instead, it uses different techniques to gather information. This haphazard "methodology" creates crucial problems:

1. Police forces in different regions of Britain use different standards to gather data regarding hate crimes.

2. Police forces in Britain are presently in the process of revising how they collect their hate crime records so that data from one year may show different results from data from a different year even if the number of hate crimes remains constant.

3. The CAA basically gathers information on the volume of incidents recorded that it considers to be anti-Semitic. But the CAA itself is actively engaged in increasing this volume. It frequently reports incidents to the police and urges other members of the Jewish community to follow suit. An interested body that actively contributes to the rise of reported anti-Semitic incidents cannot also claim to be objective in its "audit" that measures the rise of anti-Semitism.

4. While the CAA's audit of anti-Semitism shows a nationwide rise of 14.9 per cent in anti-Semitic incidents between 2016 and 2017, this is based on data gathered by the CAA half of which shows wild year to year fluctuations of up to 1050 per cent. Such fluctuations defy any rationale. These statistical anomalies beg careful analysis that the CAA not only fails to apply – the CAA fails to address this drastic shift in number of reported incidents. The CAA's study aggregates divergent data collected in different ways and calls that an "audit" of anti-Semitism in Britain. The flawed study was released to the British public with the help of the disgracefully gullible British media. The BBC, Sky, the *Guardian* and others reported the amateurish statistical "audit" to the British public without raising a single question as to its reliability.

The 2016 audit

In July 2017 the CAA published its 2016 annual audit of anti-Semitic crimes in the UK. The audit's first pages raise serious questions as to its reliability:

On page 4 it reads: "2016 was the worst year on record for anti-Semitic crimes", reporting a 14.9 per cent rise in crimes "targeting Jews" nationwide. But a few lines below, the audit states that during the same period "violent anti-Semitic crimes fell by 44.7 per cent". This difference in incidences appears contradictory.

The CAA admits that it doesn't have an explanation for the drop in violent crimes: "We have considered various explanations; however at this point we do not find them persuasive." (page 6). This drop occurred even though the CAA inflated the number of "violent incidents" by expanding the Home Office definition of violent incidents. (page 16) The CAA defined violent anti-Semitic acts as the combination of the Home Office categories of "homicide" or "violence with injury", and the heretofore non-violent "assault without injury" and "racially or religiously aggravated assault without injury".

This means that the audit conveyed the good news that, even using the CAA's inflated category, the number of "violent anti-Semitic incidents" dropped. Strangely, the Jewish pressure group does not write that the drop in violent anti-Semitic crime is a positive finding.

Fishing for J words

Since the CAA doesn't have an access to each police force's records, it derives its statistics from police reports. When a police force does not flag anti-Semitic incidents, the CAA asks that police force to conduct a keyword search of its files:

Some police forces made the CAA aware that their keywords method is not a reliable way to find anti-Semitic crime. "Not all incidents where 'Jew' is mentioned are anti-Semitic," wrote the Northumbria police force. It also refers to the CAA exercise as a "fishing expedition". The CAA ignored this caution and simply used as the number of incidents the data they had been warned were incorrect.

Duplicity vs methodology

The CAA employs inadequate and inconsistent methods of information gathering not only in its audit, but in its information gathering from Jews.

In 2017 the CAA made some shocking revelations:

- "One out of three British Jews were considering leaving the kingdom."
- "Four out of five Jews saw anti-Semitism disguised as comments about Israel."
- "Four out of five saw Labour as anti-Semitic."
- "Half of British Jews didn't trust the Crown Prosecution Service."

And the source of these disturbing feelings? They came from the results of an online questionnaire found on the CAA's website. The CAA's findings were not even from as unbiased sample as the average FaceBook poll. Instead of revealing what British Jews think, the CAA "survey" revealed the opinions of its Zionist readers. It is outrageous to label the results of this exercise "statistics". In fact, Jewish leaders who criticised the CAA's duplicitous use of the "poll" were brutally silenced and slandered. Probably the most problematic result of the poll was that the British press reported it but did not point out that the CAA's findings were based on a self-selecting sample.

Stupidity or duplicity?

Is the CAA a dysfunctional body of incompetent and clueless characters or is the CAA a group of consciously deceptive Zionists who deliberately deceives the British public? The following evidence suggests the latter.

As discussed above, the CAA 2016 anti-Semitsm audit is methodically and factually a problematic document. The CAA was warned of this by different law-enforcement bodies such as the Northumbria police. The CAA audit uses its questionable data to show an increase in the volume of reported anti-Semitic incidents but still fails to prove an increase in anti-Semitism. Does that mean that the CAA intended to produce a deceptive audit?

The CAA audit's raw data (from page 24 onward) reveals extreme fluctuations in anti-Semitic incidents reported by police forces from 2015 to 2016, with year to year increases of up to 1050 per cent in some categories and drops of 80-90 per cent in others.

In Derbyshire, for instance (page 34), the audit shows an increase of 1050 per cent in non-criminal anti-Semitic incidents: from two in 2015 to 23 in 2016. This would mean that non-criminal anti-Semitic incidents rose in Derby 70 times more than the CAA's own nationwide rate of 14.9 per cent. On paper, the situation in Derbyshire is almost a *Shoah* scenario. Did the CAA try to verify, as even elementary statistics would require, this enormous increase? Was there a pogrom reported in Derbyshire?

In Hertfordshire (page 44), they show an increase of almost 400 per cent in anti-Semitic crime and a surge of 800 per cent in non-criminal anti-Semitic incidents. Again, there is no indication that the CAA tried to look into the cause of this improbable increase.

The explanation of the unreasonable rise was known to the CAA. West Yorkshire police notified the CAA that the recent rise in numbers of hate crime incidents "is predominantly associated with administrative change in relation to force crime-recording processes". It was an administrative change, not an increase in anti-Semitism that led to the huge increase in the number of hate crimes recorded. So, despite the CAA's knowledge of the reasons for the wild fluctuations, the CAA still dispensed the misleading numbers to the British public.

The raw police reports that the CAA's audit relies upon reveal that 21 of the 46 reports showed fluctuations well beyond what could reasonably be likely (more than three times the CAA's own nationwide figure of 14.9 per cent rise in anti-Semitic incidents). The CAA could claim that its mistakes were due to incompetence, that they simply copied and pasted police reports without thinking. But the last page of the audit reveals that this is not the case.

The CAA does admit that the numbers reported by Wiltshire police (page 73) were unreliable, as they showed a radical rise from one incident in 2015 to 139 incidents in 2016. This is an increase of 13900 per cent in anti-Semitic incidents in a region with fewer than 540 Jews. The CAA discarded the data from Wiltshire as unreliable. But by deciding not to include the Wiltshire police report the CAA reveals that it doesn't just copy and paste police data.

So, the CAA included some data and discarded others with no apparent standards. What statistical methodology did the CAA use when it decided to discard a rise in 13,900 per cent in anti-Semitic incidents in one jurisdiction and to include a rise in 1000 per cent, 400 per cent or even 50 per cent in others?

It is a basic tenet of statistical analysis that statistics from different sources cannot be combined or meaningfully compared without properly adjusting for different data gathering systems and methods. Deriving an overall percentage increase by averaging data derived by different systems is patently absurd. Nor is it accurate to compare different years from the same data source unless the gathering methodology is the same. The CAA's audit compiles apples, oranges and bananas and treats them as identical. The extreme fluctuations in police reporting reveals that police force systems did exactly as the police force said it did and underwent significant reporting changes as the CAA admits in its introduction (page 3).

The alerts from the police forces that collection methods had changed means that the CAA should have known that its audit was flawed. This was also pointed out to the CAA by experts within the Jewish community who were highly critical of the audit.

Michael Pinto Duschinsky, a well-respected political scientist, wrote a devastating commentary in the *Jewish Chronicle* about the CAA. As a holocaust survivor, Duschinsky writes, I have two commitments: "to combat anti-Semitism and other forms of racism and to avoid trivialising it by misleading allegations". Duschinsky denounced the CAA for its "deeply flawed", "misleading" and "amateurish" methods.

Of the self-selected CAA poll, Duschinsky wrote:

> It was completely predicable that the questionnaire would produce the conclusion that one in four British Jews had considered leaving the UK... This was because the questions were so slanted and tendentious and because anyone who wished could complete the questionnaire... Not only did CAA incorrectly characterise its amateur questionnaire of Jewish opinion as a "poll" (thereby suggesting a statistically-valid sample), it then used overblown language in reporting it results.

Abuse of the judicial process

The hysteria over alleged anti-Semitism has led to trials and convictions for the crime of "anti-Semitism". Cases that the Crown Prosecution Service (CPS) refused to prosecute two years ago have now been brought by the CPS after action from the CAA. Is the change in prosecutions a sign that the CPS now realises that it can obtain convictions it thought unlikely, does it result from a change in what the state considers to be "speech" crimes, or is the CPS placating the CAA?

Gideon Falter and the CAA have been instrumental in utilising a variety of techniques to force prosecution of "anti-Semitism". Their campaign to restrain speech previously thought permissible has been successful in England as the following sampling of cases shows.

Jeremy Bedford Turner

Turner was recently sentenced to a year in jail after a jury convicted him of stirring up racial hatred during a 2015 speech in which Turner criticised Shomrim, a Jewish-only police unit funded by

Britain, whose job it is to protect only Jewish neighbourhoods. Turner further opined the racist sentiment that he wanted Jews out of England.

The CPS declined to prosecute Turner's speech as incitement to racial hatred. There is an "incitement to racial hatred" clause in the statutes but it is not all-encompassing, and it did not come close to making "anti-Semitism" illegal. The CPS's policy guidelines on cases involving "incitement" clearly state that the language employed by a defendant must have been "threatening, abusive or insulting". The courts have upheld the right to freedom of speech even when behaviour is, as in this case, "annoying, rude or even offensive without necessarily being insulting".

Falter requested a "victim's right to review" in response to the CPS's decision not to prosecute. The request was denied on the basis that Turner hadn't mentioned Falter, Falter did not personally hear Turner's speech and therefore Falter couldn't claim victim status. The CAA then instituted the process for judicial review of the CPS over its decision not to prosecute and, on the eve of a hearing in the High Court, the CPS agreed to quash its original decision, put a more senior lawyer on the case and proceeded to prosecute and convict Turner.

CAA head Falter claimed the verdict was a "damning indictment" not only of Turner, but of the CPS and its outgoing head, Alison Saunders. Falter said: "The real question is why the director of public prosecutions and CPS got this so dismally wrong." Falter's question conflates a jury verdict of "guilty" with proof that the CPS was misinterpreting the law.

Further in 2015, when Turner gave his speech, the United Kingdom had not yet signalled its willingness to stifle speech by adopting the "international definition" of anti-Semitism.

Alison Chabloz

Alison Chabloz, singer, 54, of Derbyshire, was recently convicted on two counts of causing an offensive, indecent or menacing message to be sent over a public communications network. District Judge John Zani said he was satisfied the material was grossly offensive and that Chabloz intended to insult Jewish people.

The CPS initially declined to prosecute Chabloz's speech, presumably because it was both satirical and political. The CAA launched a private prosecution against Chabloz. Private prosecutions are undertaken in the British system as a direct way for a citizen to institute a criminal case. The rules are intricate, but until recently such prosecutions generally dealt with complex business questions.

Under constant pressure from the CAA, the CPS took over the prosecution of Chabloz. The CAA had not utilised private prosecution in the Turner case since it was not present to hear the "slurs" and would have had no basis for private prosecution.

The songs that provoked Chabloz's prosecution had been performed at a London Forum event (hardcore nationalist gathering) in 2016 and uploaded to YouTube. They included one song describing the Nazi concentration camp Auschwitz as "a theme park" and the gas chambers a "proven hoax". This is a pretty clear example of provocative speech that most of us disagree with. However, does the state need to criminalise such speech? Won't the "marketplace of ideas" call out Chabloz? I suspect the internet world would not allow her lyrics to go unchallenged.

Prosecutor Karen Robinson told the court: "Miss Chabloz's songs are a million miles away from an attempt to provide an academic critique of the holocaust. They're not political songs. They are no more than a dressed-up attack on a group of people for no more than their adherence to a religion."

But is it a legal requirement that political song lyrics provide an "academic critique"? Must political satire be clearly defined as found by a court? It's not clear that "Alice's Restaurant" or "Fortunate Son" would pass this test.

Adrian Davies, defending, argued that: "It is hard to know what right has been infringed by Miss Chabloz's singing." The singer has defended her work as "satire", saying many Jewish people found the songs funny.

The focus of the private prosecution brought by Falter was Alison's comments criticising the narratives of Elie Wiesel, Irene Zisblatt and Otto Frank, in her song *Survivors*.

The authenticity of the tales of these three holocaust victims has been the subject of academic debate. The Anne Frank foundation recently admitted the diary had not been solely authored by Anne. Elie Wiesel's wartime saga has been called into question over a number of issues. Under cross-examination, Falter was forced to admit that he had not actually read Zisblatt's book, and so knew nothing about its accuracy, despite having brought a private prosecution to protect it from ridicule.

There are no specific laws against holocaust denial in the UK, even if that is what this was. Britain has resisted attempts to enforce a European Union directive outlawing holocaust denial. Falter seemed to differ from the Crown which said that the prosecution was not against mere questioning of the holocaust. Falter indicated that those who question the new holocaust religion should be prosecuted under the law and attacked professionally: that is, ruined financially.

Falter also claimed that it was "intrinsically offensive" for Chabloz to refer to Palestine being reclaimed "from the river to the sea". But, of course, the question of whether Palestine ought to be reclaimed for its indigenous people is a political question and not one of race, so what exactly was her crime? Falter openly stated that he is intent on shielding Israel from criticism, and said of the pro-Palestinian aspects of Chabloz's songs: "You want to silence her and stop her putting those messages out."

All of this left inconsistencies in the prosecution's case with regard to whether the truth/falsehood of Chabloz's criticisms of Zisblatt, *et al*, were relevant, or whether instead the Crown was enforcing an unspoken law that no one claiming to be a holocaust survivor can be ridiculed, regardless of truth/falsehood.

Adrian Davies, Chabloz's lawyer, told Judge Zani that his ruling would be a landmark one, setting a precedent on the exercise of free speech. This is a particularly egregious precedent limiting speech since it is not clear what speech led to Chabloz's conviction and the case therefore provides no insight to others on what speech must be avoided.

Gilad Atzmon

The case against Atzmon illustrates that in the present environment in Britain, you can be liable not only for anti-Semitism, but for questioning the methodology by which anti-Semitism is determined.

Falter appeared on *Sky News* on 16 July 2017 to explain how he, on behalf of the CAA, had brought a law suit against the Crown for failure to prosecute the anti-Semitic speech supposedly uttered by Jeremy Bedford-Turner. Falter further complained that his statistics on the incidence of anti-Semitism showed far more anti-Semitic incidents than the CPS claimed. Falter claimed, "our view [on anti-Semitism] is right and the Crown is wrong".

Writing in response to Falter's appearance, Atzmon wrote on his own website that: "We are asked to choose between two versions of the truth, that delivered by Falter who leads the CAA and basically makes his living manufacturing anti-Semitic incidents and the judicial approach of the CPS: a public body, subject to scrutiny and committed to impartiality."

Atzmon pointed out that "Falter interprets condemnation of Israel and Jewish politics as 'hate crimes'". Atzmon commended the CPS for upholding "freedom of expression", and this in free speech's most cherished exercise – political speech.

Atzmon noted that Zionism also benefits from anti-Semitism (even though it does not intentionally cause it) since Israel claims that it exists to provide shelter to all Jews. Comparing Falter and the CAA to Israel, Atzmon noted, "since a decrease in anti-Semitic incidents [could have] fatal consequences for Falter and his CAA's business plan. They need anti-Semitism and a lot of it."

Falter filed a suit against Atzmon, claiming libel and defamation. Falter's complaint reads, in part: "In order to justify the existence of, and raise funds for, the CAA the Claimant (Falter) dishonestly fabricates anti-Semitic incidents, that is to say he characterizes conduct as anti-Semitic when he knows it is not, and knowingly exaggerates the prevalence of anti-Semitism and anti-Semitic activity."

Falter complains that he was called a "devious fraud and a hypocrite", even though neither word appears in Atzmon's article. Falter further interprets Atzmon: "He [Falter] publicly campaigns against anti-Semitism but in reality his business plan is that he wants Jews to be hated so that he can make money." In fact, Atzmon made the claim that Falter is a covert Jew hater who pretends to campaign against anti-Semitism.

In addition, Falter claimed that unless restrained, Atzmon would continue to publish similar words. Here Falter openly reveals that his lawsuit is not only against the words complained of, but an attempt to muzzle Atzmon.

The first stage of the lawsuit was a hearing before Justice Nicklin of the British High Court to define the issues created by the language complained of. In his ruling, the judge went beyond the complaint to determine that Atzmon's words said that the claimant obtained funds through "fraud".

Atzmon had not claimed that Falter committed fraud, and it was not clear that Falter's misuse of statistics rose to the level of fraud, i.e. involving a criminal intent. The ruling made clear that a further defence before this justice would be pointless. The parties settled: Atzmon had to issue an apology and pay Falter £7500 in damages, plus an additional amount in legal fees. The irony of forcing Atzmon to pay Falter based on the allegedly false claim that Falter seeks money for anti-Semitism begs recognition.

The Nazi pug

Earlier this year Mark Meechan, aka "Count Dankula", was convicted and fined £800 for posting on YouTube a video of a dog he had trained to give a Nazi salute in response to the phrases "gas the Jews" and *sieg heil*. In case viewers worried that he was trying to turn canines into Nazis, one pug dog at a time, Meechan stated in the video that he wasn't himself a Nazi but thought that what he had done was funny. It is a reasonable interpretation of this video that it ridiculed Hitler supporters as much as it was offensive to others.

The Scottish police arrested Meecham and charged him with posting "grossly offensive, anti-Semitic and racist material". Sheriff O'Carroll said the right to freedom of expression was very important but "in all modern democratic countries the law necessarily places some limits on that right".

Meecham pleaded not guilty but was convicted under the Communications Act in a crime that the court found was aggravated by "religious prejudice". Although Meecham's video was certainly tasteless and offensive, it is not clear how it fell into the obscure category of "religious prejudice".

Meecham's lawyer, Ross Brown, stated of Meecham, his difficulty, "it seems, was that he was someone who enjoyed shock humour... and went about his life under the impression that he lived in a jurisdiction which permitted its citizens the right to freely express themselves". This perception is understandable; British humour is famous for its tastelessness. *Monty Python* mocked the church, *Little Britain* mocks the disabled and so on.

Why did Scottish law enforcement prosecute a silly offensive video of a dog? Is Scotland so crime-free that this is a matter worthy of its crime-fighting resources? It's hard not to wonder if the same case would have been brought five years ago.

The First Amendment

In the United States, our freedom to speak is guaranteed by the First Amendment, which forbids Congress from making a law abridging free speech (now held to apply to the states as well). The First Amendment was enacted primarily as a defence against government power. The founders were concerned that the federal government exercise only enumerated powers and no more. Still, free speech is not unlimited: the United States limits some speech, including false commercial speech, defamation and incitement to violence.

No reasonable person enjoys confronting hate speech, but allowing free speech, even at its most obnoxious, frees us from self-appointed guardians of the discourse. Who would any of us choose to decide what speech ought to be allowed? Congress? Trump? Obama? The FBI? The NSA? Scientists? The courts? Or the CAA or ADL (Anti-Defamation League)?

The United States government has spent more money on Israel than on any other foreign country, and it is reasonable for Americans to be free to comment on where their money is spent. And yet we have laws that punish those who speak out against Israel, even though we have no such laws for criticising our own government or to protect the people whom we formerly enslaved.

While speech against Israel is not illegal *per se*, the US government, and states such as New York and Texas (among others) have chosen to punish criticism of Israel as anti-Semitic. They do this by prohibiting state funding or business with any group that advocates boycotting Israel.

Canada also protects speech, but not "hate" speech. Under the urging of B'nai B'rith, Canada has prosecuted "anti-Semitic" speech as hate speech. As in the cases in England, it is difficult to ascertain which particular speech was forbidden. In a trial against blogger Arthur Topham, the prosecution cited all of Topham's writings that were unfavourable to Israel or Jewish culture and hoped some of them stuck. They did, and Topham was convicted.

Despite Canada's enforcement of its hate speech laws, Falter urged Canadian Jews to follow his example of aggressive prosecution. He stated, "I believe that Canadian [Jews] increasingly will be looking at their situation and asking, 'Do we have a future in this country?' And that's a question they shouldn't be having to ask at all."Where is Falter's evidence that Canadian Jews are asking if they have a future in Canada? Is he trying to lay seeds of alienation so that Jews in Canada will feel less like a part of Canada?

This raises the question of whether the CAA intensifies anti-Semitism by urging Jews to find anti-Semitism everywhere and to prosecute perceived anti-Semitism and "to ensure ruinous consequences, be they criminal, professional, financial or reputational". The CAA uses the judicial system to achieve its aims, but its use of the law seems cynical as in its legal machinations the CAA deliberately disrespects the principle of freedom of speech that is ingrained in the law of Britain, the United States and Canada.

8

Enough Tropes to Hang Themselves

The Lobby, Part 1
YOUNG FRIENDS OF ISRAEL
Produced by Al-Jazeera Television
Narrated by Clayton Swisher (CS)
Speech recorded using secret filming is shown in italics; narration in bold; interviews are shown in plain text.

CLAYTON SWISHER: How Israel influences British politics…. We reveal from the inside how the Embassy penetrates different levels of British democracy.

In the first of four programs, the battle for Britain's youth.

CAPTION: THE LOBBY

Following decades of violence, a new challenge has emerged to Israel's occupation of Palestinian lands – called BDS. That's the global movement to boycott, divest and impose sanctions on Israel – and expose it as an apartheid state. The Israeli government has responded with a campaign to influence and re-brand the country's image.

BENJAMIN NETANYAHU: The reason we should fight BDS is because it's wrong. It is a moral outrage.

CS: It's an operation run by the secretive Ministry of Strategic Affairs.

YOSSI MELMAN, ISRAELI JOURNALIST: They recruit mainly former intelligence officers. Its main task is to counter BDS worldwide.

CS: Using an undercover reporter, Al Jazeera's Investigative Unit exposes Israel's clandestine activities in London, a city that's become a major battleground.

ILAN PAPPE: The BDS campaign in many ways germinated in Britain.

CS: You'll meet the people working to challenge BDS at every level of British politics.

MICHAEL RUBIN: We work really closely together. But a lot of it is behind the scenes.

CS: One of Israel's main targets is the Labour Party. For the first time its leader is a champion of Palestinian civil rights.

BEN WHITE: They would be very happy to see Jeremy Corbyn no longer leader of the Labour Party, for sure.

CS: It's a covert action that penetrates the heart of Britain's democracy.

PETER OBORNE, JOURNALIST: It is outrageous interference in British politics, it shouldn't be permitted.

CS: A battle of ideas - seeking to change not only how Israel is portrayed, but how it is even debated. Our undercover reporter grew up in Germany and creates an identity as a graduate planning to live in Britain. Robin sets himself up in London as an aspiring Labour Party

activist with strong sympathies toward Israel. After over a month of attending party functions, he stood out as a friend of Israel. And before long, he recognized a familiar face.

Shai Masot is a Senior Political Officer at the Israeli Embassy

It's a meeting of the Labour Friends of Israel or LFI – members of the British parliament who lobby for Israel. Shai later explained to Robin the problems the LFI is facing.

SM: Not a lot of young people want to be affiliated. Obviously when they become MPs they won't be affiliated and then that's it, the chain is done. Because for years, every MP that joined the parliament, the first thing that he used to do is go to join the LFI. They're not doing it anymore in the Labour Party. In the CFI they are doing it automatically.

CS: Britain's ruling party also has a lobby group – the CFI or Conservative Friends of Israel.

SM: Out of the 40 new MPs who just got in at the last elections… all of those ones were in the CFI, Conservative Friends of Israel. In the LFI it didn't happen, obviously.

CS: Robin tweeted and wrote articles about Israel and the Labour Party, building up his online identity. He discovered numerous groups that support Israel, and which identify themselves as independent, grassroots movements. One is the Sussex Friends of Israel. They organised a march to protest against the pro-Palestinian movement to boycott Israel. Robin had joined them.

Shai later described the Embassy's role in some of these movements:

SM: There is a grassroots organisation such as Sussex Friends of Israel that… you went to their demonstration. There is Israel Britain Alliance, there is BICOM. There is so many, there is We Believe in Israel, there is so many.

CS: Shai had helped establish a youth group within the Conservative friends of Israel.

ROBIN: They have a young section of the Conservative Friends...?

SM: CFI, yeah... CFI started one year ago because of my idea. Then when I tried to do the same in the Labour, they had a crisis back then with Corbyn. Every group have a different idea. Specifically, LFI young people doesn't exist. That's the only place where there is a vacuum. The moment it will become 100 people, 200 people. Then it's starting to become a real organisation. But this could take a year.

ROBIN: Have you ever built something, like a group?

SM: Yeah I did several things like that yeah.

ROBIN: O.K In Israel?

SM: In Israel and here.

ROBIN: Ah, here as well.

SM: Yeah

SM: Nothing that I can share but yeah.

ROBIN: Nothing you can share?

SM: Yeah, because there are things that you know happen, but... It's good to leave those organisations independent. But we help them to actually...

ROBIN: To establish?

SM: Yeah.

CS: Our investigation linked the Embassy's Senior Political Officer with a series of pro-Israel groups – the Parliamentary Friends of Israel, Young Conservatives, lobbyists as well as grassroots movements. In addition, Shai is involved with the youth arm of the Fabian Society, an influential Labour Party think-tank.

MARTIN EDOBOR: I know Shai, Shai is a good guy. Yeah he's good friend of mine.

CS: Martin Edobor was chairman of the Young Fabians, 2015-16.

ME: When we engage with the Israel Embassy they gave us a programme that was very neutral. I met Shai through the process and Shai you know in himself he's a very balanced guy. If you talk to the Israel Embassy, they're not going to throw at you propaganda.

CS: It appears the Israeli diplomat's mission is to build support for Israel at all levels of the Labour party.

SM: There's a lot of groups that are educating the MPs. But there's no-one who's educating the grassroots of the party. That's the idea. Specifically in the Labour. Conservatives doesn't need it.

CS: Shai says he knows nearly all the Fabian Society activists.

SM: There's no more than that, there is two-hundred.

ROBIN: This is all?

SM: This is all in London, around 200 that are active. That are campaigning, that are active. I know almost all of them. I took a Fabians group to Israel.

CS: Martin Edobor was in that group and others. He explains how foreign government support helps the Fabian membership.

ME: Shai is good in terms of manpower and he's got great contacts on both sides… both in Palestine and in Israel as part of his job experience. He's a great guy. He's very helpful and very supportive as well. And he's very balanced.

PETER OBORNE: I went on one of the trips of the Conservative Friends of Israel to the Middle East. It was brilliantly well arranged. Very well looked after. You got fantastic access. You did meet Palestinians. If all you did was rely on that one trip, you would have a very one sided point of view.

ME: Recently I saw something on Facebook that… some really wild thing that the Israelis are not giving… weren't giving Palestinians water or something during Ramadan. I know that's false.

CS: According to *Ha'aretz* newspaper, Israel, which controls all water sources in the Occupied West Bank, did cut supplies, even if the reason was contested.

ME: I've been to Israel going to the delegation, seeing what the system is actually like. I know that's false, and I know that's propaganda. You will only understand that if you actually go to the country.

CS: Our undercover reporter discovered that Shai Masot played a role in another key Labour Party organization, the Jewish Labour Movement, or JLM. Robin attended a summer BBQ organised by the JLM. Much of the small talk turned to the Israeli Embassy.

MEMBER: Oh you know Shai? Interesting. I work with Shai.

ROBIN: Oh, you work with Shai?

MEMBER: I work for the ambassador.

JEREMY NEWMARK: At this moment I wanted to also formally welcome Ella to her new post as director.

CS: Jeremy Newmark is the Chairman of the Jewish Labour Movement.

JN: Ella was by no means the person on that pile of CVs that had the most Labour Party and political experience. But there was something we felt on the JLM executive as trustees mattered far more, which is that she's one of you. She's seen this stuff from the inside. She's fought the campus battles alongside you. Which is why we took the step of appointing Ella to this role because we think she's going to go on and play an incredibly critical role at the lead of the struggle against anti-Semitism in the Labour Party.

ELLA ROSE: Hi folks, I've been introduced. I'm Ella, the JLM's barbecuer-in-chief and new director.

CS: Ella Rose is the Director of the Jewish Labour Movement.

ER: Let's go out, let's change the Labour Party for the better and let's hopefully influence the future of this country for the better with a progressive, strong, fair society.

CS: What came next surprised our undercover reporter. Shai had asked Robin to become part of the Israeli Embassy's plan to attract young Labour Party members.

SM: LFI is Labour Friends of Israel. They are trying... they want to establish a branch of Young Labour Friends of Israel. The idea is to establish a kind of a branch that will work with young people. So what I'm saying is that if you have free time and you would like to get engaged. Then I guess they are looking for someone who will launch it, and run it. We need to try to think about what can you do?

CS: Shai then suggested that as well as setting up the Young LFI, Robin apply for a job at the Israeli Embassy. He was invited to a private meeting at a London Hotel. It included embassy staff and British supporters of Israel. An Israeli diplomat takes Robin to one side.

MICHAEL FREEMAN: We're looking for workers. Someone to work in the Embassy. I don't know if that is something that might interest you.

CS: Michael Freeman is Head of Civil Affairs at the London Embassy.

ROBIN: Shai talked to me about that actually. So I handed him my CV.

MF: That'll be it.

ROBIN: Yeah, that's it. Exactly. And we're also looking for somebody to work on the whole BDS piece, doing research into the different BDS movements... who they are, what they are, a little bit of strategy on that whole piece. I don't know if either of those things might appeal to you.

CS: Ella Rose, the new director of the Jewish Labour Movement was pleased to hear of Robin's plans to set up a Young LFI.

ER: I used to work at the Embassy here. I can definitely help you out. And I'd love to come to any and every event you're hosting. Please consider me your number one fan.

CS: The guest of honour was a Minister from the Israeli government.

GILAD ERDAN: I grew up with the ideology that the land of Israel totally belongs to the Jewish people. Not any compromise, morally. Biblically. The land of Israel belongs to the Jewish people.

CS: Gilad Erdan is Israeli's Minister for Strategic Affairs. The primary role of Israel's Strategic Affairs Ministry is to counter the BDS movement.

GE: It is a strategic threat for the future of Israel because if we will allow them to continue with all the lies that they are spreading against Israel... We will lose this fantastic young generation. And maybe from here, there will be the next leaders of the UK or other countries and they will think that Israel is a very bad country.

CS: During another meeting with the Embassy's Senior Political Officer, Shai tutors Robin on setting up a new pro-Israel group.

SM: Basically, the people who are affiliated with the Labour Party, they are young. How do you approach them? So first of all I think that you need something to sell. Right? Theoretically maybe LFI will agree to do a delegation to Israel. That's always a good start. Second, maybe you need an interesting speaker. That's when the Embassy can help or the LFI can help. If you are volunteering to be the chairman of it, you theoretically need someone to do social media. And someone that will take care of speakers or events, or someone who will be the chairman of the delegations to Israel. And then you just... then people become the new structure then it's not just your responsibility. Then you have another six people with responsibility somehow and they are the committee of the organisation. That's it. That's the way to establish an organisation.

ROBIN: *Who should I contact, what do you think?*

SM: *Michael. Rubin. Michael Rubin.*

ROBIN: *Michael Rubin?*

SM: *Tell Michael you have an idea, you want to take it forward*

ROBIN: *What's his position in the LFI?*

SM: *He's parliamentarian officer.*

MR: *I recently started at LFI. I worked for the Labour Party before that. I was chair of Labour Students. Let's take advantage of the sunshine whilst it lasts.*

CS: Michael Rubin is Parliamentary Officer for the Labour Friends of Israel.

MR: *We've talked about having a launch event, like a drinks reception like hiring out like the upstairs of a pub like this, putting a little bit of money behind the bar to get people there. You could get some parliamentary supporters, people like Joan Ryan. She could come along and speak and it gives people the chance to meet her.*

CS: Joan Ryan is an MP and Chairperson of the LFI.

ROBIN: *And she's in contact with Shai as well?*

MR: *Yes, yeah. We work with the ambassador and the Embassy quite a lot. So she'll speak to Shai most days.*

CS: The LFI appears to be looking beyond Labour's present set of MPs.

MR: *The Labour Party at the moment is not in a good place to say the least. There are lots of young people coming through who are moderate, who have good views on Israel. I think we haven't really paid much attention to those people... people who are going to be in parliament in 10, 15 years' time.*

CS: Robin tells him about the Israeli Embassy's interest in recruiting him.

MR: I know there are job openings available quite frequently. So you should chat to Shai.

CS: He gave an example of how a job at the Embassy could further a career in British politics.

MR: Ella Rose, she was president of UJS which is the Union of Jewish Students a couple of years ago. She works in the Embassy. But she's leaving the Embassy to work as a Jewish Labour Movement new staff member.

ER: A new guard came in. And they sort of thought at some point "okay, we're gonna hire someone to like help with stuff." And then all the anti-Semitism stuff kicked off, and JLM vastly increased its profile. They thought we should probably hire someone political who actually knows... what they're doing. Before that I was at the Embassy working with Shai.

ASA WINSTANLEY, JOURNALIST, ELECTRONIC INTIFADA: Around about the same time... that the JLM reemerged under the leadership of Jeremy Newmark, who would later hire Ella Rose as the Director of the JLM, the big story was about a young student in Oxford who made allegations that the Labour Party and most of the student Left at Oxford was anti-Semitic. He didn't present any evidence at all, the only thing he said was that they had promoted the Israel Apartheid Week, which is a well-known event which takes place on campuses around the world.

CS: The national chairman of Labour Students at that time was Michael Rubin.

MR: There were allegations of anti-Semitism at the Labour Club. So I did the investigation, I was Chair of Labour Students. It was a Labour Students report but like there are some people sort of obviously asking questions about it because that was kind of a first instance of anti-Semitism.

AW: There was lots of media leaks and talks about how anti-Semitism was being covered up.

CS: British newspapers repeatedly ran stories of anti-Semitism in the Labour Party. One of the next targets was Malia Bouattia, the newly elected leader of Britain's National Union of Students.

MR: She described Birmingham as a Zionist outpost because it has a large Jewish society. So it was pretty bad. In NUS and student politics in the UK, the anti-Israel rhetoric is pretty bad. Like Zionism is an awful thing. Like if you call yourself a Zionist, you would get ripped apart. They say they're anti-racist, they say they don't discriminate people. But if anti-Zionism goes so far, I would say it becomes anti-Semitism.

CS: With each year of Israel's expanding occupation, support for BDS has spread on college campuses around the world. In Britain, the Israeli-Palestinian conflict defined the 2016 election for the NUS presidency.

CHANNEL 4 INTERVIEWER: Israel where it exists now, is that a problematic to you?

MALIA BOUATTIA: Israel as it behaves, is problematic to me.

PRESENTER: You would feel that it is OK for you to say about yourself that you were anti-Zionist?

MALIA: Yes I would.

MR: Bouattia. She's really bad. Do you know Robbie Young? Have you heard of Robbie Young? Malia is NUS president and Robbie is one of the vice presidents. He's a Labour Student and he is like really good on Israel. He been out on a trip so he's seen Israel, seen it first-hand. He's really pro-Israel, so there are some people in the NUS which are quite balanced and good.

CS: Another vice president, Richard Brooks, took the unusual step of publicly claiming that Bouattia's criticisms of Israel amount to anti-Semitism.

RICHARD BROOKS: I could never have an elected leader who's racist. NUS's internal structures don't usually allow a vice president to go and publicly criticize the president on national radio. But you got to do what you got to do.

RADIO 4 PRESENTER: When we look at what Malia Bouattia has been saying, she says her criticisms are a political one. She talks about Zionism, not about people who are Jewish.

RB: I think the real important thing here and something that the student movement has to face up to is that it is for Jewish students to define what anti-Semitism is and in the runup to national conference nearly fifty Union of Jewish Student presidents of societies made it clear that they had concerns about some of the rhetoric.

CS: Brooks never mentioned that weeks before that interview, he'd been taken to Israel as part of a delegation from the Union of Jewish Students.

RB: I got educated on all this kind of stuff and like spoke with people in UJS. I got taken to a trip to Israel with UJS. That was about two months ago. So I kind of learned loads on that and from there on in I felt confident enough to start talking about some of the stuff more seriously. Obviously Malia is awful. I was at the conference where she got elected. We were campaigning for the person running against her. Because we didn't want her to win. Obviously didn't work.

CS: During the run up to the election, Richard Brooks had held private meetings with Russell Langer, the campaign director of the Union of Jewish Students. Also attending the meetings was Michael Rubin.

RB: Michael was chair of Labour Students last year I worked with… there was me, him and Russel from UJS. We'd have our little secret purpose meetings where we'd plan how to get moderate people with good politics and any number of things… elected to certain places. Like I said me and him worked quite closely together last year.

CS: After being introduced by the Israeli Embassy as a Young LFI volunteer, our undercover reporter explores the possibility of ousting the pro-Palestinian NUS president with the help of Richard Brooks.

ROBIN: So how can we get in touch with the people who are trying to oppose her?

RB: You can speak to me. I've been organising them, so yeah. Yeah, so just drop me a line whenever you want to have a conversation or you want to speak with someone inside a geographical area I'll point you at the right people.

CS: Our investigation also revealed that the Union of Jewish Students – who sent critics of Malia Bouattia on trips to Israel - has received money from the Israeli Embassy.

ADAM SCHAPIRA: The Israeli Embassy in the UK gives money to the Union of Jewish Students. Once you're involved with the Union of Jewish Students, they then get you.

My sister worked for the embassy for a bit, as her first job. It's a good platform do to for like a year.

CS: Adam Schapira, a student at University College, London. In 2016 Schapira launched an unsuccessful bid for the presidency of the Union of Jewish Students. He also received donations from Israel to set up a new campus-based think tank. He established the Pinsker Center, with former University College student, Elliot Miller.

ELIOT MILLER: I just spent a year working in the government in Israel. I was doing a fellowship at the foreign ministry, in the congressional affairs department, so all Congress, AIPAC stuff. There's a guy behind me, he's in Israel. He's the main guy. He's the sort of guy who can walk into a room with the donor, and the donor will give him a cheque for £25K. Just like that. He's a genius.

CS: They also confirmed for the first time that the powerful American pro-Israel lobby, AIPAC, is channelling money to British campuses through the Pinsker Centre.

RB: I think AIPAC gave some money.

EM: We went to AIPAC in March, and we got involved with AIPAC London.

CS: Eliott Miller remains vocal in the cauldron of London student politics.

EM: You don't respect women! You don't respect gays!

AS: Elliott and I have set up the Pinsker Center, our aim to reframe the rhetoric on UK campuses. I feel like a lot more needs to be done in the educational field, bringing over diverse speakers from across the political spectrum on campus, present another narrative.

EM (to supporters of Palestine): It's a violent religion!

CAPTIONS: AL JAZEERA APPROACHED ALL THOSE FEATURED IN THIS PROGRAMME.

THE ISRAEL EMBASSY, SHAI MASOT, THE **YOUNG FABIANS** AND **LABOUR FRIENDS OF ISRAEL** WERE AMONG THOSE WHO DID NOT RESPOND TO OUR FINDINGS.

WE BELIEVE IN ISRAEL DID CONFIRM THAT, WHILE IT WAS NOT CONTROLLED FINANCIALLY OR OTHERWISE BY ISRAEL, IT WORKED WITH A RANGE OF SHAREHOLDERS INCLUDING THE ISRAELI EMBASSY.

THE **JEWISH LABOUR MOVEMENT** DENIES THAT IT HAS WORKED CLOSELY WITH SHAI MASOT

The Lobby, Part 2

CAPTION: The Training Session

CS: Our undercover reporter has held meetings with the senior political officer of the Israeli Embassy in London. Shai Masot wants Robin to help set up a new youth movement allied to Britain's Labour Party. Shai Masot is a Senior Political Officer at the Israeli Embassy. It will soon be time for the party's annual conference and he's keen that Robin attends.

SM: We are going to be there a huge group. From the embassy there are going to be about five people and there going to be an MK (parliament member) from Israel and eight young Labour (members) from Israel.

CS: He suggests Robin liaise with the heads of other pro-Israel movements.

SM: So Luke Akehurst is the director of We Believe in Israel. He's a great guy.

ROBIN: So you know him?

SM: Of course!

SM: So Luke is great guy. I know him, he's a great friend. We Believe in Israel is sitting together in the offices of BICOM.

ROBIN: But it's not the same organisation.

CS: Luke Akehurst is head of the Britain Israel Communications and Research Centre, BICOM and *We Believe in Israel*

SM: He's a great campaigner, he's one of the best in the inside. In all the party. Seriously, there is not a lot of people like him. And Luke... ask him if he is keen to...

ROBIN: Can I mention your name towards Luke?

SM: Yeah.

CS: Shai also suggests that Robin contact Michael Rubin to take forward the idea of attracting pro-Israel young people to Labour.

SM: Drop Michael an email. Tell him you are keen to do that 'we just need your umbrella'. Then you need a business card. That's it.

CS: Michael Rubin is Parliamentary Officer for the Labour Friends of Israel.

ROBIN: Ok, can I claim that I have your support?

SM: You can tell him that I suggested to…contact him but not my support because LFI is an independent organisation. No one likes that someone is managing his organisation. That is really the first rule in politics.

MR: The Embassy helps us quite a lot. When bad news stories come out of Israel the Embassy sends us information so we can counter it. Getting it directly from the horse's mouth, as it were, is quite helpful. We work really closely together. But a lot of it is behind the scenes. We got to be careful because I think there are some people who would be happy to be involved in a Young LFI but wouldn't necessarily be happy if it was seen as an Embassy thing. Having Shai helping in the background, yeah. I think definitely keeping Shai up to date and let him know what we're doing. I think we just have to be careful that not to be seen as Young Israeli Embassy like… we want it to be distinct by itself. So we do work really closely together, it's just publicly we just try to keep LFI as a separate identity to the Embassy of course. Being LFI allows us to reach out to people who wouldn't want to get involved with the Embassy. Keeping it as separate thing is actually best for everyone because ultimately we want the same end goal of getting more people to be pro-Israel and understand the conflict. It's just how you do it.

CS: It's time for members of the Labour Party to travel to their annual conference in Liverpool. Robin sits with the Israeli delegation. Shai announces plans to establish another organization in Britain – this time with links to AIPAC, America's powerful pro-Israel lobby.

SM: I'm arranging a, I'm establishing a group, it's called 'The City Friends of Israel'.

And basically we are doing like a small lunch with a congressman from America. We are doing it, I am doing it with AIPAC.

CS: Our investigation has already established this Israeli diplomat's links to numerous political groups in Britain, including the parliamentary lobby group, the Labour Friends of Israel, or LFI. At the Conference, Shai introduces our undercover reporter to LFI members at their stall.

ROBIN: Hi, nice to meet you.

JOAN: Hello.

ROBIN: Robin, nice to meet you.

CS: The Israeli diplomat advises the chair of the LFI about Robin's new role within her organization.

SM: So you've just met. So Robin is volunteering for the LFI as well and he's doing the.. trying to get the young people…

JOAN: Excellent, welcome.

CS: Joan Ryan is an MP and Chairperson of the Labour Friends of Israel.[*]

SM: He's trying to arrange another delegation maybe, activists from LFI.

JOAN: That'd be really good.

CS: They discuss paying for influential MPs to take a government-run tour of Israel.

JOAN: What happened with the names that we put into the Embassy, Shai?

---

[*] On September 6th, 2018, she failed to survive a vote of no confidence in her constituency. [KS]

SM: Just now we've got the money, it's more than one million pounds, it's a lot of money.

JOAN: I know, it must be.

SM: And now I've got the money so from Israel so… it's not physical, it's an approval.

JOAN: I didn't think you had it in your bag!

YOSSI MELMAN: The Government of Israel has already budget, allocated to various ministries which can use it as they like, to bring foreign delegations to Israel. It's part of the information campaign, you may call it propaganda campaign.

CS: The deputy Israeli Ambassador to the UK arrives at the stall and is introduced to our undercover reporter.

SM: This is Robin. He is volunteering in the LFI to bring young people to the Young LFI.

MARTIN: And he is a Young Fabians as well!

SM: And the Young Fabians as well.

RYAN: I hope that doesn't mean you're getting rid of us older ones though!

CS: Shai networked with pro-Israel Labour activists. He offered assistance to the Jewish Leadership Council, an influential umbrella group of Jewish organizations in Britain.

SM: And he told me there is a couple of things that you asked… you JLC, asked to arrange? So I gave them a draft schedule.

CS: Russel Langer, the former leader of the Union of Jewish Students, is now Public Affairs Manager with the Jewish Leadership Council

RL: My understanding is it was just more of an offer from us to them to help facilitate anything they need with some suggestions of what to do.

SM: She wrote to me...

RL: But I don't know anything more than that at this point.

SM: Yeah but they were amazing. This is the best piece, "Shai, do whatever you want in Israel".

RUSSEL: Ah well, that's good.

SM: And I love when people tell me that.

CS: While in Liverpool, Shai's confidence in Robin grows. The Israeli diplomat goes so far as to introduce him as the chairman of the Young Labour Friends of Israel.

SM: He's the Young LFI chairman.

UNKNOWN MAN: Nice to meet you.

MIKHAL: Robin is establishing now the LFI part of the youngsters.

ROBIN: Young LFI.

MIKHAL: Yeah....and Shai is the Head of the Delegation.

KAREN: Hi Robin I'm Karen, nice to meet you.

MIKHAL: And he is establishing now Young LFI.

KAREN: Ah, you're heading up the Young LFI. Brilliant.

CS: Robin learns that pro-Israel activists are planning to attend a meeting organized by the Labour Friends of Palestine and the Middle East – the LFPME. On the way he spots Luke Akehurst - the prominent pro-Israel operative within Labour - who Shai had told Robin to contact.

ROBIN: Excuse me Mr Akehurst.

LUKE: Hi.

ROBIN: Hi, I'm Robin. I'm the guy setting up the Young LFI.

LUKE: Oh well done, good good.

ROBIN: We have a little progress now. We have the first signing up, 22 people on the mailing list.

LUKE: Good, good, excellent.

ROBIN: Are you going to any events?

LUKE: To the LFPME thing? Yes I am. Because I need to take notes on that one.

ROBIN: Oh, are you going to write something?

LUKE: No, no, just for internal, for BICOM*.

CS: It becomes clear that as well as Akehurst, other pro-Israel activists will be discretely recording the event.

RL: There's the Labour Friends of Palestine and the Middle East one at 2:30, which I'll be going to, so…I need to charge my phone up so I can get some more recordings.

CS: Ahead of the Palestine event, one member of the Israeli delegation contemplates wearing a T-shirt promoting Israel.

MALE STAFFER: It's brave.

FEMALE STAFFER: She's dying for some action. Yes, yes, it's good!

MALE STAFFER: I wouldn't if I were you…

FEMALE: You wouldn't if you were me.

ROBIN: Akehurst is gonna write a report anyway.

MALE STAFFER: These are our spies, which is why you can't wear that T-shirt becauae then everyone will know.

MICHAEL RUBIN: You don't want people to shout at you.

FEMALE STAFFER: Well you know I was an Intelligence Officer so…

---

* Britain-Israel Communications & Research Centre

ROBIN: Oh.

MIKHAL: ...a spy.

FEMALE STAFFER: ...for four years.

FEMALE STAFFER: I can get the intel for you no worries.

CS: While the Palestine event passed without incident, controversy did follow a private training session organised by the Jewish Labour Movement. Mike Katz is Vice Chairman of the JLM.

MK: My name's Mike Katz, I'm one of the National Vice Chairs of the Jewish Labour Movement.

CS: Mike Katz works under Jeremy Newmark, the Chairman of the Jewish Labour Movement. Newmark recently appointed Ella Rose as the JLM's new director.

MK: The title of today's session is: 'Confronting Anti-Semitism and Engaging Jewish Voters'.

CS: The training session was arranged following allegations of anti-Semitism within the Labour Party. It became a highly-publicised matter for Jeremy Corbyn after an incident involving the former Mayor of London.

MAN SHOUTING AT LIVINGSTONE: You're a Nazi apologist, a disgusting Nazi apologist

CS: A barrister, Shami Chakrabati, launched an inquiry and concluded that despite an "occasionally toxic atmosphere", anti-Semitism was not endemic within the Party.

MK: Anti-Semitism as a phenomenon across the world. Here's an example... in 1992 Buenos Aires, the Israeli Embassy, 29 killed, 242 injured. 2012 Toulouse school attack... 4 killed. Obviously 2014, shortly after the awful Charlie Hebdo attack, we had the attack in a supermarket in Paris...

CS: The private JLM training session was about to have very public consequences for one attendee.

JACKIE WALKER: At the start it seemed relatively relaxed. It was simply a training session and I think some of us had gone along there with the idea that it was kind of strange because in some ways this was going against what Shami Chakrabarti had actually advised so we wanted to see what was going on.

MK: The Community Security Trust, they recorded 557 anti-Semitic incidents across the UK in the first six months of 2016.

CS: The Community Security Trust, a charity that monitors anti-Semitism in Britain.

MK: That is an 11% increase in the period in 2015. 2014 was the most anti-Semitic year on record.

CS: One member of the audience challenges how the list was drawn up. Christine Tongue, Labour Party Member.

CT: I'm wondering if I'm now going on that list, because my MP actually sent a letter to Jeremy Corbyn asking him to bar me from a rally in Ramsgate because I was an example of anti-Semitism. Because his office had trawled through my Facebook page and found an article that I shared by Norman Finkelstein.

CS: Norman Finkelstein is a Jewish American academic who defends the rights of Palestinians. Finkelstein wrote – in what many considered a humorous post - that one way to deal with the occupation of Palestinian land, was to move Israel to the United States.

ILAN PAPPE: In the past anti Semitism was hating Jews for being Jews, uh, now Israel tries to extend it to say that this is any criticism about what Jews are doing, is also anti Semitism.

If you question the right of Israel to be a Jewish state, uh, then you are not different from these classical anti Semites.

JACKIE WALKER: This goes back to the training session. They do this by saying most Jews relate to Israel as being as an important part of their identity.

MK: What we need to do is recognise that Israel is an integral part of the vast majority of the Jewish community's identity.

JW: Therefore, if you attack Israel you are attacking their identity.

MK: You've got to create a welcome, a debate that is fair. I think you need to be careful with your language, think about the references to the Holocaust and what you might say actually delegitimises that right of Israel, that basic right of Israel as a country to exist. That is not appropriate. Zionism, Zio, is not a term you should use, and that is in any Labour Party conversation.

CS: Zionism is the political ideology that Israel has the right to exist as an exclusively Jewish homeland in historic Palestine. Graham Bash, Labour Party Member.

GB: I'm Jewish and I don't agree with the concept of a Jewish state because it gives me the right to live in Israel whereas a Palestinian who's been displaced has a lesser right than me. So when you say it's not appropriate, are you really saying it's not appropriate for us to have a political discussion?

ILAN PAPPE: The Jew of Europe had the right to look for a safe haven. There is no doubt about, when they were persecuted by anti-Semitic governments and movements. And definitely the Jews had to save themselves when this anti-Semitism has turned into this Nazi machine of destruction and genocide. The question is do people who were persecuted in Europe have the right to displace people of another place? Can the abused become AN abuser?

JW: If you are saying effectively that Zionism, is not open to debate as a concept, then that is really worrying. Anti-Semitism, like any form of racism is deplorable and my feeling about how to tackle this is for Jews to be standing firmly and squarely alongside our

Black comrades, our Muslim comrades, who are much more at the moment the target of racism thankfully at the moment we are.

CS: As well as our undercover reporter, someone else was secretly recording the debate.

JW: I am laughing because by the time the row actually broke out I was on my way home. I mean none of us thought anything about this training session. I was in the car and suddenly I started to get these tweets coming through to me and these phone calls from the BBC. A secretly recorded clip was leaked to a news outlet. What was actually leaked were certain little segments that would be as controversial as possible.

JW IN MEETING: In terms of Holocaust Day, I would also like to say wouldn't it be wonderful if Holocaust Day was open to all peoples who experienced Holocaust, and if the Jewish....

??: It is...

JW: As I spoke If you like there was a ripple in the room and I was just constantly interrupted...

JW IN MEETING: Well actually... in practice it's not actually circulated and advertised...

JW: I am not just Jewish, I am black and my ancestry is of African enslavement. Only this year I spoke at slavery Remembrance Day and I spoke to a crowd in Trafalgar Square about the African Holocaust and that is what we call it. You can disagree with me as to whether I should call that a Holocaust but it is not anti-Semitic for me to call what happened to African people in the diaspora a Holocaust.

JW IN MEETING: I was seeking information, and I still haven't heard a definition of anti-Semitism that I can work with.

JW: How it was reported and how it was tweeted was I was basically saying I can't find anywhere a definition of anti-Semitism to work with. That's total nonsense. I am an anti-racist trainer. I have been an anti-racist trainer for forty years. I have been fighting fascists and anti-Semites on the streets for decades.

CS: The incident caused uproar in the British media. The Board of Deputies of British Jews called Walker a "an unapologetic Jew-baiter." Walker was suspended from the Labour Party pending an investigation. Shortly afterwards Robin meets the embassy's senior political officer.

ROBIN: What do you think of that woman, Jackie Walker?

SM: Yeah, she is problematic. What can we do?

ROBIN What can we do?

SM: Do not let it go. That's all that you can do. Do not let it go.

ROBIN And report every time she...

SM: Not just her. All of the party. Do not let it go. That's... the key.

YOSSI MELMAN: In recent years, there is a growing tendency within the government to smear people who are anti-Israeli, or anti- Zionist, also to be anti-Semite. But not all anti-Israelis, and anti-Zionists are anti-Semites. On the contrary.

JW: If they accuse anybody of anti-Semitism it is basically as bad as kind of accusing somebody of being a paedophile or a murderer and it is really hard to come back from that one.

CS: Meanwhile, our undercover reporter spots Ella Rose across the road. News had broken of Ella's former job at the Israeli Embassy - which had not been widely known. She's in tears because of what she considers anti-Semitic harassment. Ella Rose is the Director of the Jewish Labour Movement

ROBIN: Are you all right?

ELLA: It's been a tough week.

ROBIN: I'm sorry to hear that.

ELLA: It is all right. Essentially Electronic Intifada released that I worked at the Embassy before JLM and Jackie Walker has been slamming me online all week. I just had to stand in front of her. It was really hard, it was really hard. It's over. I'm going to run a rally so fuck you, fuck you, fucking anti-Semites, the lot of them.

JW (watching the video) : Oh my god.

CS: When our undercover reporter next met Ella she had regained her composure.

ELLA: I saw Jackie Walker on Saturday and thought: you know what, I could take her, she's like 5'2 and tiny. That's why I can take Jackie Walker. Krav Maga training…

CS: Krav Maga is a hand to hand combat technique developed by the Israeli Military. Yeah. I'm not bad at it. If it came to it I would win that's all I really care about. all I really care about.

JW: Oh my gosh… Well, I am kind of… that says it all. I mean you know I don't even speak about people like that in that way. You would take somebody! You would take somebody out! And she is speaking about another Jewish Labour member in this way. I think that's breath-taking. It is absolutely breath-taking. I am just stunned.

CS: The report that Ella worked at the Israeli Embassy had appeared in the Electronic intifada, a pro-Palestinian news website.

ASA WINSTANLEY; Ella Rose had been working for a year at the Israeli Embassy in London, something that wasn't widely known at all, that had been as far as I could ascertain had been essentially covered up.

ELLA: Ahh, Asa Winstanley. He was the one that wrote the douchy things about me. He's a dickhead.

AW: They know they can't win when the debates are open, so they have to do these things behind closed doors. So when I'm outing her as an Officer at the Israeli Embassy and she didn't want that to be publically known, yeah she's not gonna like that, she's gonna lash out

ELLA: Look, at the end of the day these people are sad, sad tossers. They're completely pathetic, and leave them in their corner where they belong. I'm very over them and their existence. As far as I'm concerned they can go die in a hole.

AW: She's worked for the Israeli state – the Israeli state talks about a "war" against organisations like us – it is a threatening thing to hear about, absolutely.

JW: What we need to have is some investigation of this from the Labour Party and I will be making a formal complaint against both Ella Rose and the Jewish Labour Movement.

ELLA: Shit happens… People are going to hate me no matter what, and they're always going to find something. It was all very anti-Semitic to be honest. I'm a Zionist, shoot me.

CAPTIONS: THE ISRAELI EMBASSY AND SHAI MASOT DID NOT RESPOND TO OUR FINDINGS.

WE BELIEVE IN ISRAEL DID CONFIRM THAT WHILE IT WAS NOT CONTROLLED FINANCIALLY OR OTHERWISE BY ISRAEL, IT WORKED WITH A RANGE OF STAKEHOLDERS INCLUDING THE ISRAELI EMBASSY.

ELLA ROSE STATED THAT SHE HAD BEEN OPEN ABOUT HER PREVIOUS EMPLOYMENT WITH THE ISRAELI EMBASSY.

THE LABOUR FRIENDS OF ISRAEL SAID THEY WORK ALONGSIDE MANY ORGANISATIONS – BOTH ISRAELI AND PALESTINIAN - AS WELL AS THE ISRAELI EMBASSY. THEY SAY SHAI MASOT WAS CLAIMING INFLUENCE HE DID NOT HAVE AND THAT ANY YOUNG LFI GROUPING WOULD BE ORGANISED BY THE LFI AND NOT THE EMBASSY. THE LFI ALSO STATE THAT THE CONVERSATION BETWEEN MR MASOT AND their chairperson, Joan Ryan, concerning £1M had nothing whatsoever to do with LFI delegations. The LFI say that no payment of £1M was offered, given or received by them and the names of individuals supplied by Ms Ryan were for a visit arranged, advertised and paid for by the Israeli Embassy. At the time of transmission no one has clarified to whom the £1M was to be paid.

The Lobby, Part 3

CAPTION: An anti-Semitic trope

CS: One of Israel's main targets is the Labour Party. For the first time its leader is a champion of Palestinian civil rights.

BEN WHITE: They would be very happy to see Jeremy Corbyn no longer leader on the Labour Party, for sure.

CS: It's a covert action that penetrates the heart of Britain's democracy.

SM: Can I give you some MPs that I would suggest you would take down?

PETER OBORNE: It is outrageous interference in British politics, it shouldn't be permitted.

CS: It's a battle of ideas – seeking to change not only how Israel is portrayed, but how it is even debated.

JOAN RYAN: It's anti-Semitic, it is, it's a trope.

JEAN: No it's not anti-Semitic...

CS: The Labour Party is holding its annual conference in Liverpool. For the first time, the leader of a major British party is an outspoken critic of Israel. The Israel Embassy has sent its senior diplomats to canvass opinion. Our undercover reporter attends a private meeting of sympathetic Labour activists. The ambassador, Mark Regev, tells them what to expect.

MR: Some of the people here are more Palestinian than the Palestinians. The fashion if you are on the left today you are probably very hostile to Israel, if not anti-Semitic.

CS: Ambassador Regev suggests a message that should be delivered to other Labour Party members.

MR: Why are people who consider themselves progressive in Britain, supporting reactionaries like Hamas and Hezbollah? We've gotta say in the language, I think, of social democracy, these people are misogynistic, they are homophobic, they are racist, they are anti-Semitic, they are reactionary. I think that's what we need to say. It's an important message.

CS: Jeremy Newmark, the chairman of the Jewish Labour Movement, reveals how the message worked – with a close ally of Jeremy Corbyn.

JN: Just to get Clive Lewis as one of Corbyn's key lieutenants onto an openly Zionist JLM platform took a lot of heavy lifting.

CS: Clive Lewis, MP for Norwich South is the Labour Party's spokesman on defence issues.

CL: Look, it is a real pleasure to be here tonight...

CS: Lewis's decision to condemn anti-Semitism at a JLM event was viewed as a tactical victory for the faction inside Labour that opposes Jeremy Corbyn. Corbyn is the party's first openly pro-Palestinian leader. The faction that supports him is called Momentum.

JM: We already have intelligence that from the Momentum political directors meeting last night. They passed a vote of censure on Clive Lewis, just for coming to our meetings and speaking.

CS: At the time, Jackie Walker was vice-chair of Momentum. She believes that reports of a crisis of anti-Semitism were a consequence of the same ruthless party infighting.

JW: Some of us would say it was mostly a constructed crisis for political ends. I would say, there is a crisis in the way the anti-Semitism is being manipulated and being used by certain parties not just in the Labour Party but other parties and the media to discredit Jeremy Corbyn and a number of his supporters. I mean let's disagree politically. I am anti-Zionist, they are pro Zionists, let's have that argument. Let's have that argument not this what is going on at the moment no.

JN: So everything is wheels within wheels, you know? It has created a bit of division within Momentum.

JW: The day before I had a debate with Jeremy Newmark. At one point he turned his back on the audience and whispered to me "you are a court Jew". Now anybody that who is Jewish understands what that means. If you are being abused as a black person in the same way you would be being called a house nigger.

CS: Did you report it to anyone in the Labour party----?

JW: I told my partner, and told some friends that had happened. It is very hard to use a system which is so discredited, which the Compliance Unit is.

CS: Shai Masot - whose job at the embassy includes liaising with pro-Israel groups in Britain - ends the meeting with a summary of his achievements.

SM: This year we did more than 50 events on the campuses and universities from the Embassy. There are more than 100 events that happened by the Israeli societies, by themselves that they arranged in the campuses. In addition to that, we did more, than I think eight receptions for young people in the Embassy, including three receptions of 300 people that came from the parliament.

CS: Back at the LFI stall Shai and the Israeli delegation continue to debate whether to wear the Pro-Israel t-shirts.

FEMALE STAFFER: Shai has a dream, I'm going to make it come true today. He wants me to put on the T-shirt. But you know ,as Robin is my witness...

SM: Robin can put a shirt on as well.

FEMALE STAFFER: I was going to put on that T-shirt today and...

SM: I have a dream that an activist will not be ashamed of what he's representing.

FEMALE STAFFER: I'm not ashamed by what I'm representing.

SM: So put it on.

FEMALE STAFFER: It's a T-shirt and it's fucking cold.

SM: It's such a huge message.

FEMALE STAFFER: I'm what?

SM: It's such a huge message.

CS: One party member was attending her first conference.

JEAN FITZPATRICK: I heard there was a Labour Friends of Israel stall and I thought this'd be a really good opportunity, to have a dialogue with a group I know who have a lot of influence and it'd be very interesting to hear their ideas, so I found where their stall was.

JEAN: Can I just ask you if you're very anti the settlements, what is Labour Friends of Israel

JOAN RYAN: We make our view clear and we meet with people at all levels in Israeli politics and diplomatic circles etcetera and we make it absolutely clear we're not friends of Israel and enemies of Palestine, hence our new campaign launching next month and that we're showcasing here. We believe in a two-state solution and the coexistence and

self-determination for both people and that's really important.

JEAN: And how will that come about do you think?

JOAN: Well our job is to support any possible means that can bring it about and facilitate…

JEAN; So what sort of support can bring it about?

JOAN: Well what we are supporting is coexistence projects which is what this is about.

JEAN: I had no idea, quite honestly, who was behind the stall. There was a woman behind the stall.

CS: Joan Ryan is an MP and Chairperson of the Labour Friends of Israel.

JEAN: My first series of questions from memory was simply to say I was very interested to know how a two-state solution would come about, what would be the details? Not a slogan but the details.

JEAN: But what about Israeli occupation?

JOAN: Well what we want is a two-state solution and the reason we've not got it now at the moment is the distinct lack of security for Israel.

CS: Supporters of a two-state solution believe that a peace deal based on national boundaries that existed in 1967, before Israel's occupation, will one day lead to lead to a viable Palestinian state. But the continued growth of Israeli settlements on occupied land has made an independent state all but impossible.

BEN WHITE: If you look at a map of the West Bank and East Jerusalem today, you are looking at a fragmented territory that Israel has colonized now for almost half a century. Practically speaking, a two state solution is just not possible under these conditions.

JEAN: I was actually, seeking some reassurance that a two-state solution, if that's what they were promoting, was still possible.

JOAN: This is a big picture situation and we want a two-state solution that is good for all.

JEAN: No, I know, you've said that a number of times, but what steps?

JOAN: Well I've told you what steps we're taking

JEAN: So the Labour is saying...

JOAN I'm not going to defend or criticise...

JEAN: But it seems you are defending Israel.

JOAN: No. I would defend Israel, I defend Israel's right to exist, I defend Israel as a democracy and a social democracy.

JEAN: But at what expense?

JOAN: I think we have to be very, very careful not to let our feelings about this morph into anti- Zionism.

JEAN: So no feelings come into account? No I'm not being anti-Zionist...

JOAN: You have to be very careful...

JOAN: Don't we all want a two-state solution based on coexistence and peace?

JEAN: I said time and again, "I'm here to talk about the two-state solution which you are promoting and this is what I'd like to learn about,"

BEN WHITE: It's clear that the Israeli state, no matter which party is in power, has got absolutely no desire or inclination to relinquish the territories occupied after 1967. But the questions that that throws up are the kinds of questions that people don't want to ask or don't want to answer

JEAN: But I'm asking you how you are bringing about...

JOAN: ...so you make your effort and we make ours.

ILAN PAPPE: Anyone who supports Israel has to ask himself or herself the following question. There are two possible scenarios and only two possible scenarios. Either I support the new state of Israel which is an ethnic apartheid state or I support a change of regime in Israel namely that this...the state and the country as a whole would go through a genuine process of democratisation as did apartheid South Africa. There is no third option.

JOAN: Thank you Jean, I've enjoyed the conversation, I'm leaving it there.

JEAN: No, no, I'm asking you about settlements...

JOAN: Well I'm not answering it any more, sorry Jean.

JEAN: They've totally atomised the whole of the West Bank. I'm asking you, I'm really genuinely interested how a two-state solution...?

JOAN: I'm just working for a two-state solution.

JEAN: But how can it come about if the whole of the West Bank is atomised?

JOAN: We're trying to do everything we can to support and facilitate that solution.

JEAN: Okay, but in practical terms?

JOAN: That's what we're doing as Labour Friends of Israel, if that's what you're doing as Palestine Solidarity Campaign, that's good isn't it.

JEAN: No but I'm asking in terms of the West Bank is atomised – where will the state be?

I mean that is a genuine, genuine question. Where will the state be?

ILAN PAPPE: The activist who came to ask her tough questions about settlement activity, that was her main point. She didn't ask her about Judaism or the existence of Israel, she just wanted a straight answer for how does, uh, anyone who supports Israel, uh, explain the settlements, or justify the settlements.

JEAN: We go over there, we witness, but nothing chances.

JEAN: I was quite interested in whatever funds they had and influence they had, how would this bring about a two-state solution? That was my very basic question.

JEAN: You've got a lot of money, you've got a lot of prestige in the world.

JOAN: I don't know where you get that from.

JEAN: Sorry?

JOAN; Labour Friends of Israel have got a lot of power, a lot of money... that's just not...

JEAN: Well I think so, that's what I hear that, you know, it's the stepping-stone to good jobs. A friend of mine's son's got a really good job at Oxford University on the basis of having worked for Labour Friends of Israel.

JOAN; If you just believe rumours then I…

JEAN: It's not a rumour, it's a fact.

JOAN: It's anti-Semitic. It is. It's a trope. It's about conspiracy theorists.

JEAN: No it's not anti-Semitic, it's not (repeats).

JOAN: Sorry, it is. Anyway, that's my view and I think we'll have to agree to differ.

JEAN: No, I don't think we do have to agree to differ.

JOAN: Well I'm agreeing to differ and I am ending the conversation because I am not really wanting to engage in a conversation that talks about get involved with this and then you get a good job in Oxford or the City or… and that is anti-Semitic, I'm sorry.

CS: Joan Ryan falsely claimed that Jean referred to jobs in the City – London's financial centre.

ILAN PAPPE: It comes very clearly in the discussion that you have filmed, that the woman was not anti-Semitic. They know it. She didn't talk like an anti-Semitic person. She was a typical pro-Palestinian person who was worried about the violations of human, of the Palestinian human and civil rights.

CS: Ryan repeated the reference to banking – a traditional anti-Semitic trope – as she left the conference hall with our undercover reporter. But Jean had never mentioned it.

JOAN: It's an anti-Semitic…you heard her say, you know, 'join you lot and you get into Oxford and you get into working in the bank or…' That's anti-Semitic.

JEAN: At no point did I ever say that, Labour Friends of Israel will get people jobs in banking in the City. I did say, which is absolutely true, that I know the son of a friend of mine who, he believed himself that having some connection with Labour Friends of Israel didn't harm his career at all.

CS: That evening at a rally to combat anti-Semitism organised by the Jewish Labour Movement. Joan Ryan described her day at the stall.

JR: We have also had three incidents of anti-Semitic harassment on our stand, to the people who are staffing that stall today. And that, I think, tells you something about why we need to be having this Against Anti-Semitism Rally.

CS: By the following day, word had spread about Jean's exchange at the LFI stall. Several MPs came by and expressed concern, including Jeremy Corbyn's former challenger, Angela Eagle.

MICHAEL RUBIN: We had a couple of problems yesterday but...

ANGELA: Yeah, no I saw that.

RUBIN: ...today's been better where we did have one person towards the end of the day come and say the anti-Semitism was just being used to crush Jeremy and that the allegations are made-up to certain extent, which is obviously awful but compared to the stuff yesterday it's sort of not as bad.

CS: Michael Rubin is Parliamentary Officer for the Labour Friends of Israel.

MR: Somehow that sort of stuff that has become normalised, sort of less shocked about that than I was about what happened yesterday.

ANGELA: That's bollocks.

RUBIN: I know. How are you anyway, are you okay?

ANGELA: I'm absolutely loving it.

CS: As well as Jean's case, other alleged incidents of anti-Semitism involve the attempt to replace the Labour leader, Jeremy Corbyn. Another prominent Corbyn opponent arrives at the stall and hugs Jennifer Gerber, the Director of the LFI. Labour MP Chuka Umunna asks for an update on the anti-Semitic incidents.

CHUKA: So what exactly happened?

JENNIFER: Oh God, yeah...

RUBIN: So one nutter came up and basically said the "coup" was run by Jews and Jewish MPs and Jewish millionaires and Angela Eagle's husband is Jewish...

JENNIFER: He's Jewish.

RUBIN: You couldn't make it up could you? But we reported it.

CHUKA So that was incident one, what were the other two?

JENNIFER: Joan, you were, Joan dealt with the other incidents, the other incidents yesterday.

JOAN: I reported that incident with that woman, yeah. She took a video of me then... "Joan Ryan Labour Friends of Israel walking away, won't answer the questions". She didn't show any of the bits where I said "you're being anti-Semitic". So I made a formal complaint.

JEAN: I am very shocked about the way she described my words to other people. I am very worried, I'm very hurt, I feel very anxious that she has taken my words, to making it into something entirely different and that she should be misinterpreting me totally to other people I find that very very worrying.

JOAN: Well I mean I wrote down honestly what she was saying about him being rich and powerful and then when he went to Oxford and the next minute he's got a big job in banking, you know... and I said... classic anti-Semitic tropes aren't they.

JEAN: I have no idea how she got from A to Z going from my comment, which was what it was, to then saying he got a, a big job in banking. Maybe she believes her own trope, if that's the word they use.

JENNIFER GERBER: We had a woman saying: "I've never seen anti-Semitism, my Jewish friends haven't, well I said it is real, is it real is it really real... "It's just being used to crush Corbyn.

RUBIN: Yeah, to undermine Corbyn.

JENNIFER: And I said you know as a Jew, would you say that to any other... I haven't experienced homophobia but I don't deny it.

JENNIFER: But anyway it's only a few I guess, that's the way to... outlook.

CS: Jennifer Gerber is the Director of the Labour Friends of Israel.

RUBIN: Most people have been positive, we signed up lots of people, so.

JENNIFER: Yeah, do you know what most people have been positive and nice and kind of like... people are coming up and like solidarity. it's like 'solidarity' guys.

CHUKA: It's disgraceful. We'll prevail, we'll prevail in the end.

JENNIFER: I like that optimism.

ILAN: It's in a way pathetic, but it's also worrying how such a pathetic, uh, evidence can, and we know, can be used to, uh, intimidate Jeremy Corbyn into, establishing an inquiry commission in making daily confessions that he's not anti-Semitic and so on.

JENNIFER: That is I think gonna be the defining narrative actually now which is anti-Semitism. And you know what that denies, you know, what I found, I said to her, you heard me a couple of times saying I find that upsetting that as a Jew you're telling me like, and she didn't give up.

RUBIN: Yes.

JENNIFER: Like I think it's, if an anti-Semite comes up, you know, somebody says to me: "Jews, they're all fucking big noses and control the world." I'm like wow you're an anti-Semite, that's terrible. Someone like her worries me more because is she an anti-Semite, I don't know, but she basically denies the fact that it exists, she just thinks it's made up.

CS: The group discusses which act of alleged anti-Semitism was worse. Rubin believes that Jean's discussion with Joan Ryan was amongst the most serious.

RUBIN: I know, I know, I know. It's just that the stuff yesterday was explicit anti-Semitism.

JENNIFER: A difficult moment was when that woman who told us that anti-Semitism you know is being concocted to crush Corbyn. That is what she said and I think people, like if we're not getting it out there…

RUBIN: Yeah, yeah.

JENNIFER: Is that anti-Semitic guys, I don't know, like…?

RUBIN: I don't know where the line is anymore… I think it's different to yesterday.

ALEX RICHARDSON: I think if it makes you feel uncomfortable I think that's the point which you call it out and report it, and that's why Joan convinced me to report the one yesterday because I was made to feel uncomfortable and although nothing anti-Semitic was said I'm sure there were undertones of it and it was brought up on that context.

CS: Alex Richardson is Joan Ryan's Parliamentary Assistant.

JEAN: I thought Labour Friends of Israel were talking about Palestine because they were promoting a two-state solution. Now I find they don't want to talk about Palestine, and if you do talk about Palestine it would appear you're kind of sucked into having an accusation of anti-Semitism brought against you.

ALEX: At the end of the day if you feel offended by it and uncomfortable for it this should be a safe space and anything that breaks that should be reported I think. But there is that line obviously, I don't know.

ILAN PAPPE: So they are really scratching the bottom of the barrel to make a list of two and a half cases of anti-Semitism, … two of, two out of the three, uh, they themselves are not totally sure that they fall into their own strict definition of anti-Semitism.

CS: Jean was unaware that her exchange with Joan Ryan had made national news and that a complaint of anti-Semitism was lodged.

JEAN: I felt overwhelmed by being at the conference I had no idea that there would be so many things to go to, so many interesting workshops to go to, seminars at the same time as people speaking in the main hall. My husband had not been very well so we actually left a day early.

CS: Shortly after, Joan Ryan's assistant emailed Robin asking him to be a witness to Jean's alleged act of anti-Semitism.

ALEX: I kind of feel it was an anti-Semitic trope, against Israel. Like Jews controlling and having power and money. I thought it was... I know she didn't say Jews and she said Israel.

It is definitely on the line, do you know what I mean? If she had said the word "Zionist" I would have said one hundred percent. A hundred percent.

CS: Despite being unsure of what he had witnessed Richardson had no qualms about the expulsion of a fellow Labour party member.

AR: How it works is that you make the complaint within the Labour Party, within their own rules will decide. I suspect, I don't know but I suspect that this woman might be potentially banned because she said something that was anti-Semitic.

CS: After Jean had left the conference, she was contacted by a Labour Party investigator. He would only say it was about a serious incident.

JEAN: I was thinking had I seen a fire take place, had I seen someone throw a bottle, had I seen a fight break out. I was really racking my brain thinking what incident had I seen, was I aware of, was I a witness to something. And almost by return came an email that is was my conduct that was being investigated.

IMAGE OF EMAIL BEGINNING "The following allegation has been brought against you regarding your conduct at the Labour Party Conference.

JEAN: I was totally shocked! That was like a real bombshell.

CAPTION: AL JAZEERA APPROACHED ALL THOSE FEATURED IN THIS PROGRAMME.

JEREMY NEWMARK SAID HE DID NOT DESCRIBE JACKIE WALKER AS A 'COURT JEW' OR SAY OR UTTER THOSE WORDS IN ANY CONTEXT WHATSOEVER AFTER THEIR PANEL DISCUSSION.

NOR DOES MR NEWMARK BELIEVE THIS WOULD BE A FAIR OR ACCURATE DESCRIPTION OF MS WALKER.

JOAN RYAN STATED THAT IT IS THE DUTY OF ALL LABOUR PARTY MEMBERS TO REPORT LANGUAGE THAT THEY BELIEVE TO BE RACIST OR ANTI-SEMITIC. SHE BELIEVES HER ACTIONS WERE ENTIRELY APPROPRIATE.

MS RYAN ADDED THAT REFERENCES TO GROUPS HAVING 'LOTS OF MONEY' AND 'LOTS OF PRESTIGE IN THE WORLD' AND SUGGESTIONS THAT THEY ADVANCE PEOPLE'S CAREERS APPEARED TO EVOKE CLASSIC ANTI-SEMITIC TROPES.

NEITHER THE ISRAELI EMBASSY OR SHAI MASOT RESPONDED TO OUR FINDINGS

The Lobby, Part 4

Caption: The Takedown

CS: In this final episode of *the Lobby*, Shai Masot's activities paint a troubling picture. Few foreign embassies in London are this engaged in Britain's democratic process. And at what point does it cross the line? The annual conference of Britain's opposition Labour Party is continuing in Liverpool. The gathering is important for Israel, because for the first time the party leader is a supporter of the BDS movement. Robin, our undercover reporter, has been with members of the Labour Friends of Israel. Shai Masot had conceived a plan to attract young, pro-Israel Britons to the Labour Party – what he called the Young LFI. He promoted Robin as their chairman. Now it seems the Young LFI is about to become operational.

MICHAEL RUBIN: Shai spoke to me and said the Israeli Embassy will be able to get a bit of money which is good.

CS: Michael Rubin is Parliamentary Officer for the Labour Friends of Israel. He's happy to sort of help fund a couple of events so...

MR: It makes it easier, so I don't think money should be a problem really, it's just getting organised and off the ground now really.

CS: By now our undercover reporter had become a trusted confidant of the Israeli embassy's senior political officer. But suddenly he wants a private word.

SM: I wanted to speak with you, I wanted to do it over coffee but let's do it on the way to the event. It appears that something has changed. When I was drunk or whatever, I introduced you like as working with Young LFI. Actually it's not an official position yet.

CS: Shai had earlier introduced our undercover reporter as the new 'chairman' of the Young LFI.

SM: It was an idea, it is an idea that I cannot implement because I'm not a Young Labour Friend of Israel, or young British guy. It's not relevant to me at all, I am an official. I can give you an idea, and I can help you with everything, but I'm not relevant to you at all. Just I'm a tool to you to help you, if you want to do it. If you decided to get the idea.

ROBIN: So you don't coordinate too much with them?

SM: I'm coordinating a lot of things with them. But I'm not their boss. My position is that if you need help... to connect you to the groups, to be in different places, I can do that.

But you cannot be affiliated with me, and you cannot like... use me as someone that said something. It's not relevant. I'm not relevant to anything, I'm just working in the Embassy.

CS: On the following day, *Haaretz* newspaper reported on a leaked cable from the Israeli Embassy in London. The memo accused an Israeli government ministry – Strategic Affairs.- of 'operating' British Jewish organisations 'in a way that could put them 'in violation of British law'.

Headline: Ministries feud over anti-BDS warfare in U.K.

Israeli diplomats complain the actions of another Israeli ministry is in potential violation of British law

YOSSI MELMAN: The ministry of strategic affairs may use local groups, which are entitled as British civilians, to counter BDS. They may be in touch with them, they may instruct them, they may support them. But they would be very very careful not to violate as a state, the laws and the sovereignty of other nations.

SM: You cannot say 'Yeah Shai said that it's fine that I will volunteer to you' because I'm not the one taking the decisions at the LFI.

ROBIN: I'm sorry if I brought you into trouble.

SM: No, I'm totally fine.

ROBIN: Ok, good

SM: It's just important that you know it is clear. So if I'm giving you like ideas, it is like friendly ideas. It's in a friendly way, it's off-the-record, it's not something that you can use...

ROBIN: So but then, there is I mean...

SM: If you feel that you like the idea, so you got an idea from a friend to do in the LFI, it's fine that I'll be that friend. But the bottom line, it's not like... It's not like... that I have a say in that idea.

ROBIN: Yeah ok sure.

SM: Do you get it? That's politics.

PETER OBORNE: If you were trying to fool the British people by setting up a front organisation which masquerades or says that it is genuine Friends of Israel but actually is run from Tel Aviv that's troubling. Just imagine it being sort of apparently spontaneous pro-Iranian organisation in Britain and it turned out that it was run from Tehran or inspired by Tehran. That will be outrageous.

CS: The annual event run by the Labour Friends of Israel was one of the most anticipated at the conference – the party leader always attends. The LFI Chairperson kicked off proceedings.

JOAN RYAN: We must campaign flat-out against the BDS movement and all those who seek to demonise the state of Israel. But to single out uniquely the world's only Jewish state and call for it to be boycotted. That is anti-Semitic and we should say so loudly...

ILAN PAPPE: It is very surprising that people suddenly were talking about fundamental issues of anti-Semitism in the Labour Party once a certain person was elected as its leader.

JR: Ladies and gentlemen, the leader of the Labour Party, Jeremy Corbyn.

ILAN PAPPE: That's the only reason people were looking for anti Semitism and you know if you look for something you will always find it whether it exists or it doesn't exist

CORBYN: I want to thank Joan Ryan for all the work she has done...

CS: The sudden onset of anti-Semitic claims led Jeremy Corbyn to publicly engage with Labour's pro-Israeli groups.

JC: I say this, the Labour Party is not a home for anti-Semitism in any form. I do not intent to allow it to be. We have produced a report...

JEREMY NEWMARK: I can kind of live with that for the time being. It will get us through for another year.

CS: In the past, Israel has grown used to unchallenged support from across the British political establishment. That cross party consensus allowed Israel a free hand enabling it to build illegal settlements on Palestinian lands.

JOAN RYAN: I am sure many people are pleased to hear your commitment to a two state solution and your commitment to fight anti-Semitism wherever it appears in our party or in wider society...

CS: In private – Israel has another message. Corbyn – and the global BDS movement that he supports – threatens the political status quo that has tolerated Israel's occupation of Palestinian lands for half a century.

SM: Corbyn is a crazy leader. One of the things he doesn't understand,.. he doesn't get is that the moment you get the leadership, you need to drop all the weirdos. The extremists. It's good that they were your campaigners. You cannot build a government from extremists. And he doesn't want to do that. He wants to stay with all of those weirdos.

CS: Back at her London home, the woman who confronted Joan Ryan over the construction of Jewish only settlements had received a message. She had become the subject of a formal Labour Party investigation.

JEAN: So, 'The following allegation has been brought against you regarding your conduct at the Labour Party conference 2016

JOAN :Thank you Jean, I've enjoyed the conversation, I'm leaving it there.

JEAN No, no, I'm asking you about settlements...

JOAN :Well I'm not answering it anymore, sorry Jean.

JEAN: When the lady who I now subsequently learned, but only very subsequently, was Miss Ryan, um... accused me, the allegations was that I was being anti-Semitic, I was just appalled.

JEAN:They've totally atomized the whole of the West Bank. I'm asking you, I'm really genuinely interested how a two-state solution...

JOAN: I'm just working for a two-state solution.

CS: The complaint alleged that Jean constantly suggested that the LFI had "lots of money and power," when in fact she had said once the LFI has money and prestige. Nor did Jean mention a "high paying job."

JEAN: As a concluding paragraph, the summary says: 'The above incidents and allegations le, levelled at me left the complainants feeling victimised, intimidated and both felt the incident contained what they both described as incidents of anti-Semitism.

JOAN: I reported that incident with that woman. I made a formal complaint.

CS: After several weeks, the investigation cleared her name.

JEAN: That they should be the ones to feel victimised and intimidated from a member of the public, a member of the Labour Party approaching a stall where they're purporting to give information and presumably wanting to discuss the two state solution, I, I just find that almost, I mean, laughable, if it weren't so Affecting of me. I know now that it can absolutely impact on people's lives. I am just a regular citizen who is concerned about what is happening in the Middle East and not to be able to talk about that without being accused of being anti-Semitic I find deeply worrying. I think that is quite shameful.

CS: Back at the Israeli Embassy in London, Shai Masot remained keen to find a role for Robin. He invited our undercover reporter to meet an experienced parliamentary operator – Maria Strizzolo.

MS: You must have arrived one second after me.

CS: Both were on time for their meeting. As they waited for Shai to emerge from the Embassy, it turns out that Strizzolo has met two of Shai's superiors in Israel.

MARIA STRIZZOLO: The one time I was late ... actually she is Shai's boss ... I met her in Jerusalem when I was there in the summer, the one time I was late she was one time! Last year I met her with her boss a couple of times with my then boss because they wanted to discuss things like, you know, problems... with the UK Government.

ROBIN: Yeah, who did you work for then?

MS: I used to work for an MP, a Minister really.

ROBIN: Who is that?

MS: Robert Halfon.

CS: Robert Halfon is Britain's Minister of State for Education and former Deputy Chairman of the Conservative Party. The British civil servant began to educate our undercover reporter on how the Israel lobby works inside Parliament – and especially the Conservative Party.

ROBIN: How many of the MPs from your party are in Conservative Friends of Israel?

MS: Oh, pretty much all of them. When there is the annual lunch which is just before Christmas, basically the Whips always make sure that like the votes come after to the CFI event because it's like all the party's there.

CS: Whips are party loyalists who ensure MPs turn up whenever they are needed to vote.

SM: And the PM.

MS: And the PM, and the Chancellor, and the Foreign Secretary and everyone.

PETER OBORNE: When we are talking about the construction of British policy towards the Middle East, towards the Palestinians, toward the Israelis that you can't describe that without taking into account the fact the Israeli government has a very powerful ally in the shape of the Conservative Friends of Israel and they do play, they do brilliantly a brilliant job at getting the Israeli point of view across.

CS: The parliamentary officer described the ease with which the CFI's information was accepted by MPs

MS: If at least you can get a small group of MPs that you know you can always rely on, when there is something coming to parliament, and you know you brief them, you say: "you don't have to do anything, we are going to give you the speech, we are going to give you all the information, we are going to do everything for you." Then I think it becomes easier. And from that little group it might grow and grow. So if you prepare everything for them, it's harder for them to say: "Oh no, I don't have the time..." So if they already have the questions to table for Prime Minister's Question Time, it's harder to say "Oh no, no, no I won't do it."

CS: Strizollo boasted how her efforts once made an immediate impact on the national debate.

MS: I was in Israel with CFI when...they found the three kids that had been kidnapped in 2014. And I was on the phone with Rob to convince him to table a question for Prime Minister's Question Time for, paying tribute...

SM: Did he do it?

MS: Yeah. And also table in an urgent question to... to get a statement from the Government on the three kids.

SPEAKER IN PARLIAMENT: Mr Robert Halfon!

HALFON: Thank you Mr Speaker. For the world to see the tragic and brutal murders of three Israeli youngsters, most probably by Hamas. Will my honourable friend give the Israeli Government every support, possible support at this time? And does he not agree with me that far from showing restraint, Israel must do everything possible to take out Hamas terrorist networks, and will he give the Israeli Government support in this?

DAVID CAMERON: It is very important that Britain will stand with Israel as it seeks to bring to justice those who are responsible.

CS: By now the Senior Political Officer at the Israeli Embassy had become a trusted confidant of our undercover reporter. Shai invited Robin to attend a meeting organised in part by the City Friends of Israel –a group he earlier said that he was establishing.

MS: Looks like you get along with the Israelis. You have this thing with Israelis, you're quick to get along. That's amazing how you do that.

CS: Maria Strizzolo was also there. Discussion turned to Donald Trump.

SM: So he's an unpredictable person. The only thing you know you can, from an Israel perspective.... you can think that he is steady in this area is the fact that his daughter is Jewish. She converted to Judaism.

CS: The meeting had been coordinated with AIPAC, the American Israeli Public Affairs Committee, perhaps Washington most powerful lobby group. It is not widely known that AIPAC has a presence in London.

SPEAKER: As a European and someone who lives in the Western world and enjoys its individual freedoms, I also view, and I hope most of you do as well, I view Israel as the battleground where modernity and Western values meet the forces that want to destroy that way of life.

CS: Joe Richards from AIPAC's Wall Street Division summed up their operations.

JOE RICHARDS: Today, we are a robust organisation, we have one single mission, which is to make sure the United States and Israel remain very close together in their relationship in many different ways. The way we do that is by relationship building with our 535 members of Congress. 100 in the Senate, 435 in the House.

CS: AIPAC's guests explained to Robin their interest in Britain.

JR: The strategic goal is to get the UK to be more like the US than Europe, when it comes to Israel. Pull them, tug them into the US sphere....

CS: By this point, Robin was well aware of the Israeli diplomats close ties with America's pro-Israel lobby.

SM: I went to AIPAC last year because I organised the American - British Delegation to AIPAC. It was me and the British donors... around thirty, forty rich families that sponsored CFI, the Conservatives were with us and some from the Labour as well and we all went together to AIPAC. But the bottom line we had a donor meeting with the Head of Strategy at AIPAC and he met us basically to teach us, you know, give us some ideas for Britain.

CS: Shai then announced another audacious plan - involving a front company set up by the Ministry of Strategic Affairs, whose mandate is to fight BDS.

SM: The Strategic Affairs they asked me, they are establishing a new company... a new private company that basically will work for the Israeli Government. A kind of outside company...

CS: The Ministry of Strategic Affairs has called it a 'secret war' – potentially involving what this prominent Israeli reporter described as 'Dirty Tricks'.

RM: When I say dirty tricks... they can smear people, or activists, BDS activists or others. They can, um, hack their emails in order to collect information about what's there are... what they are up to. They can you know trash people.

SM: It's going to be an office of twenty people, so... the position that they suggested to me to do is to be the liaison for the international communities around the world. So it's good sometimes because you know it's good to work with AIPAC and all the others, CFI and LFI it is cool, it's good. The last position that I applied for that there is a slight chance that I will get it actually, is to be the Head of the Foreign Affairs Department of the Intelligence Department in Israel. I'm not a career diplomat, I am political posting which means that I can just run one position to assist in political issues that are specific, sometimes you need someone to take care just of them, to be focused on them. That's what I do.

CS: At ease and with the trust of his dinner companions, Shai floated the idea of a parliamentary plot...

SM: Can I give you some MPs that I would suggest you would take down?

MS: Well you know, if you look hard enough I'm sure that there is something that they're trying to hide.

SM: Yeah. I have some MPs.

MS: Well let's talk about it.

ROBIN: Yeah.

SM: No, she knows which MPs I want to take down.

MS: Yeah it's good to remind me.

SM: The Deputy Foreign Minister.

CS: Sir Alan Duncan is Deputy Foreign Secretary. He has been critical of Israel's policy on illegal settlements in the West Bank.

PETER OBORNE: This exchange between the political officer of the Israeli Embassy and the parliamentary staffer about "taking down" is the phrase used Alan Duncan is outrageous, it is shocking. This is a clearly deliberate attempt by a foreign government to interfere in the workings of British democracy and to secure the destruction of career of a minister in the British government.

ALAN DUNCAN: We recognized Israel in 1950 when they didn't have any clear borders, they didn't have a capital city. And now it is high time we did the same for Palestine

MS: You still want to...?

SM: It doesn't matter

MS: You still want to go for it?

SM: No, he's doing a lot of problems.

MS: It sounds like a conspiracy!

MS: I thought you had neutralised it just a little bit, no?

SM: No.

MS: Ah, why is this?

SM: Boris. Even if he's good...

MS: He's solid on Israel.

SM: ...yeah he just doesn't care. He's busy with everything else, Boris is busy you know.

CS: Boris Johnson is Britain's Foreign Secretary and Sir Alan Duncan's boss.

SM: You know he is an idiot but so far... he has become the Minister of Foreign Affairs without any kind of responsibilities. So technically if something real happened it won't be his fault.

CS: The parliamentary officer then recalled how Sir Alan Duncan had once confronted her boss, the MP Robert Halfon.

MS: Rob was writing articles...

MS: He was doing everything, asking questions in parliament about the terrorist salaries....

SM: When he was an MP?

SM: Ah, when he was a Minister in DFID

(Department for International Development)

MS: Yeah, and after a while though Rob was doing a lot of it, and Alan Duncan took him like I think but I don't remember exactly where... but he took him to one side and threatened him. "If you don't stop this I'm going to ruin you, I'm going to destroy you" and all of that shit, and Rob told the Whips, and the Whips just told him to calm down.

SM: Okay.

MS: Yeah, you know, never say never.

SM: Never say never, yeah but...

MS: A little scandal maybe? Anyway, please don't tell anyone about our meeting!

SM: No, no, no; to who would we tell?

PETER OBORNE: I certainly think that she needs to explain what she was doing. We want to know whether any further steps were taken towards getting rid of taking out Mr Duncan. I think we need a lot more about the background to this. What else was going on to damage the foreign office minister? it strikes me that this is the sort of job which, which the intelligence services should do to have a good look at what is going on

CS: Britain's domestic spy agency, MI5, includes in its definition of espionage: "Seeking to influence decision makers and opinion formers to benefit the interests of a foreign power."

CAPTIONS:

Since this programme was made, the Israeli Ambassador to the UK, Mark Regev, has apologised to Sir Alan Duncan. Mr Regev said that Shai Masot's comments were "completely unacceptable".

Mr Masot returned to Israel and has now resigned from government service.

Maria Strizzolo has also resigned from her post as a British civil servant.

Joan Ryan believes it was 'entirely appropriate' to make the complaint against Jean Fitzpatrick. Ms Ryan said that it was the duty of all Labour Party members to report language that they believe to be racist or anti-Semitic.

9

Who will Edit the Editors?
Kerry-Anne Mendoza

Britain's three most prominent Jewish weekly newspapers – *Jewish News*, the *Jewish Chronicle* and the *Jewish Telegraph* – published a joint front page describing Labour leader Jeremy Corbyn as an "existential threat" to British Jews on 25 July. Stephen Oryszczuk is foreign editor of *Jewish News*. Here, he speaks exclusively to *The Canary* in a personal capacity about why he feels the attack was wrong. But beyond that, he suggests how we can come together to fight the scourge of antisemitism, and how to do so without hindering free speech and justified criticism of Israel.

PART I – Who is Stephen Oryszczuk?

Q: Could you introduce yourself?

A: I'm foreign editor at *Jewish News* (JN), the UK's largest Jewish newspaper, one of the three papers that just published a shared front page attacking the Labour Party over antisemitism. That random assortment of consonants after my first name is Ukrainian origin. I've been in this role for six years, and speak here in a personal capacity. Before the JN I was an editor at a Jewish news TV channel based abroad.

Q: But you're not Jewish, I understand?

A: Nope, although there may be some J-genes back there on my dad's side, probably the ones that manifest as love of food.

Q: How did you come to work for a Jewish newspaper?

A: By complete accident! I've been covering the Jewish world for a long time now, particularly Israel. The boss of the TV channel actually preferred his journalists to be non-Jews. He said we could be more objective. I'm not sure that's true, but that was his take on it. I've always been taught to look at things objectively, to keep my head when all about are losing theirs. It's so important given the passions on the subjects I cover. Unfortunately, last week passion became apoplexy.

Q: Do you report on antisemitism too?

A: Yes, it seems to be taking over my life at the moment. I've reported on every kind of antisemitism – far-right, far-left, Islamist ideology, Christian theology, or just plain old tweeted ignorance. In the current media climate you can lose touch with the fact that it comes from everywhere. If you speak to the Jewish community's most prominent anti-racism campaigners, they say there's a resurgence in far-right/white supremacist antisemitism that's being missed in all this.

Q: I understand you have issues around the shared front page?

A: Some of the phraseology I take a giant step back from, vicious personal phrases like "Corbynite contempt for Jews," which is one step away from calling him a Jew hater. It's repulsive. This is a dedicated anti-racist we're trashing. I just don't buy into it at all. Who knows, I may change my mind, something may yet out, but for now it seems completely unfounded. The rhetoric doesn't match the reality. But – and it's a big but – I'm not Jewish. The papers are for the Jewish community. I'm speaking for me but they speak for the Jewish community, and many Jews have echoed Dame

Margaret Hodge in calling Jeremy Corbyn an 'antisemite', so if the community is beginning to feel that way, I respect my paper's right to reflect that, just as my editor and news editor respect my right to dissent. Fair play to them.

Q: So you don't share your paper's views?

A: Some bits I do, but I don't share this frothy-mouthed obsession with adopting the IHRA definition and its examples word-for-word if you think you can do better at contextualising it. I do agree that this must be a shared exercise with the Jewish community, not just lip-service. If the full definition is then accepted with accompanying notes, fine. And if the parties can't agree, that's fine too, but at least try! I also don't share the papers' vitriol. In fact I think it's counter-productive. I do understand the rage, but I vehemently oppose the personal nature of the attack, just as I opposed Hodge's attack, although it's her choice to do so. For me, it was a profoundly unjust accusation, to say the least, and more than proves the point that when applying the label of 'racist' it should first be warranted.

Q: Talk us through this new antisemitism definition and your take on it.

A: Your readers may already know this. The IHRA is a relatively new multi-state body. The UK's delegate is former Tory minister Sir Eric Pickles, who also chaired Conservative Friends of Israel. Their definition includes 11 working examples, seven of which relate to Israel. As a journalist covering Israel, what can and can't be said in this regard is of direct relevance to me – it affects my day-to-day work. More broadly, the question of what is or isn't antisemitic is highly relevant to our reporting. So I take a professional interest, but as with most journalists, I'm a big believer in free speech, so there's a personal interest too.

Q: What's your take on it?

A: The main definition is vague, the examples lack context and qualification, and those campaigning so hard for its verbatim adoption, with their strident opposition to context, at the very least need to explain why they're so against giving it depth, given how many leading barristers have raised concerns about it. Many Jews share those worries but their voices are not being heard. Increasingly, if anyone does voice it, they are seen as antisemitic for doing so! I would be truly fearful for our country and the right to free speech if that were the case.

Beyond that, I understand the urge to tighten up and update – antisemitism is an old hatred with new masks, and when people say 'Israelis' or 'Zionists' they can often mean 'Jews'. Like most people, I feel I know antisemitism when I see it. You sense it, you smell it. Howard Jacobson described it as "a toxin you taste on your tongue". That kind of instinctive gut feeling doesn't sit comfortably with the clamour to define it, but I know that it's completely subjective if you don't, and like most people my starting position is to support whatever helps tackle the scourge. That said, this definition is causing so many problems that I sympathise with those who want to rip the whole thing up and introduce a new one with just two words: 'Jew hatred.'

Q: Are you surprised that it's come to this situation, that it's become such an issue in the Labour Party in recent years?

A: Yes and no. Yes because it's a progressive party with a history of defending minorities. No because the party leadership now hails from the left, rather than the centre-left, and you get a lot of strident criticism of Israel on the left of British politics, which can sometimes cross the line.

Q: The papers, yours included, said 'United We Stand,' – is that correct?

A: Yes, the big Jewish mainstream organisations back it, as do many councils and public authorities, and Labour should have taken this more to heart, but it's important to say that some Jews don't back it. They're a minority but not an insignificant one. A petition against the papers' stance had about 700 Jewish signatories in its first 2-3 days. It's no surprise, clearly not every Jew thinks alike, certainly not on Israel.

Q: Why haven't we heard from them in the publications making these claims?

A: It's partly our fault, in the mainstream Jewish media. We could – and arguably should – have done a better job at giving a voice to Jews who think differently, for which I personally feel a little ashamed. I should have done more. We are, after all, called 'Jewish News.' I'd like to think we could be braver and risk the wrath of the many to give voice to all, because we're just an echo chamber otherwise, and that creates its own problems. But ultimately it's not my call – it's not my paper, it's not my community. There are various factors to consider and I respect that, I respect my editor hugely. But it does sadden me. There's a Jewish saying: 'two Jews, three opinions' – possibly a conservative estimate! It expresses the wealth of views held on any given subject, voiced on any given Friday night. It's a tradition I love from a people I love, and I think they'd say that habit has served them well over many hundreds of years. But on Israel today, what you hear publicly tends to be very uniform.

Q: Why is that?

A: From what I know, it goes back 50 years, to the war Israel fought in 1967. A century ago, it was different. British Jews openly held vastly different visions for the Jewish future, from complete immersion and assimilation, to the full withdrawal from non-Jewish society. Zionism back then was just one competing idea, and not too popular. Even after the war, when support for Zionism was boosted by the horrors of the Holocaust, there was still widespread Jewish resistance to the Zionist project and bitter divisions in the Zionist camp. There's an excellent recent book on the different opinions of British Jewry by Jewish sociologist Keith Kahn-Harris called *Uncivil War*, in which he traces the change. From 1967, he says:

> Support for, and loyalty to Israel became a taken-for-granted feature of almost all Jewish communal institutions. The argument that Jews should not undermine Israel through public criticism became mainstream. The institutional infrastructure of western Jewish communities was transformed to reflect the centrality of Israel... Support for Israel became a Jewish political priority, with the growing strength and importance of lobbying groups... and the defence of Israel taking a central role in UK umbrella institutions such as the Board of Deputies.

That situation persists today, and I think it is important to understand the Labour-Jewish community stand-off at least partly through that prism i.e. constitutional support for Israel.

Q: How does the IHRA definition threaten free speech?

A: If you have a system that automatically labels someone as antisemitic for voicing potentially legitimate thoughts and opinions, that's a huge threat to free speech, and it's not weird to think so. It stains people whose arguments would automatically trigger a suspension, an investigation, their naming and shaming in the press, all sorts of trouble, if it's simply an IHRA box ticked with little consideration around it.

Q: What part of the definition do you think endangers free speech?

A: It's more of a worry with some of the examples, if they're applied or interpreted broadly and without context, or if they're misunderstood. For instance, there's one sub-example that says it's antisemitic to claim Israel is a racist endeavour. There's a subtle but important difference between claiming Israel is racist and Israel is a racist endeavour. The IHRA example refers only to the latter, but they're not easy to prise apart, especially since some Israeli laws form its constitution, so you can understand how it's confusing. One is arguing that the policies and practices of the state of Israel are racist; the other is arguing that the very state itself is racist. Most Jews would deem the first fair comment, the second a big no-no, and it's the second that the IHRA prohibits. Hands up who could easily tell the difference?

Then there's the counter-argument: that we've long been able to debate and take a view on the basis and foundation of states, so if you feel Israel was set up along racist lines, despite the Declaration of Independence saying what it does, then you should be free to argue that. Jon Lansman addressed this in his *Guardian* piece, in which he said it raised the most alarm bells on free speech. He said:

> It cannot possibly be antisemitic to point out that some of the key policies of the Israeli state, observed since its founding days, have an effect that discriminates on the basis of race and ethnicity.

A day later, Israel passed the 'Nation State Bill,' which even Israel's defenders said risks discriminating against its non-Jewish minority. So it's a live issue and people must feel able to discuss it without being labelled racist themselves. That's my main concern: the IHRA definition, in its original form, was intended to defend against antisemitism, and I hope it still does, but in so doing it could prohibit reasoned arguments on Israel that are genuinely made.

Q: Do you think Lansman's argument is valid?

A: Valid or not, the question is: if I made it, should I be labelled a Jew hater, if I sought to argue it legitimately and reasonably, and applied the same principles to other states? You have to consider context and intent.

Let's say I made my argument with reference to Jerusalem. You'd ask if I'd held Israel to a higher standard, which is another IHRA example, but Israel is unique in so many ways – where else in the world do you find a situation like Jerusalem?

My point is that this isn't tick-box stuff, it's far more complex. I'm not saying all these things aren't antisemitic. They often are, but only an idiot would argue that this isn't now becoming an absolute minefield for those who mean well, which by its very nature will scare people away from making legitimate criticism. That's the negative impact on free speech I'm worried about, that's my concern. I'm as keen as anyone to get rid of racists, but it should be the racists, the antisemites, not all the rest who get caught up in the dragnet. That's why I think you need context and explanation, and that's what the Labour Party sought to add.

Q: Are there any examples of that impact on free speech you mentioned?

A: One example is that a Jewish peer has been writing letters to university vice-chancellors on behalf of a pro-Israel organisation in the UK, advising them to cancel Israel Apartheid Week activities or risk falling foul of the IHRA definition. At least one university did so. It saddens me that the IHRA definition and its examples are already being used to silence potentially legitimate criticisms of Israeli policy that have, for many years, been considered a student's right to voice. Has the IHRA now silenced that? If so, what will it silence next? That's my worry. If you push the IHRA [definition] verbatim, it seems that this is what you get. We all need to protect against that.

Q: So in your view, what is 'legitimate' criticism of Israel?

A: That's the million-dollar question! When it comes to that fine line on Israel and some of these examples, one person's legitimate criticism is another person's antisemitism. I hope they can agree something most can live with. I think it's possible. For me, as with so much else when it comes to antisemitism, it boils down to context and intent.

Q: Can you explain what you mean?

A: OK, so imagine if I'd said what Kahn-Harris said – that British Jews' political "priority" is to support Israel. I'd be reported for antisemitism for suggesting Jews are more loyal to Israel than the

UK, one of the IHRA tick-boxes. I'd be antisemitic. Would it make a difference if I was repeating what I'd read in a book? What if I was a PhD student researching identity choices of ethnic minorities and this was my conclusion after two years studying statistics and interviewing hundreds of Jews? Likewise, if I were to talk about Jewish lobbying, as Kahn-Harris does, that too would make me antisemitic, because that too could tick an IHRA box. Yet I think it's a good thing, it's legitimate and Israel needs a robust defence in the world of public opinion, so am I still antisemitic? In the context of Kahn-Harris's book, which explores the way Jews think about Israel, none of this is antisemitic, it's just factual, his intent is to inform. But taken out of context and placed in the wrong hands it could be nasty if the intent is to hurt – you need only think of those age-old myths and tropes about Jews controlling the world, or being parasites in a host country, to understand why. The point I'm making is that context and intent don't just matter, they're crucial. And tick-boxes don't give you any of that. So screaming that you only want the tick-boxes and nothing else doesn't crack the nut, it cuts the whole tree down.

Q: Perhaps a more common example these days is Nazi comparison?

A: Sure, and I would hope that most sane people could understand why Jews feel deep pain when someone likens Israel's treatment of Palestinians to the Nazis' treatment of Jews, when there can be no equivalence whatsoever. So like the other examples, it seems on the face of it to be always antisemitic. But on the day we published our joint front page with other Jewish newspapers, a Jewish reader wrote to us explaining how his Jewish father personally believed that Jewish people in Israel had ended up committing similar types of atrocities against Palestinians as Hitler committed against the Jews, how the irony of these parallels was not lost on many people, and how his Jewish father never considered saying so to be antisemitic. If his father thought as he did because he cared about Jewish values, was he an antisemite? Likewise a woman in my village in Devon, in her mid-80s, who wouldn't harm a fly, spoke to me back in 2014 – when Israel was bombing Gaza – and said something like: "Of everyone, you'd have thought Jews wouldn't do this to another people, given what they went through with the Nazis. It's like it's happening again." Is she an antisemite? I'm pretty sure the thought of it would make her cry, but the IHRA definition says she's a racist, pure and simple. It's about context and intent again. And Labour sought to add that.

Q: How do you determine what is and isn't antisemitic at the paper?

A: From my perspective I've always heeded the advice of the Community Security Trust (CST), which defends the Jewish community and which I admire. They taught me that context is crucial. For example, if a former mayor with a history of baiting Jews using wealth stereotypes mentions Hitler supporting Zionism as an historical aside while defending someone accused of antisemitism, the context suggests it might be not be benign, even if he's avoided ticking an IHRA box. If the leader of a country vowing to "wipe Israel off the map" asks questions about the Holocaust, it's unlikely to be scholarly research. And if 327 Holocaust survivors and their descendants invoke the well-known Holocaust phrase 'never again' over Israel and Gaza, context tells you that they're unlikely to be Jew haters, despite them ticking an IHRA box. It's the same with that Jewish Auschwitz survivor Corbyn hosted in parliament. Plenty would say that if the Nazis had killed his family and almost killed him, he surely has a right to speak. If he draws parallels then who are we to say otherwise? Is he antisemitic? If it's a tick-box then he is, but it's not black and white. The CST recognises the action alone may not tell the whole story, so why can't Labour? The times when you don't even need to ask second questions are the times when people tell you that you're writing your editorials for Mossad, a familiar charge at the JN! That's when you don't need to dig too much deeper!

Q: So you're saying that the IHRA definition reduces antisemitism to a tick-box exercise?

A: Absolutely. All definitions listing supplementary examples run this risk. Are you telling me something so complex as antisemitism can be reduced to that? If that's your argument, the onus is on you to prove it. And if you're going down that road, you need to make damned sure they stand up, that they're contextualised, and that they're not too broad as to capture lots of potentially legitimate criticism, because you'll tie yourself up in sifting and stain a lot of people in the process. In other words, you need to show, or be convinced of, underlying Jew hatred, or "intent," before you deem someone a Jew hater, because it can affect people's jobs, people's lives. You need to know that what they're saying or doing is hatred towards Jews, not just hatred towards Israel. Not only do I not apologise for saying so, I can't say it loudly enough. If I could megaphone it to every Labour MP currently plotting how best to screw Corbyn on this, I would. So, you have to be sure that someone's an antisemite before the formal process triggers. If that means setting the bar a little higher, as the Home Affairs Select Committee recommended, then so be it. I worry that some people forget what an awful label it is to attach to people, not to be done lightly. The IHRA itself recognises the importance of accompanying suggestions. It explains that antisemitism "employs sinister stereotypes and negative character traits". The CST also recognises this. Just last week it discounted hundreds of incidents as 'not antisemitic,' including anti-Israel activity that did not involve "antisemitic language, imagery or targeting". So the CST – charged with defending the Jewish community against antisemitism – knows you need something else, some "evidence," as a spokesman said. So I ask: why all the fuss about Labour's code? It's rarely difficult to find. Antisemites tend to show their true colours sooner or later, whether it be in "antisemitic language, imagery or targeting," as per the CST, or elsewhere in the context of what they've done or said.

Q: Do you have any other concerns with the IHRA definition?

A: I think the core definition itself is appalling. To call it woolly and vague is an understatement. It defines antisemitism as "a certain perception of Jews" that "may" be expressed as hatred towards Jews. How on earth is that a decent definition? Imagine a police officer pulling you over for having a certain perception of speed that may or may not be expressed as speeding. It's ridiculous. Then there are the IHRA examples, with no explanatory notes, so widening the scope. The bigger the box, the more ticks it will get, and the more difficult it will be to find those who need ticking off, those who need casting off, and those who were simply piping off legitimately. In the meantime, it stains anyone who falls within its reach.

Q: So you're in favour of the Labour Party amending it?

A: They didn't amend the definition. They drew up a code of conduct that took most of the definition as its basis but added bits to make it more useable and explanatory and removed the bits they disagreed with. They're entitled to do that, but they didn't really consult. I feel that what Dame Margaret Hodge said about Jeremy Corbyn was awful and wrong, but what she said later – on *Woman's Hour* I think – was a fair idea. She said Labour could have said yes to the definition in its full form, then got together with Jewish representatives to pull together guidance that contextualises it, to be read in accompaniment with it, or words to that effect. But they didn't do that, so Jewish leaders were left furious. They thought Labour had no right to tinker. They also felt the code had loosened the definitions to such an extent as to allow antisemitism. I can see it from both sides. I certainly understand why Labour did it, just as I understand why the Home Affairs Select Committee, in 2016, was concerned enough to recommend that the definition came with qualifiers. The MPs suggested adding to the definition to say that Israel criticism needed antisemitic intent. That's what Labour did. They also filled in gaps, including derogatory terms for Jews, stereotypical tropes and negative physical depictions, which the IHRA missed.

Q: Were you pleased that they did this?

A: I wasn't pleased or displeased – I just felt they needed to. I felt they had understood the importance of context and intent. I also appreciate that they built on the definition elsewhere. I felt Labour needed to draw a clear red line for its membership and say 'don't overstep this mark or you're out', but I also felt that mark needed the qualifiers, as per the MPs' recommendation. Yet for mainstream Jewish representatives and for Jewish media outlets – my newspaper included – that was tantamount to treason, a grave insult to Jews, an existential threat, and all the other dramatic phrases we heard. I believe Labour tried to do the right thing, but that it did it in absolutely the wrong way in not consulting widely before putting its code out there. Why on earth would you not make sure those most affected by it were OK with it first? I just don't understand that. Offering to consult now feels like an after-thought. It was a real snub, even though the code itself is on the right lines.

Q: Do you believe Labour and Corbyn are an existential threat to the Jewish community in the UK?

A: Of course not, but it's not for me to say, I'm not part of the Jewish community in the UK. I speak to many Jews day-to-day and many are genuinely concerned. I do believe that we would see some leave the UK if Corbyn was elected, which for me goes beyond sad. So yes, when Jews say the conversation around the dinner table on a Friday night is one of fear for the future, I believe them. As well as foreign editor, I'm also the newspaper's leader writer. That's the weekly editorial section – ours is called 'Voice of the Jewish News.' I've been doing that for about three years now. It's an honour, especially for a non-Jew. I don't believe they'd ask me if I wasn't tuned in to the thoughts of the community.

Q: So you don't think Corbyn warranted the abuse?

A: No, because I don't believe he's antisemitic, nor do most reasonable people. He's anti-Israel and that's not the same. But it says something that I even have to say that in 2018. Yet again, context is crucial, and the context to the accusation is the last three years, the constant examples of antisemitism in the Labour Party, the suspensions not expulsions, the Chakrabarti recommendations not being implemented, the lack of ownership or responsibility from the top... Jews feel Corbyn has failed to properly own up to the problem and assure them he's going to get on top of it. So I really don't think he can be surprised by the rage. To say he's been slow on the uptake is putting it mildly. I have a great deal of sympathy for Britain's Jewish community, especially left-wing Jews. They're exasperated, and now, to top it off, they see Labour raising the burden of proof on Jew hatred, introducing this element of 'intent.' You can understand the disbelief and upset. They see Labour making it more difficult for Jews to shout 'racism' and they're asking why should it not be less difficult, given the difficulties to-date. They say Jews should be allowed to define their own racism, with the antisemitic label in the hands of the victim.

Q: As a journalist at the centre of this story for three years, what do you say to those who think there has been a smear campaign against Jeremy Corbyn?

A: A 'smear' is the spreading of falsehoods, of 'fake news,' and we've (*Jewish News*) never done that, not intentionally anyway. But I do understand why people would think along those lines, because of the sheer volume of news about it. I too have questioned the timing of some of these 'findings' of very old clips, which always seem to be released at crucial moments. Is it by chance that news of him hosting an event linking Nazis to Gaza came out now? Is it by chance that news of him suggesting Holocaust Memorial Day be changed to Genocide Memorial Day came out now? Is it by chance that their support for the anti-Zionist network came out now? 'Now' being when he's under maximum pressure. I'm just saying: ask the question. As journalists we're taught to be sceptical.

The question is whether there is an intention to taint him. Some are certainly out to get him, but without revealing sources, all I can say is that it's sometimes questionable where these things come from. At the end of the day, most Jews just want Corbyn to get on top of Jew hatred.

For me, criticism is fine, but this has sometimes felt like character assassination, and I've always thought we were better than that. I'd much rather we stuck to our core business of news. That may be cover-to-cover Corbyn and Labour for all I care — if it is newsworthy then it is justified. But to keep doing these front pages attacking him is starting to feel uncomfortable, and not just for me. Several Jews, independently and privately, have told me in recent days that they're worried all the noise is "turning people against them", that it is becoming counter-productive. The other concern I've heard, particularly in relation to Hodge, is that she risks "crying wolf" at a very sensitive time. So of course all this hysteria worries me. These are a people I love, and a people with fears. I want them to make their point forcefully, and for it to register, but to be mindful that over-making it can blunt it.

Q: Is the picture completely bleak or is there hope?

A: I still think this code of conduct can be discussed this summer and more agreeable wording thrashed out. Lansman says that of the four IHRA examples Labour didn't replicate word-for-word, three are covered by its code, including accusations that Jews are more loyal to Israel, holding Israel to higher standards, and making Nazi-Holocaust-Israel links. If that is the case, the gap between the parties should be far smaller than all the screechy rhetoric and endless column inches suggest, so let's see if Labour can tighten these elements up. Likewise, most Jews value free speech, so I would hope that Jewish representatives could recognise the risk of curtailing legitimate criticism and help Labour find a way of catching genuine antisemitism while leaving politics free. What I'm saying is, there's wiggle room on both sides. The question is whether they'll wiggle. With mediation from a conflict resolution specialist, they could find something acceptable to both. But that requires vast amounts of bitter animosity being put to one side.

Q: If you were the mediator, what would you advise both parties?

A: I'd advise Corbyn to start by recognising the failing to date: the delayed disciplinary processes and their sometimes disastrous outcomes, the lack of transparency, the production of a code of conduct without wider consultation that's now distrusted by those most affected by it, and so on. But I would also advise the Jewish side to better recognise Labour's albeit belated progress, including the appointment of a QC, the drafting of a decision-making framework, the new time limits on disciplinary cases, the rollout of training, the continued sole recognition of the Jewish Labour Movement despite its attacks, the increasing public assertions that antisemitism is not welcome in the party, the recent speed with which antisemites are being suspended, even the attempt to clarify what it is the party deems antisemitic while incorporating the advice of the Home Affairs Select Committee – despite doing it all wrong. Both have to see that the other has a valid point. You can't just keep throwing bricks. I'd recognise that Corbyn probably felt Jewish leaders were bullying him over the IHRA [definition] and that Jewish leaders probably felt Corbyn was deaf to their concerns, so I'd ask both parties to prove those assumptions wrong to the other. I'd then tell them success relies on cool heads, reasonable demands and a common goal – that being the best definition of antisemitism to distribute while still protecting free speech. Then I'd keep all my fingers and toes crossed, and triple check the meeting wasn't being recorded for someone to leak it later.

Q: What do you think will happen if they don't reach agreement by 5 September?*

A: I think both sides will press the nuclear button. The Jewish community will declare Labour "institutionally racist" and pursue legal action against it however it can. MPs like Luciana Berger, Ruth Smeeth and John Mann will probably walk, maybe others. Likewise, Labour could declare that it now considers the Board, the Jewish Leadership Council and the Jewish Labour Movement to have prioritised their efforts to protect Israel from criticism over their efforts to help Labour define genuine antisemitism in the party, and move to end all relations. It may then institute new relations with groups like Jewish Voice for Labour. I hope it doesn't come to that. God bless the peacemakers!

Q: Finally, why did you decide to speak out, and to speak out to *The Canary*?

A: I don't know that it's speaking out so much as speaking up. But no, it wasn't an easy decision for me to do this, because I'll take a lot of flak for it. Still, if it helps cool even one head in this sorry saga then it's worth it. There's a personal reason too, a promise I made to my grandfather – who was almost killed by both the far-left (the Soviets) and the far-right (the Nazis) – to stay out of politics if you're able, even given the area I cover. So that editorial was a real problem for me and I wanted to say 'that's not where I'm coming from.' This is the first time I've ever said anything outside my news outlet, so I don't make a habit of it. The other reason is to appeal to your readers, those who haven't made their minds up yet, to say there's nuance in this debate but also that it's not just philosophical – it's having real world consequences. Jews are scared. Antisemitism has gone up precisely because of the debate.

---

* Agreement by Labour's NEC to adopt the whole definition was reached on September 5th. Nevertheless, this wasn't enough for some members of the Jewish community, and the criticism continues.

There's a middle ground to be had, and if cool heads prevail, if the Labour MPs itching to stick it to Corbyn hold back and let the right outcome be reached, then that right outcome can be found and Labour can get rid of the right people, protect free speech and win back trust. It takes an effort on both sides, and the first priority is to say 'hold on' to those bullying the leadership into accepting the IHRA examples verbatim. I know the left must currently be feeling attacked and that it is likely acting as anyone would in those circumstances. Just remember that Jews are not the enemy. They were there at the very foundation of the Labour movement, playing a part. It's been their natural home for decades. They've fought the battles Labour has fought. Hang on to that great vision of seeing them side-by-side once again to fight the battles of the future.

10

The Conduct of Baroness Tonge[*]

Committee for Privileges and Conduct

The conduct of Baroness Tonge, 7th Report of Session 2016–17

Summary of the complaint and investigation

1. On 25 October 2016 Baroness Tonge hosted and chaired a meeting in House of Lords committee room 2A in the Palace of Westminster. The meeting was organised by the Palestinian Return Centre to launch the "Balfour Apology Campaign". The meeting was filmed and photographed; both were published on the internet, including on the website of the Palestinian Return Centre. Journalists were present. Two days later *The Times* reported on the meeting under the headline "Jews blamed for Holocaust at 'shameful' House of Lords event". It was also reported in the *Jewish Chronicle*. Both newspaper articles mentioned a blog by David Collier, who attended the meeting. A transcript taken from the recordings of the meeting is in appendix A.

---

[*] The notes at the end of this report refer to documents and appendices not included in this book. They can be read in the full report on the Parliamentary website, referenced before the Notes on p. 230.

2. On 31 October 2016 I received a complaint from Karen Elizabeth Leon about the meeting. The complainant suggested Baroness Tonge breached the Code of Conduct because discussion at the meeting was "very anti-Semitic with the usual comments made about non-Israeli Jews"; was an "anti-Jewish litany and holocaust deniers' rant"; that Baroness Tonge "did not rebuke her speakers or stop them at any time"; and that "blatant racism and anti-Semitism was made ... public by her meeting and her speakers."

3. I also received a letter dated 27 October 2016 from Mark Regev, the Ambassador of Israel. He expressed "alarm" about the event, suggesting that its content involved "disseminating antisemitism, promoting Holocaust revisionism and encouraging support for Hamas". He commented that remarks that "Jews themselves had caused the Holocaust" and "the 'Zionist movement' holds power over Parliament" were "clearly grounded in bigotry and hatred". He referred to paragraph 9 of the Code of Conduct,[7] which requires members to act on their personal honour. The Ambassador did not identify an individual alleged to be in breach of the Code; his letter was about the event. Therefore the letter could not be treated as a formal complaint, but as it was relevant to the complaint already received I disclosed it to Baroness Tonge.

4. I carried out a preliminary assessment of the complaint. On the basis of it I decided there were two matters which warranted investigation. First, whether in hosting and chairing the meeting Baroness Tonge may have not acted on her personal honour. Secondly, whether she may have breached the Code by not acting in accordance with a rule on the use of facilities agreed by the House: that permission should be obtained for such an event to be filmed and photographed.

5. I wrote to Baroness Tonge on 8 November 2016 seeking her response to the matters under investigation. She replied on 21 November 2016.

6. On 17 November 2016 I received a further complaint, from six members of the House: Lord Beecham, Lord Carlile of Berriew, Baroness Deech, Lord Mitchell, Lord Palmer of Childs Hill and Lord Stunell.[11] They complained that the meeting was "host to appalling antisemitic comments and Holocaust denial by audience members"; that the audience "applauded statements ... that Hitler only decided to kill all the Jews after he was provoked by anti-German protests led by a Rabbi in Manhattan, and that "the Zionist movement has that power and it has that over our own Parliament". They considered comments at the meeting about the Holocaust and Zionism to be "historically and factually inaccurate" and "a classic antisemitic trope." They referred to Baroness Tonge hosting and chairing the meeting and invited me to investigate if the Code had been breached.

7. I advised the six members that I would consider their complaint as part of my investigation into whether Baroness Tonge had failed to act on her personal honour. I provided the six members with the transcript of the meeting and invited them to identify the particular remarks during the event which they considered to be antisemitic or which otherwise may have breached the Code of Conduct. At that time there was no official government definition of antisemitism for me to refer to, and as they wrote to me as members of the All-Party Parliamentary Group Against Antisemitism I was keen to get their detailed views.

8. Lord Beecham replied in an email of 24 November 2016. He referred to comments by "audience member 11" about the Holocaust and Zionism, and suggested that Baroness Tonge's failure to rebut or question those remarks breached the Code.

9. Lord Palmer of Childs Hill replied in an email of 27 November 2016. He too suggested Baroness Tonge was at fault for not "distancing herself and the meeting from very offensive remarks", particularly those by "audience member 11".

10. I wrote further to Baroness Tonge on 25 November 2016 asking questions arising from her previous response and disclosing to her the complaint by the six members. I also disclosed to her the follow-up emails from Lord Beecham and Lord Palmer of Childs Hill.

11. Baroness Tonge replied on 30 November 2016. The chairman of the Palestinian Return Centre, Majed al Zeer, wrote to me on 5 December 2016 in response to a request I had made to Baroness Tonge. I interviewed Baroness Tonge on 12 December 2016. I asked the Gentleman Usher of the Black Rod, David Leakey, who is responsible for enforcing the House's rules on filming and photography, for a statement on those rules.

IRRELEVANT CLAUSES OMITTED

Launch of Balfour Apology Campaign on 25 October 2016
Alleged failure to act on personal honour: relevant definitions

14. The Balfour Apology Campaign is designed to obtain an official apology from the UK Government for the Balfour Declaration of 1917. Here is the description of it and the meeting on 25 October 2016 from the Palestinian Return Centre's website:

"The Palestinian Return Centre is hosting an event inside the UK Parliament a week ahead of the 99th anniversary of the Balfour Declaration which will be on November 2nd. The Balfour Declaration, which had no basis of legal authority, promised the establishment of a Jewish state in Palestine, where the indigenous Palestinians amounted to 90% of the total population.

After the Balfour Declaration Palestine became the victim of colonialism and Britain's legacy is still evident today as Palestinians continue to be denied the right to self-determination and suffer from living under military occupation or as refugees. As the 100th year since the Balfour declaration approaches, the

Palestinian Return Centre has decided to re-launch its campaign which started in 2013 called Balfour Apology Campaign which asks the UK Government to officially apologies for its past colonial crimes in Palestine.

Committee Room 2a, Houses of Parliament

Tuesday 25th of October at 7pm

Hosted and chaired by Baroness Jenny Tonge

Panel Includes

Professor Manuel Hassassian, Ambassador of the Palestinian Mission to the UK

Betty Hunter, Honorary President of Palestine Solidarity Campaign, *Britain's legal and moral obligation*

Karl Sabbagh, Historian and Writer, *How successive British governments fell in love with Zionism, until it was too late*

Majed Al-Zeer, President of the Palestinian Return Centre, *On the Balfour Apology Campaign*

More speakers to be announced".

15. In December 2016 the Government adopted the working definition of antisemitism agreed in May 2016 at a plenary meeting of the International Holocaust Remembrance Alliance. It is:

    "Antisemitism is a certain perception of Jews, which may be expressed as hatred toward Jews. Rhetorical and physical manifestations of antisemitism are directed toward Jewish or non-Jewish individuals and/or their property, toward Jewish community institutions and religious facilities."[25]

16. I have used this definition and the examples which accompany it in considering the complaints.

17. As an allegation about Zionists was the subject of complaint I have used this dictionary definition of Zionism:

    "a movement for (originally) the re-establishment and (now) the development and protection of a Jewish nation in what is now Israel ... "

The Code of Conduct and personal honour

18. I have considered whether in hosting and chairing of the meeting Baroness Tonge failed to act on her personal honour. In reaching conclusions about what was said at the meeting I seek only to address this question; nothing which follows should otherwise be taken as endorsing or criticising the cause launched at the meeting or the views expressed there.

19. Under paragraph 8(b) of the Code of Conduct members "should act always on their personal honour". This is elaborated on in paragraph 7 of the Guide to the Code of Conduct, which quotes from a report of the Committee for Privileges:

> "The term 'personal honour' has been used within the House for centuries to describe the guiding principles that govern the conduct of members; its meaning has never been defined, and has not needed definition, because it is inherent in the culture and conventions of the House. These change over time, and thus any definition of 'personal honour', while it might achieve temporary 'legal certainty', would quickly become out-moded … the term 'personal honour' is ultimately an expression of the sense of the House as a whole as to the standards of conduct expected of individual members … members cannot rely simply on their own personal sense of what is honourable. They are required to act in accordance with the standards expected by the House as a whole. 'Personal honour' is thus … a matter for individual members, subject to the sense and culture of the House as a whole."

20. Paragraph 9 of the Guide continues:

> "a written Code can never cover every eventuality. Paragraphs 8(a) [which requires members to comply with the Code] and 8(b) of the Code, taken together, mean that members are required not only to obey the letter of the rules, but to act in accordance with the spirit of those rules and the sense of the House. This includes the rules agreed by the House in respect of financial support for members or the facilities of the House."

21. This case raised the question of how the requirement to act on personal honour applies to a member who hosts a meeting in the House of Lords' part of the parliamentary estate.

22. Two of the complainants referred to "deeply offensive" and "very offensive" remarks being made at the meeting. I considered whether the sense of the House would be that a member hosting a meeting on the parliamentary estate should be required to take steps to prevent grossly offensive comments being made, or to intervene once such a comment has been made. I concluded that a test of "gross offensiveness" would not be appropriate, for three reasons.

23. First, any test of gross offensiveness would be subjective.

24. Secondly, the sense of the House as a whole is likely to favour preserving freedom of speech on the parliamentary estate, both because it is important in its own right and because of the symbolism of restricting it on the parliamentary estate.

25. Thirdly, any requirement on members to monitor the content of everything said at meetings they host and/or to intervene where offence may have been caused might have a "chilling effect". Such a requirement might result in members erring on the side of not hosting meetings on the parliamentary estate; or they might become excessively vigilant in intervening during meetings, perhaps to the hindrance of the free exchange of views.

26. Instead, I consider that the sense of the House is that a member should not host a meeting on the parliamentary estate with the intention of promoting antisemitism (or any other form of discrimination based on protected characteristics) and, if a meeting on the parliamentary estate was not hosted for that purpose but was taken over by those promoting antisemitism, that the member should take steps to address that.

Consideration of alleged failure to act on personal honour

27. Applying the above test to this case, I now consider:
    (a) whether there were examples of antisemitism at the meeting;
    (b) if so, whether those examples amounted to a takeover of the meeting by those promoting antisemitism;

(c) if so, whether Baroness Tonge took steps to address the takeover.

28. I deal first with the complaints that there was Holocaust denial and Holocaust revisionism at the meeting, that this was applauded by the audience and that Baroness Tonge made no effort to stop or challenge these remarks. There are three references to the Holocaust in the transcript. First:

"There are two issues. Is Britain in general historically and politically responsible? If so, one obligation is there on today's Government to make an apology for the action of their predecessors. Let us take two examples: slavery and the Holocaust. These are issues where people, entities and groups have sought apologies in the past and received them. These are apologies not for actions that were done by those in power at the time of the apology; these are apologies for events that happened in the past, for which nevertheless their successors as politicians and statesmen have accepted there is some value and necessity to apologise in that situation."[28]

29. Secondly:

"No matter how often the truth is spelled out, by Jewish historians as well as others, the denials continue. Jenny mentioned my publishing company. We have a book that has just come out called *State of Terror*, which is an appalling catalogue of the violence and terror in the 1940s and into the 1950s when the state of Israel was founded—terror not just by small Jewish terrorist groups but supported by large numbers of Jews who lived in Palestine. It was a blatant and self-justifying attempt to get the British out of Palestine and take over the land. That needs an apology. Holocaust denial is quite rightly seen as a gross insult to the memory of millions who suffered under Nazi Germany but Nakba denial is a daily occurrence for Palestinians. It is a real obstacle to any peace settlement. To put it another way, the psychological effect of an apology would be to remove a major roadblock, proving that for the first time the Israelis were serious about addressing the injustice and arguing for a peace treaty."[29]

30. The above two quotes include nothing that could be interpreted as Holocaust denial or revisionism.

31. The third mention of the Holocaust was by "audience member 11". He was apparently a member of the Neturei Karta sect of Judaism. The sect is described thus: "Neturei Karta opposed the establishment of and retain all opposition to the existence of the so-called "State of Israel"." At the meeting he was wearing the sect's distinctive dress, apparently based on that of an 18th-century Polish nobleman. He was one of three or four members of Neturei Karta who arrived part-way through the meeting. He was not one of the invited speakers; he asked a question from the floor. The members of Neturei Karta had apparently not registered to attend the meeting. This was the exchange:

"**Audience member 11:** I'm not wanting to distract from the situation in Palestine, but surely one of the best ways to atone for the mistakes of the past is to prevent the same type of thing happening in the future. I am referring specifically to the situation now in Syria and Iraq. Just as the so-called Jewish state in Palestine was created by—it doesn't come from Judaism [*inaudible*]—so this Islamic state in Syria is nothing to do with Islam. It is a perversion of Islam, just as Zionism is a perversion of Judaism which serves certain non-Semitic interests. It is just carrying on. Just as the main victims—I'm again not wishing to belittle in any way the suffering of the Palestinians, the Arab and Christian Palestinians and Muslim Palestinians at the hands of the Zionists.

I once said to a daughter of one of the Palestinian refugees who had to leave after the '48 war [*inaudible*] ending up having to leave Palestine, I said, not wishing to belittle the sufferings that they had had at the hands of the Zionists and these victims [*inaudible*] spiritually and physically at the hands of the Zionists due to the Holocaust, one of the main Zionist speakers in America, so-called Rabbi Stephen Wise, a Reform heretic so-called rabbi, is quoted in the *New York Times*, I think it was 1905, "There are 6 million"—note the number—"bleeding and suffering reasons to justify Zionism." Thirty years later he made the boycott on Germany, the economic boycott on Germany, which antagonised Hitler over the edge to then want to systematically kill Jews wherever he could find them, as opposed to just a Judenrein, to make Germany a Jew-free area of land, which is enough. But that isn't noted by one of the rabbis. That's what pushed him over the edge. His personal secretary Ribbentrop was in Nuremberg during the trials. He said to Rabbi [*inaudible*], "Well this is what, he became a madman after this boycott. Judea declares war on Germany." In Manhattan, they had I think 100,000 or more people marching for the economic boycott in 1935. It was the same Reform heretic rabbi who holds that 30 years prior put the number 6 million in the *New York Times*. Again, it doesn't come from Jewish interests. It's not promoting the whole ideology—

Baroness Tonge: Thank you very much. I think it's very important that the word "boycott" has come up, because BDS, the campaign to boycott Israeli goods and services and for divestment from Israel, a lot of us think—most of us think—that it's very, very important indeed. [*Applause.*] In this year of apologising for Balfour, that is one really effective action we can make stronger and stronger and stronger to show the Israeli government that we do not like them, they are not a good thing and they have got to stop what they're doing and leave the Palestinians. I mean, Karl is a non-two-state-solution man, because he feels that it's gone, I think, too far now and it's a bit difficult when you go out there to see that two states. But whether it's a two-state solution or one state, the Palestinian people have to have total freedom and equal human rights and political rights and physical rights and they have to have their homes and lands back. I mean, there's no question about it and BDS is the thing we can do to put pressure on Israel. We can put pressure on our Government to apologise for Balfour, but we can put pressure on the Israeli government by BDS. Now, more questions."

32. This contribution by audience member 11 is more problematic than the previous two. It is unclear what points the speaker was trying to make. Baroness Tonge said while audience member 11 was talking she "could barely hear what he was saying and I was looking for an opportunity to interrupt and go on to another contributor, which I did when I heard him use the word 'boycott'. I used this to move the meeting on to discuss the BDS movement (Boycott, Divestment, Sanctions). At that point the audience clapped in relief and we moved on."[35] Baroness Tonge repeated in a subsequent letter to me and at our interview that she had not understood what audience member 11 was saying at the meeting, or even after reading the transcript of it.[36] Others present stated that they had trouble understanding the speaker, saying he was "garbled" and "unintelligent".[37] Thus my findings are based on the transcript of what audience member 11 said, the purpose, and even the meaning, of which is unclear.

33. Having read Mr Collier's blog, I understand that the reference to "Rabbi Stephen Wise, a Reform heretic so-called rabbi, is quoted in the *New York Times*, I think it was 1905, 'There are 6 million'—note the number—'bleeding and suffering reasons to justify Zionism.'" is a device used by Holocaust deniers to seek to show that the numbers of Jews killed in the Holocaust was exaggerated. The complaint by the six members of the House said this was a "classic anti-semitic trope." I accept that reference to this apparent mention of six million in 1905 is used by Holocaust deniers and is antisemitic when used in this way.

34. However, the rest of audience member 11's contribution appears to show that he accepted the reality of the Holocaust. The fact that Holocaust deniers use this device cannot be evidence that someone who accepts that Hitler wanted "to systematically kill Jews wherever he could find them" is a Holocaust denier.

35. The Israeli Ambassador complained that the event promoted "Holocaust revisionism" and that remarks that "Jews themselves ... caused the Holocaust" were "clearly grounded in bigotry and hatred".[38] The six members of the House complained that the audience "applauded statements ... that Hitler only decided to kill all the Jews after he was provoked by anti-German protests led by a Rabbi in Manhattan".[39] These complaints clearly arose from the contribution of audience member 11. The allegation that Jews caused the Holocaust is an example of Holocaust revisionism and clearly fits within the official definition of antisemitism.

36. However, this is not what audience member 11 actually said. He referred to an economic boycott led by Rabbi Wise, but he did not say that the boycott was by Jews or Zionists.

37. Mr Collier's blog makes a link with neo-Nazi websites that claim that the economic boycott of Germany was carried out by Zionists who were therefore to blame for the Holocaust. I have no reason to doubt Mr Collier's claim. People who monitor such neo-Nazi websites are likely to be aware of this type of Holocaust revisionism. But those who do not have this specialist knowledge cannot be expected to decode incomplete references to allegations which do not, in the words used, appear to be antisemitic, or even anti-Zionist.

38. Complaints were made that the audience applauded the remarks of audience member 11, and that Baroness Tonge made no attempt to stop him speaking. As noted above, Baroness Tonge said she was looking for an opportunity to interrupt audience member 11, and did so when he used the word "boycott". The video and transcript bear out her recollection; they show that she interrupted him and that the applause followed her reference to the current boycott campaign, rather than the remarks of audience member 11.

39. I note from the recording of the meeting that the next speaker was sitting in the same part of the room as audience member 11, and that Baroness Tonge had to ask her to repeat her question.[40] This supports the suggestion that audience member 11 was inaudible as well as incoherent.

40. Another specific complaint was that a reference was made to the Zionist movement having power over Parliament.[41] The complete quote (from audience member 8) is:

> "The trouble is that 100 years on, and I'm not talking about world Jewry, I'm talking about that segment which we call the Zionist movement, which has that power. It has it over our own Parliament. It has been able to put people into a very invidious situation.
>
> When I look around middle-class society, there is a lot of awareness of what's gone on. I can see this when I talk at the churches, at the political parties, even to my own family. There is a massive fear factor of being outed or denigrated or, to put it in the words of Sir Alan Duncan, of being "trashed, traduced and bullied" because you speak up for Palestinians. We have created that situation for ourselves and we need to tell people that. Ultimately we will pay for this in suppression of free speech and the ability to discuss things openly among ourselves. We cannot have the sort of open debate that we had about Scottish independence, which horrified me—the idea of tearing our country in two—but it was carried out in a relatively civil manner if you compare it to the sort of nastiness you get if you stand up for the Palestinians and the smearing that can come not only from Zionists and people who are not even Jewish but who are playing that game—there are some of them here in Parliament. So please let's take that message out to the people as well. [*Applause.*]"[42]

41. It is clear that what was being alleged was that those who speak up for Palestinians can be denigrated, which creates a fear of speaking out and results in free speech being suppressed.

42. One example of antisemitism is that of:

> "Making mendacious, dehumanizing, demonizing, or stereo-typical allegations about Jews as such or the power of Jews as collective—such as, especially but not exclusively, the myth about

a world Jewish conspiracy or of Jews controlling the media, economy, government or other societal institutions."

43. Audience member 8's allegation of controlling Parliament is not made against Jews, but against Zionists and non-Jews who "smear" those who support Palestinians. The issue of whether anti-Zionist criticism is coded antisemitism is contentious, must be situation-specific and is not one on which I can give a general answer. However, as the speaker explicitly stated that he was not referring to world Jewry, and as he did not criticise Jews as such or the power of Jews as a collective, I do not think that this remark fits within the definition of antisemitism.

44. There were also non-itemised complaints that the event was "very anti-semitic;"[43] was an "anti-Jewish litany";[44] involved "disseminating anti-semitism";[45] and was "host to appalling antisemitic comments."[46] In light of these I have considered whether anything else was said at the meeting to justify these complaints.

45. While reading the transcript I noticed that the remarks of at least one speaker were not recorded.[47] At several points remarks were unable to be transcribed so are marked "inaudible". The recording was in three parts, and it seemed there were gaps between them. I was concerned that there was a possibility that antisemitic comments could have been made during a gap in the recordings or transcript.

46. I have checked the recordings (which are online) against the transcript to see if I could hear what the transcribers found inaudible. I was not able to distinguish clearly any of the words labelled inaudible, but at most they were a few words long and part of longer sentences which were not about the Holocaust or antisemitism.

47. In case there were antisemitic comments that could have been made in the gap between the second and third recordings, I

looked at all the specific examples given in Mr Collier's blog. He referred to "four incidents that I need to describe, to expand on this issue of growing antisemitism".[48]

48. One was the comment by Mike Abramov (see footnote 47). The others were all captured in the recordings, and included the contributions of audience member 8 and audience member 11, both considered above.

49. The remaining "incident" referred to in the blog was the comment by one of the invited speakers, Betty Hunter, that "Israel is not a democracy."[49] Ms Hunter also referred to "the colonialism of the Israeli state" and said that "the new colonialism of Israel was all based on violence", particularly against Palestinians.[50]

50. The official definition of antisemitism makes clear that "criticism of Israel similar to that levelled against any other country cannot be regarded as antisemitic." Ms Hunter's criticisms of Israel were that that "violence ... is waged on the Palestinian people daily";[51] that "more and more land" is being confiscated, with settlements "encroaching all over the West Bank and in East Jerusalem";[52] and that not all of its citizens "have the same rights."[53] Whether or not these criticisms are justified, they are clearly similar to criticisms levelled at other countries, including at the meeting, and including by Ms Hunter, who was critical of racism in the United States and elsewhere.[54]

51. I fully understand that supporters of Israel may find these criticisms hurtful and unfair, but I do not consider that her remarks fit the definition of antisemitism above as they refer to alleged political decisions.

52. Many of the criticisms at the meeting that were not directed at successive British governments were directed at alleged Israeli political decisions which have adversely affected Palestinians. As with my finding with regard to Ms Hunter, I do not consider that these criticisms fit the definition of antisemitism above.

53. The definition of antisemitism states that it can also be expressed by the use of "sinister stereotypes and negative character traits." I heard and read no such stereotyping at this event. When talking about the views and actions of Jews, official speakers and audience members acknowledged that Jews in Israel, in Britain and around the world have a variety of political opinions, including differing opinions about Israel and its policies. There were no suggestions that Jews have particular characteristics that distinguish them from others. Speakers also referenced support for Zionism by non-Jews, which indicates that Zionism is recognised as a political or religious cause, not a Jewish trait.

54. One of the complainants alleged that the event involved "blatant racism".[55] Although no comment was identified in connection with this allegation, it may have been connected to Mr Collier's remark in his blog about the contribution of audience member 14. That person spoke at the end of the meeting and said:

> "Just to say thank you. It is marvellous work. Keep it up. We belong to large groups all over the world. Not necessarily one specific community but religious groups at large are totally upset with everything around Israel, whether it's being antagonistic against the Palestinians, harming them and indeed harming the Jewish religion itself. So you keep it up. You should never be impressed and fear that the Israelis will come back to you and say you're an anti-Semite, which they will. It is their best tool. Don't look at it. Ignore it. It is not true. If anybody's anti-Semitic, it's the Israelis themselves. [*Applause.*]"

55. It was claimed in the blog and the newspaper articles that the last sentence of this received applause. I have set out the whole quote so that the last sentence can be put in context.

56. The sentence itself is offensive and untrue. However, in context I do not believe it amounts to racism, as it is clearly directed at those whom the speaker believes make untrue allegations of antisemitism against those who support the Palestinian cause.

Finding on alleged failure to act on personal honour

57. It is clear from the transcript that the event as billed—to launch the Palestinian Return Centre's Balfour Apology Campaign—was what took place, and that the event was not intended to promote antisemitism. I find that there was no takeover of the event by people promoting antisemitism, and that therefore Baroness Tonge was not obliged to deal with any such takeover.

58. For the above reasons I find that Baroness Tonge did not breach paragraph 8(b) of the Code of Conduct in her hosting and chairing of the meeting on the parliamentary estate on 25 October 2016.

IRRELEVANT CLAUSES OMITTED

Summary of findings

76. In this report I find that Baroness Tonge:

   (i) did not breach paragraph 8(b) of the Code of Conduct in respect of the meeting in committee room 2A hosted and chaired by her on 25 October 2016; (*the first meeting*)

   (ii) breached paragraph 10(c) of the Code of Conduct by not obtaining permission for that meeting to be filmed and photographed—a breach admitted by Baroness Tonge;

77. This is the first occasion on which a member has been found in breach of the Code for failure to comply with the rules on filming and photography. I therefore consider it appropriate to refer the case to the Sub-Committee on Lords' Conduct.

Lucy Scott-Moncrieff, CBE

Commissioner for Standards

NOTES:

References in the notes to Appendices refer to the Appendices in the original report which can be found online at https://publications.parliament.uk/pa/ld201617/ldselect/ldprivi/142/14202.htm

[1] The Times, 27 October 2016.

[2] Jewish Chronicle, "'Shameful' House of Lords event condemned after audience 'blames Jews for Holocaust'", 27 October 2016.

[3] Appendix E.

[4] I am grateful to House of Lords Hansard for producing the transcript.

[5] Appendix C.

[6] Appendix B.

[7] Fifth edition: July 2016.

[8] I asked the Ambassador if he intended to make a formal complaint about Baroness Tonge and, if he did, if he could clarify which particular remarks during the meeting he considered may have breached the Code of Conduct. The Ambassador's office replied that he did not wish to add to his original letter.

[9] Appendix D.

[10] Appendix E.

[11] Appendix F.

[12] Appendix G.

[13] Appendix H.

[14] Appendix I.

[15] Appendix J.

[16] Appendix K.

[17] Appendix L.

[18] Appendix M.

[19] Appendix N.

[20] Appendix O.

[21] Appendix P.

[22] Appendix Q.

[23] Appendix R.

[24] http://www.prc.org.uk/portal/index.php/activities-news/workshop-seminar/3523-launch-of-the-balfour-apology-campaign-join-us-in-the-house-of-lords

[25] The definition was accompanied by examples of antisemitism, which are at this link: https://www.holocaustremembrance.com/sites/default/files/press_release_document_antisemitism.pdf

[26] Oxford Dictionary of English, second edition (Oxford University Press).

[27] Appendices H and I.

[28] Appendix A, opening speech by Karl Sabbagh.

[29] Ibid.

[30] Appendix E.

[31] www.nkusa.org/aboutus/index.cfm

[32] Appendices E, K and M.

[33] Appendices E (blog by David Collier), L and M.

[34] Appendices L and M.

[35] Appendix E.

[36] Appendices K and M.

[37] Appendix K (statements by Jonathan Coulter and Jocelyn Hurndall).

[38] Appendix B.

[39] Appendix F.

[40] Appendix A, contribution by audience member 12.

[41] Appendix F.

[42] Appendix A, audience member 8.

[43] Appendix C.

[44] Ibid.

[45] Appendix B.

[46] Appendix F.

[47] After the contribution by audience member 6, Karl Sabbagh refers to another contributor's comments, which Mr Sabbagh described as "the picture of the Israeli parliament as a haven of peaceful co-existence, with the Arab MPs and Israelis." (Appendix A.) I could find no prior comment about the Israeli parliament. However, Mr Collier's blog did refer to a contributor, Mike Abramov, who "spoke up for Israel". (Appendix E.)

[48] Appendix E.

[49] Appendix A, made in response to audience member 7.

[50] Appendix A, made in Betty Hunter's opening remarks.

[51] Ibid.

[52] Ibid.

[53] Appendix A, made in response to audience member 7.

[54] Appendix A, made in response to audience member 7.

[55] Appendix C.

[56] Minutes of the meeting of the Administration and Works Committee on 11 February 2014 (available on the parliamentary website).

[57] "Rules on filming within the House of Lords", Handbook on facilities and services for Members and their staff (October 2015), page 56.

[58] Editions 44 (August/September 2014) and 57 (June/July 2016).

[59] A predecessor of the House of Lords Commission.

[60] House of Lords Offices Committee, (3rd Report, Session 1995–96, HL Paper 83); agreed by the House on 3 June 1996 (see LJ (1995–96) 442–43 and 464).

[61] Op. cit.

[62] Appendix N.

[63] Appendix N.

[64] Appendices E and M.

[65] Appendix M.

[66] Appendix E (email from Islam Ali, AJM Correspondent, Mubashar Channel, to Baroness Tonge).

[67] House Committee, Banqueting rules (1st Report, Session 2014–15, HL Paper 8).

[68] They were agreed on 30 July 2014.

[69] Appendix Q.

[70] One in the Mosaic Rooms, the other in SOAS University of London.

[71] Appendix Q.

[72] Appendix R.

Conclusion

I intended to conclude the book with some advice for three groups which, for the sake of euphony, I will call: supporters, reporters, and distorters. But I couldn't resist including three pieces of evidence, one in the news and the other two, for understandable reasons, unpublicised at the time of going to press, which seem to sum up the message of the book.

But first the advice:

Advice to people who are not antisemites, but wish to support the Palestinians:

I'm tempted to say 'be brave' but in fact it should not require courage to say what you know is right. And whatever you have heard about the iniquities of Israel's treatment of the Palestinians is likely to be right. There is no Palestinian equivalent to the Israeli hasbara – an organised, well-funded and mendacious propaganda machine. Apart from the fact that we are not among the world's best-organised people and don't have the funds, the Palestinians have enough evidence of a hundred years of injustice without needing to make things up. Our problem is where to start.

Let me give you seven myths about the birth of Israel, taken from a book called *The Birth of Israel* by Israeli historian Simcha

Flapan[*]. I hesitate to recommend a book published thirty years ago, but as I look at these myths they are as relevant to today's discussion as they were then, and there has been much more research since which only strengthens Flapan's argument. Take it from me, these have no factual basis, and you may bring them out with impunity in any discussion, and refer them to the book, by a Jew, if anyone wants the evidence:

1. Zionists accepted the UN Partition Plan and planned for peace

2. Arabs rejected the Partition Plan and launched a war.

3. Palestinians fled voluntarily intending to reconquer their land.

4. All the Arab states united to expel the Jews from Palestine.

5. The actions of the Arab armies made war inevitable.

6. Defenceless Israel faced destruction by the Arab Goliath.

7. Israel has always sought peace but no Arab leader has responded.

All of these statements are myths propagated to support the story Israel would like you to believe, and are false.

Another piece of advice – offending people is not a crime. I have been attacked by well-meaning Jews who could not believe that what I was saying was true. And these people were genuinely offended. But the blame for them being offended lies with the people and organisations who told them lies in the first place, not in someone who puts them right.

And remember, as we have seen in some of the accounts in this book, and certainly in the emails that I and other have received, while genuine antisemites are nasty and often stupid people, there are nasty stupid people among Zionists and supporters of Israel as well.

---

[*] *The Birth of Israel: Myths and Realities*, Simcha Flapan, Pantheon Books, 1987

Advice to media professionals:

Do your job. Treat apologists for Israel as you would spokesmen for the pharmaceutical industry, the anti-vaccination movement, or climate-change deniers. In other words, don't just reprint press releases. Any journalist being given figures for how many Jews think X, Y, or Z, or how many antisemitic incidents there have been, should at least investigate the methods used to gather those figures. And what's the worst that could happen if you, as a journalist, are targeted by the Board of Deputies or Margaret Hodge? Wear this as a badge of pride. If you write something about Israel and are not attacked, you may need to check to see if you have got the story right.

I sometimes wonder why it is that no one in an editorial position seems to understand the true nature of the Antisemitism Wars. Take the interview given by the former Chief Rabbi, Jonathan Sacks, to the *New Statesman*. When the man spouts obvious nonsense, with no solid evidential basis, about a third of British Jews wanting to leave the UK, why does everyone print it, or rather why does everyone print it under headlines which take it at face value, rather than saying '*Former Chief Rabbi Speaks Nonsense in Interview*'?

Advice to Zionists:

Read some of the many books written by Jewish academics, some mentioned in the Further Reading section, which give accurate, rather than tendentious, accounts of the history of Palestine and of the actions of the state of Israel. It is an odd fact, which I have mentioned earlier, that the best source of truth on these matters is often Israel publications, particularly the newspaper *Ha'aretz*, and books which use official Israeli archives.

Israeli statesmen, soldiers and intelligence operatives often say things that would be disbelieved by Zionists if repeated in writings or talks by supporters of Palestine. I'll give one small example, mentioned in my book *A Modest Proposal…"*

Israel has always said that it was compelled to launch the Six-Day War because it was under existential threat from Egypt. This is a myth, as Mordecai Bentov, a member of the Israeli government which launched the war, confirmed when he said: "In 1967, the entire story of the danger of extermination was invented in every detail and exaggerated *a posteriori* to justify the annexation of new Arab territory."

And now, as they say on fast-moving news programmes, 'this just in.'

In the week I am putting the last touches to the manuscript of this book, I see on the news that a British union leader, Mark Serwotka, has said, admittedly to a Palestinian support group rather than on a public platform, that Israel created the antisemitism row. "Now I'm not a conspiracy theorist," Serwotka said, "but I'll tell you what – one of the best forms of trying to hide from the atrocities that you are committing is to go on the offensive and to actually create a story that does not exist for people on this platform, the trade union movement or, I have to say, for the leader of the Labour Party."

The significance of this statement is not that it is news. To any objective observer of the events of the last years or so, or, I would hope by now, to any reader of this book, the roots of the Antisemitism Wars are clear. But Serwotka's statement could be seen – and I hope it *is* seen – as a crack in the dam holding back protest and anger at the activities of the false accusers of antisemitism. Of course, the manufactured accusations will continue, and – of course – when there is genuine antisemitism it will be identified and condemned. But in parallel with this, I hope there will be more Serwotkas who will say, like Peter Finch in the film *Network,* "I'm as mad as hell, and I'm not going to take this anymore!"

Secondly, a piece of irrefutable evidence that the fears of many who believe that the IHRA definition of antisemitism is a threat to free speech are justified:

Baroness Jenny Tonge is a doctor and a member of the House of Lords. She is chair of the All Party Parliamentary Group on Population, Development and Reproductive Health, President of the European Parliamentary Forum on Population and Development from 2011-15, and more recently an Honorary Fellow of the Royal College of Obstetricians and Gynaecologists for services to women's health in the UK and in developing countries. All this would suggest that she was a very suitable person to be invited to speak as a panellist at an event about inequality in maternal care to be held in London on October 4th, 2018. And indeed the invitation was issued, by the organisers of the event, B!RTH, a partnership between and the Royal Exchange Theatre, Manchester. Then, on September 14th, 2018, Baroness Tonge received a letter from the director of the Liverpool School of Tropical Medicine *dis*inviting her. The letter claimed that she presented a 'high risk' of 'distraction, albeit unintentional, onto broader and highly contentious public debates.' What did they fear Baroness Tonge would say that would be so counter to the aims of the B!RTH project? Would she call for a world ban on breastfeeding, compulsory caesareans for all women, and freedom to abort foetuses if they are the wrong sex?

But if course, that was not what the organisers feared. In fact, any disrupting would not be done by Baroness Tonge but by the Keystone Cops of the Antisemitism Brigade, who believe that anyone critical of Israel should be banned from speaking *anywhere* about *anything*. It is similar to the attempts to prevent Thomas Suárez playing his violin because of his views on Israel. But instead of taking action against the real cause of potential problems – the people or organisation which had approached them threatening disruption – the director of the Liverpool School of Tropical Medicine took action against the easier – and irrelevant – target, Baroness Tonge.

This spineless reaction was ascribed to "very recent media reports and allegations of anti-Semitic sentiment which are contradictory to our organisational ethos."

Clearly, another thing that is contradictory to their organisational ethos is resisting assaults on academic freedom.

And finally, a group of local left-wingers in London applied to the Kings Cross Brunswick Neighbourhood Association to hold a meeting on their premises on September 21st, 2018. The meeting was to be called "Labour, Corbyn and anti-Semitism: why is solidarity with Palestine under attack?" Armed only with this title, an official of the Board of Deputies of British Jews, Philip Rosenberg, a man with skills of clairvoyance second to none, apparently told the Association that the meeting "will be antisemitic" and ordered them to cancel it. In an echo of events thirty years before, where Jewish readers of *World Medicine* were told to complain about an article they hadn't read*, Rosenberg apparently also called upon supporters of the Board of Deputies to contact the venue to complain about the meeting.

So Zionists and supporters of Israel have reached a stage where not only critical comments about Jews are antisemitic, not only criticisms of Israel are antisemitic, but even *discussion of antisemitism* is antisemitic.

Can anyone now deny that the Antisemitism Wars are a living threat to freedom of speech in the United Kingdom?

---

* See *Viscious (sic) propaganda*, p. 41

Authors

Cyril Chilson was born in Petakh Tikva, near Tel Aviv, Israel, into a family of holocaust survivors. He was educated at the first Hebrew secondary school in the world, Ha-Gymnasiya Ha-Ivrit Herzliyah in Tel Aviv and spent his military service in the occupied West Bank. He read Classics and History at the Hebrew University of Jerusalem and worked as a journalist in the printed and electronic media. He now teaches at Blackfriars Hall, Oxford.

Tony Greenstein is a Jewish anti-Zionist and a founding member of Palestine Solidarity Campaign. He is a long-standing anti-fascist activist and author of *A History of Fighting Fascism in Brighton and the South Coast*.

Tony has written for many publications including *Tribune*, *Labour Briefing* and *Weekly Worker* and Hodder & Stoughton's *The Essentials of Philosophy & Ethics* (2006). Tony has also written for the Guardian's *Comment is Free*, before being censored because of Zionist objections.

Tony is a member of Brighton & Hove Trades Council and UNISON.

Karl Sabbagh is a British Palestinian documentary maker, writer and publisher. He was educated at King's College, Cambridge, worked for fourteen years as a BBC producer-director, and then set up an independent documentary production company. From 2000, he has concentrated on writing non-fiction books, about science, architecture, psychology and Palestine, and running a small independent publisher.

Thomas Suárez

Thomas Suárez was already known for his books on the history of cartography when his interest in historical research brought him to the subject of Palestine, in particular Zionist terrorism in the pre- and early post-statehood period. A professional violinist, he is a former faculty member of Palestine's National Conservatory of Music.

Appendices

Appendix 1:

Statements which would be antisemitic if applied to Jews.

"The Palestinians are like crocodiles, the more you give them meat, they want more".... Ehud Barak, Prime Minister of Israel at the time - August 28, 2000. Reported in the Jerusalem Post August 30, 2000

"[The Palestinians are] beasts walking on two legs." Menahem Begin, speech to the Knesset, quoted in Amnon Kapeliouk, "Begin and the Beasts". New Statesman, 25 June 1982.

"The Palestinians would be crushed like grasshoppers ... heads smashed against the boulders and walls." Israeli Prime Minister. (at the time) in a speech to Jewish settlers New York Times April 1, 1988

"There was no such thing as Palestinians, they never existed." Golda Maier Israeli Prime Minister June 15, 1969

"We have to kill all the Palestinians unless they are resigned to live here as slaves." Chairman Heilbrun of the Committee for the Re-election of General Shlomo Lahat, the mayor of Tel Aviv, October 1983.

"We must use terror, assassination, intimidation, land confiscation, and the cutting of all social services to rid the Galilee of its Palestinians population." Israel Koenig, "The Koenig Memorandum"

"One million Palestinians are not worth an Arab fingernail." -- Rabbi Yaacov Perrin, Feb. 27, 1994 [Source: N.Y. Times, Feb. 28, 1994, p. 1]

Appendix 2:

Emails complaining about a *British Medical Journal* article by Dr Derek Summerfield on the impact of Israeli military action on the health of Palestinians in Gaza.

The level of actual argument with the issues in Summerfield's article was very low. About a third of the emails issued blanket denials of all of Summerfield's claims without offering any contrary evidence.

The aligations are too stupid to respond to, but just to the most insulting ones I'like to comment: 80 times more Palestinians died thru the hands of Arabs (Jordan 1972=15.000 dead and Libanon approx. 4.000) than by the Israeli war against terror (approx. 1200).

The IDF, unlike the Arabs, has NEVER killed innocent civilians.

It is known that the Israeli army is one of the most moral armies of the world, and is not allowed to shoot to kill children-unless they are a direct threat to Israeli soldiers.

the great extent to which Israel goes to avoid unnecessary civilian enemy casualties is truly remarkable...a tribute to the Jewish people's long history of serving as a beacon to the world on ethical behavior.

No non-combatant child who was clearly that has ever, ever been deliberately targeted and killed or maimed by any israeli soldier. ... As a Chartered Accountant I am by nature and training not given to making sweeping statements without caveat but on this there is no doubt whatsoever.

The Institute for Counter Terrorism has clearly demonstrated that the majority of Palestinian deaths have been terrorists and armed combatants.

Just to set the record straight, the overriding majority of Palestinian casualties in this, Arafat's genocidal war against Israel, have been armed combatants and terrorists whose intent has been to kill and maim as many Jews as possible in busses, shops, cafes, schools, etc. Israel's army does not deliberately target or kill innocents with impunity.

Many of the emails betrayed ignorance about the Middle East in general, and about the Arab-Israeli dispute in particular.

For example:

> *Remember, prior to 1967 there was no mention of a "Palestinian State". The Countries of Egypt and Jordan were where most of these Arabs lived.*
>
> *The Land of Israel was mostly desolate when the British finally decided to give it back to the Jews. Swamps or desert covered much of the land. It is only now that the Jews have developed the land, that it is such an oasis of beauty.*
>
> *I might also add that the land, including the parts which had to be bought from the Palestinians by the Jews, was nothing but barren and diseased land. It was the Jews who made it flourish, and developed it into a first-world country. It is by no means Israel's fault that the Palestinians couldn't be bothered to do the same.*

In many emails, authors simply vented anger against Arabs and other critics of Israel. Examples include:

> *Palestinians ... never cared for the Holy Land until Jews came and developed the land...*
>
> *if it wasnt for israel their wouldn t be water in the gaza and israel west bank.*
>
> *their refusal to accept either the 1917 or the 1948 UN directives re the establishment of a Jewish state.*
>
> *the facts are that the Palestinians have targeted and killed more unamred Jewish and Muslim civilians than the IDF has killed Palestinians.*
>
> *The problem is they procreate like rabbits and someday they will come to kill you.*
>
> *If Israel did kill every one of the Arab Muslims there most Americans would not miss a beat. We hate Islam - we hate Arafat and you just don't get it. America hates you evil bastards - you support evil - you live evil and you will die evil.*
>
> *the bloodthirstty Palestinians, whose appetite for terror is simply insatiable...*

If you had even the slightest understanding of how the Jewish mind works, you would know how painful a statement this is...Jewish people value life...all life...not just their own. Golda Mier put it quite honestly and clearly when she said: "when the Arab mother learns to love her children more than she hates Israel, then there will be peace in the middle east.

Let us not forget that it is the Palistinians who started this intifada for the sole purpose of destroying Israel and seeking the death of all of its inhabitants.

Many emails abused the *BMJ* and/or Dr. Abbasi personally. These were often sent anonymously from Hotmail addresses (which can be set up easily and then abandoned), with the consequence that authors had the freedom to use obscenities and personal (including racist) insults without worrying about the effect on their own reputations. However, it was surprising to me that some of the abusive emails came from people who appeared to be unconcerned about signing their own names.

Clearly this idiot has no idea that the PLO recruits and trains children to do their bidding - to wear bombs and to blow themselves up to pieces, while the rich fat cats sit safely in their homes (guarded by the Israeli army, no less) - and they regularly allow their own children to be mamed and blown to pieces! This is astonishing to the entire world, except to this writer and your journal. Where have you been living - with your heads in a dung pile?

Your journal, having an editor with your clearly, mid-eastern name, the spewing of such published garbage seems inevitable

I believe as 'acting' editor of the BMJ if you are to publish political articles with an anti-Israeli viewpoint then you should make it quite clear where you as a Muslim stand on this issue. The answer appears all too clear!

Your article about Israel is bullshit. You should be very ashamed.

You miserable animal... I'm glad HonestReporting is on to your filthy hate and lies. You can spew your lies and garbage until you breathe your last breath, and then it's the fiery furnace for you, and that will be for all eternity.

Who the FUCK (very sorry about this expression) does he think he is to make biased political statements in a medical journal.

I hope you die of HIV disease like Yasser Arafat.

I am a physician in the USA for 30 years. You are a moslem terrorist sympathizer who hates Israel and the Jewish nation. You have hijacked the BMJ to publish anti Israeli garbage propaganda. Please don't show your filthy shit covered hands in this country. May you rot in hell you bastard son of a bitch.

You believe that killing chilren in self defence is moraly wrong? Give me your address, and I will pay a few kids to stone you to death. Believe me, 3-4 kids, 14-15 years old will kill you in a matter of minutes. Please give me your address. They can also kill your daughter for free. If you will not give me your address, then it means that you don't really believe that when Israely soldiers kill a kid there is anything wrong with it. Waiting for your reply. By they way, if you really piss me off, I will hunt you down myself, and kill you with rock(10-15 times hit you over the head until your brain will show up). Hey, that is ok right? as long as I don't have weapon in my arms.

Appendix 3

Labour, Antisemitism and the News
Dr Justin Schlosberg and Laura Laker

- Over 250 articles and news segments from the largest UK news providers (online and television) were subjected to in-depth case study analysis involving both quantitative and qualitative methods

- 29 examples of false statements or claims were identified, several of them made by anchors or correspondents themselves, six of them surfacing on BBC television news programmes, and eight on TheGuardian.com

- A further 66 clear instances of misleading or distorted coverage including misquotations, reliance on single source accounts, omission of essential facts or right of reply, and repeated value-based assumptions made by broadcasters without evidence or qualification. In total, a quarter of the sample contained at least one documented inaccuracy or distortion.

- Overwhelming source imbalance, especially on television news where voices critical of Labour's code of conduct were regularly given an unchallenged and exclusive platform, outnumbering those defending Labour by nearly 4 to 1. Nearly half of Guardian reports on the controversy surrounding Labour's code of conduct featured no quoted sources defending the party or leadership.

The Media Reform Coalition has conducted in-depth research on the controversy surrounding antisemitism in the Labour Party, focusing on media coverage of the crisis during the summer of 2018. Following extensive case study research, we identified myriad inaccuracies and distortions in online and television news including marked skews in sourcing, omission of essential context or right of reply, misquotation, and false assertions made either by journalists themselves or sources whose contentious claims were neither challenged nor countered. Overall, our findings were consistent with a disinformation paradigm.

We use the concept of disinformation to denote systematic reporting failures that broadly privileged a particular political agenda and ideological narrative. This does not mean that these failures were intentional or that journalists and news institutions were inherently biased. We recognize, for instance, that resource pressures combined with acute and complex controversies can foster particular source dependencies or blind spots.

Nor does our research speak in any way to allegations of smear tactics. To interrogate the root causes of disinformation would necessitate a far more wide-ranging study than was undertaken here. We start from the well-founded assumption that concerns about antisemitic hate speech within the Labour Party are genuine and not necessarily or entirely misplaced. There have been unambiguous examples of racist discourse invoking holocaust denial, generalized references to Jews in stereotyped contexts, and critiques of Zionists or Zionism that explicitly use the terms as proxies for Jews. Some of these cases have involved holders of official positions within the party, including local councillors.

Alongside such cases, there is a contested category of discourse that may be considered offensive or insensitive but not necessarily racist. Indeed, determining what counts as antisemitism lies at the heart of the wider controversy that has been played out in reams of column inches and air time since 2015, and with particular intensity during the spring and summer of 2018. We reserve judgement on this central point of contention but acknowledge legitimate views on both sides, as well as a spectrum in which relatively extreme and moderate positions are easily identifiable.

We recognize that this controversy – on the surface at least – involves prominent voices in a minority community accusing a major political party of harbouring racism directed towards them. What's more, these voices have been vocally supported by many high-profile Labour MPs. In such circumstances we expect journalists to take these concerns seriously, view them as inherently newsworthy, and not necessarily afford equal time and attention to contesting views. It is also important to stress that journalists must be allowed – on occasion – to get the story wrong: the public interest is never served by an overly cautious press.

But we do expect professional journalists to strive for accuracy, to establish essential contextual facts in any given story, and to actively seek out dissenting or contesting opinion including, in this case, within the minority group in question, within other affected minorities, and amongst relevant experts (both legal and academic). Nor do the particular complexities and sensitivities absolve journalists of their responsibility to offer a due right of reply to the accused or to interrogate contentious claims made by sources on all sides.

Overall, we found **95 clear cut examples of misleading or inaccurate reporting** on mainstream television and online news platforms, with a quarter of the total sample containing at least one such example. The problem was especially pronounced on television – which reaches far wider audiences by comparison – where **two thirds of the news segments on television contained at least one reporting error or substantive distortion.**

Underlying these figures was a persistent subversion of conventional news values:

- Several reports focused on a controversial social media post by Jeremy Corbyn omitted any mention that it was made six years ago, with some emphasising a sense of currency and recency that failed to make clear the historical context of the post.

- Journalists covering the launch of Labour's antisemitism report in 2016 routinely misquoted an activist in ways that were entirely removed from his original comment, in spite of a video recording of the event that was readily and immediately accessible.

- Above all, coverage of Labour's revised code of conduct during the summer of 2018 often entirely omitted critical discussion of the 'working definition' of antisemitism put forward by the International Holocaust Remembrance Alliance (IHRA), and wrongly characterized it as consensual and universally adopted.

In fact, we established through background case research that

- although the IHRA is an international body with representatives from 31 countries, only six of those countries have, to date, formally adopted the definition themselves.

- In spite of a call for local authorities to adopt the definition by the UK's central government in early 2017, Less than a third of councils have responded and several of those have chosen not to include any of the controversial examples contained within the working definition.

- Several high-profile bodies have rejected or distanced themselves from the working definition, including the EU's Fundamental Rights Agency (a successor to the body that drafted the original wording on which the definition is based) and academic institutions including the London School of Economics and School of Oriental and African Studies.

- Mainstream academic and legal opinion has been overwhelmingly critical of the IHRA definition, including formal opinions produced by four leading UK barristers.

Virtually none of this essential context found its way into news reports of the controversy. Instead, the Labour Party was routinely portrayed by both sources and correspondents as beyond the pale of conventional thinking on the IHRA definition.

This matters because although the manifest issue at stake is not outwardly political in nature, the controversy is inextricably linked to a wider ideological conflict that has been playing out within the Labour Party for some years, and within British politics more broadly. To that extent, such controversies bring into sharp relief the news media's role and responsibilities in nurturing inclusive public debate and contributing to an informed citizenry.

It also matters because the misreporting of antisemitism risks normalizing or distracting attention from certain forms of antisemitic discourse. Distortions also risk stirring racial tensions by provoking counter-outrage that may be misdirected at Jews on either the left or right of the political spectrum. It is notable in this respect that in 2016, a Daily Mail columnist who has been outspoken on this issue described one Corbyn supporter as a "useful Jewish idiot"; whilst in 2018, the Prime Minister's warm congratulatory words offered to her Malaysian counterpart – a leader who has openly described himself as an 'antisemite' – received barely no attention at all in mainstream news, despite antisemitism being such a salient issue on the news agenda at the time.

In sum, although our findings do not engage directly with the controversy – shedding no further light on what is antisemitism nor how prevalent it is within the Labour Party - we can say with some certainty that there have been prevalent errors, omissions and skews in the mainstream coverage.

This was no anomaly: almost all of the problems observed in both the framing and sourcing of stories were in favour of a particular recurrent narrative: that the Labour Party has been or is being lost to extremists, racists and the 'hard left'. Some of the most aggressive exponents of this narrative were routinely treated by journalists – paradoxically – as victims of aggression by the party's 'high command'.

During the summer of 2018, this controversy reached fever pitch amid claims that the Labour party had become 'institutionally racist' under the leadership of Jeremy Corbyn, and that the prospect of a Corbyn-led government posed an 'existential threat' to Jewish life in Britain. It has given rise to vocalized threats of a split within the party, further destabilizing politics and signalling a potentially profound reshaping of the British political map. At a time when the country is entering the final stages of its negotiated withdrawal from the European Union, these findings warrant urgent attention from journalists, editors, policymakers and activists alike.

The full summary and report can be found here: https://www.jewishvoiceforlabour.org.uk/app/uploads/2018/09/Labour-anti-semitism-and-the-news-FULL-REPORT-FINAL.pdf

Further reading

This is a very partial – in both senses of the word – list of books which I have found, on recommending them to others, to have produced the reaction "I'm angry that I never knew that."

For an account of historical and archaeological evidence, or rather its absence, for Jewish claims to Palestine, read *In Search of 'Ancient Israel'*, by Philip Davies, published by Bloomsbury, 2015.

Edward Said's *The Question of Palestine,* Vintage Books, is still very relevant forty years after its publication, and his collection of essays, *The End of the Peace Process*, published by Bloomsbury delivers the story promised by its title.

The best account of the Nakba, the deliberate dispossession of the Palestinians by Israel and Zionists, is *The Ethnic Cleansing of Palestine*, by Ilan Pappé, published by Oneworld, 2007.

The most comprehensive popular history of Palestine, showing that far from not existing, as many Zionists claim, it has a long history under that name, is *Palestine: A Four-Thousand Year History* by Nur Masalha, published in 2018 by the University of Chicago Press.

The best account of the Balfour Declaration and its aftermath is *Palestine: The Reality,* by J.M.N. Jeffries, and there is a companion volume, *Balfour in the Dock*, by Colin Andersen, which gives a biography of Jeffries as well as summaries and extracts of key elements of the book, both published by Skyscraper Publications in 2017.

For one view of the way in which the history of the Nazi Holocaust has been intertwined in the later history of Zionism and Jews in the U.S., see *The Holocaust Industry,* by Norman Finkelstein, second edition, published by Verso in 2003.

For an account, long out of print, of how the Zionist Lobby interferes in U.S. politics at the level of an individual candidate, read Paul Findlay's *They Dare to Speak Out*, Chicago: Lawrence Hill Books, 1989. The techniques used to influence his election to Congress have an eerie similarity to attacks on Labour candidates in the UK today.

Acknowledgments

I would like to thank all copyright holders who have given permission for use of their material.

They include:

Kathy-Anne Mendoza, the Canary website, for the interview with Stephen Oryszczuk

The Palestine Return Centre, for the Geoffrey Robertson QC opinion

The House of Lords Privileges Committee for the report on the conduct of Baroness Jenny Tonge

Redress Information and Contact, for the Eva Mykytyn article on the CAA

Stephen Sedley for his *London Review of Books* article

Dr Justin Schlosberg of the Media Reform Coalition

Al Jazeera television for transcripts of *The Lobby*

I should also like to thank Iain Chalmers for his usual wise guiding hand and eye as this manuscript has evolved very quickly, and for his staunch support in general for justice and peace in the Middle East.

I would also like to thank MEMO, Middle East Monitoring, for some financial support toward the costs of producing this book so quickly.

Endnotes

[1] http://www.palestinefacts.org/pf_early_palestine_zionists_impact.php

[2] *Guardian* 27 July2018

[3] https://www.thejc.com/news/uk-news/labour-veteran-sir-gerald-kaufman-claims-jewish-money-has-influenced-conservatives-1.60992

[4] https://azvsas.blogspot.com/2015/12/geoffrey-alderman-and-gerald-kaufman.html

[5] https://antisemitism.uk/sir-gerald-kaufman-mps-words-have-left-a-rotting-stain-on-our-institutions/

[6] https://labourlist.org/2017/01/oxford-students-cleared-over-antisemitism-claims-but-warned-over-bullying/

[7] Electronic Intifada 28.10.16.

[8] https://www.youtube.com/watch?reload=9&v=z4c_z8Jyuas

[9] https://www.independent.co.uk/news/uk/politics/labour-antisemitism-row-full-transcript-of-ken-livingstones-interviews-a7005311.html

[10] http://www.ameinu.net/publicationfiles/Vol.LXV,No.3.pdf

[11] https://www.youtube.com/watch?v=GRUTpypkV0I

[12] https://www.thejc.com/news/uk-news/anger-as-jeremy-corbyn-supporters-invited-to-speak-at-jewish-labour-event-1.53052

[13] https://azvsas.blogspot.com/2016/09/the-jewish-labour-movement-and-its.html

[14] https://www.independent.co.uk/news/uk/politics/momentum-labour-jon-lansman-jeremy-corbyn-leadership-challenge-a7339916.html

[15] https://www.huffingtonpost.co.uk/entry/israeli-pm-benjamin-

netanyahu-condemns-jeremy-corbyn-over-wreath-claims_uk_5b71b451e4b0bdd0620b88b7

[16] https://www.theguardian.com/politics/2018/mar/25/senior-labour-figures-defend-corbyn-row-antisemitic-mural

[17] https://www.thejc.com/news/uk-news/jonathan-arkush-claims-jewdas-is-a-source-of-virulent-antisemitism-1.461817

[18] https://www.bod.org.uk/president-jonathan-arkush-congratulates-donald-trump/

[19] https://www.washingtonpost.com/gdpr-consent/?destination=%2fopinions%2fantisemitism-is-no-longer-an-undertone-of-trumps-campaign-its-the-melody%2f2016%2f11%2f07%2fb1ad6e22-a50a-11e6-8042-f4d111c862d1_story.html%3f&utm_term=.7a087c86b3b0

[20] https://morningstaronline.co.uk/article/you-were-never-my-chief-rabbi-bruv

[21] https://www.haaretz.com/opinion/rabbi-sacks-why-are-you-cheerleading-for-anti-palestinian-provocateurs-1.5473150

[22] https://www.theguardian.com/commentisfree/2016/dec/28/britain-definition-antisemitism-british-jews-jewish-people

[23] https://www.lrb.co.uk/v39/n09/stephen-sedley/defining-antisemitism

[24] https://freespeechonisrael.org.uk/ihra-opinion/#sthash.fU50QvVr.dpbs

[25] https://www.doughtystreet.co.uk/news/article/ihra-definition-of-antisemitism-is-not-fit-for-purpose

[26] https://www.theguardian.com/commentisfree/2018/jul/12/labour-antisemitism-code-gold-standard-political-parties

[27] https://www.thejc.com/news/uk-news/labour-rejects-ihra-definition-antisemitism-nec-1.467291

[28] https://www.thejc.com/news/uk-news/labour-ihra-definition-antisemitism-nec-farce-1.469246

[29] https://jewishnews.timesofisrael.com/labour-backs-full-ihra-but-adds-caveat-for-freedom-of-expression-on-israel/

[30] https://www.jonathan-cook.net/blog/2018-08-16/corbyn-labour-fail-design/

[31] The author was among the people directly facing Mr. Hoffman when the security guard passively approached him. Mr. Hoffman yelled "He assaulted me." The audience laughed; there was no assault. A Youtube video records the audio but does not show the encounter.

[32] Rory Tingle, "'Zionism is a racist fascist cult': Israeli Embassy's fury after anti-Semitic hate speaker gives talk at a top London university," the *Daily Mail*, 8 November 2016

[33] Jonathan Hoffman, "Charity Commission investigating anti-Semitic Suárez meeting at SOAS", in The *Jewish News*, 17 February 2017; the "investigation" then copied by the *Independent*, in Rachel Pellis, "Jewish students told they 'do not have the right to define anti-Semitism' at SU meeting," 27 January 2017.

[34] Lee Harpin, "Board halt Israel hate author talk / Leader praises Quakers after they cancel Palestine campaign group event with State of Terror author," The *Jewish Chronicle*, 8 May 2017.

[35] Ben Weich, "Quakers row as venue is rented out to anti-Zionist," The *Jewish Chronicle*, 20 April, 2018

[36] At writing, IPSO has not yet issued their ruling in this case. IPSO shared the *JC*'s and my correspondence, and that is my source for the information and quotes here.

[37] David Collier & Jonathan Hoffman, *Hate and Errors a report on a modern antisemitic fraud*, September 2017

[38] Rory Tingle, "Corbyn is urged to cut links with Palestine charity after it hosts anti-Semitic speaker who accuses Jews of exploiting the Holocaust," the *Daily Mail*, 29 April 2017

[39] Joe Frank "The anti-Semitism of the Suárez talk is not the way to discuss the Israeli-/Palestinian conflict," The *Massachusetts Daily Collegian*, 26 September 2017

[40] Brian Choquet, "Hillel students say hate does have a home at UMass," *Amherst Wire*, 4 October 2017 (author has a screen grab of full deleted article)

[41] Isaac Simon, "Understanding commentary, Suárez and others," The *Massachusetts Daily Collegian*, 4 October 2017

[42] Rachel Frommer, "Anti-Israel Speakers Making Rounds at U.S. College Campuses," *Washington Free Beacon*, 27 September 2017.

[43] Norman Lebrecht, "A violinist attacks Israel for racism 'like Nazism'," Slipped Disc, 9 November 2016

[44] Months after the aborted talk, Mayor Marvin changed her story and said that she was against my speaking because neither I, nor my topic, was of any interest for the people of Bronxville. Her pre-talk email proves this to be untrue.

[45] *Evening Standard*: Rosamund Urwin, "SOAS students 'scared to wear the star of David and speak Hebrew'," 19 January 2017. The *Independent*: Rachel Pellis, "Jewish students told they 'do not have the right to define anti-Semitism' at SU meeting," 27 January 2017. *MancUnion*: Lily Sheehan, "Jewish students told they 'do not have the right' to define anti-Semitism," 3 February 2017.

[46] Danna Harman, "Calls to Bar Israeli Envoy From Speaking at London University Campus", in *Haartetz*, 25 April 2017. The "dead Jew" quote was

levelled at me and the Israeli anti-racist Ronnie Barkan, in David Collier, "'The Only Good Jew is a Dead Jew' (the Suárez – Barkan threshold)," the *Jewish Press*, 9 June 2017.

[47] See CPS, Racist and religious crime - CPS prosecution policy, Legal Guidance, Hate crime, available at https://bit.1y/2E6vxsk; archived here: http://webarchive.nationalarchives. gov.uk/20111115164417/http://www.cps.gov.uk/publications/prosecution/violent_extremism.html

[48] Perinçek v. Switzerland, (2016) 63 ECHR 6

[49] CICAD v Switzerland, [2016] ECHR 495 (07 June 2016)

[50] There is some confusion about the so called "MacPherson Principle" (a reference to Mr Justice MacPherson's Report into the Stephen Lawrence murder) which is often thought to require that the victim's perception of racism should prevail. But what Justice MacPherson was emphasising was that police should adopt the victim's perception that he had suffered a racist attack when recording the crime, but not necessarily after further investigation.

[51] E g BDS: How a Controversial Non-Violent Movement has Transformed the Israeli-Palestinian Debate,"The Guardian' 16 August 2018.

[52] Written Testimony to US House of Representative Committee on Judiciary, 7 November 2017, p5-7, 14

[53] By this time, the EU Group was called The Fundamental Rights Agency.

[54] See Arutz Sheva, "The Huge Importance of the Recent IHRA Definition of Anti-Semitism" 7th June 2016.

[55] See Education Act 1986, Section 43.